SUGARCANE PRICING
Policy, Procedure and Operations

V.B. JUGALE

ATLANTIC PUBLISHERS AND DISTRIBUTORS

Published by
ATLANTIC PUBLISHERS AND DISTRIBUTORS
B-2, Vishal Enclave, Opp. Rajouri Garden, New Delhi-27
Phones : 5413460, 5429987
e-mail : info@atlanticbooks.com

Sales Office
4215/1, Ansari Road, Darya Ganj, New Delhi-02
Phones : 3273880, 3285873, 3280451
Fax : 91-11-3285873
web : www.atlanticbooks.com

ISBN 81-7156-913-7

THE AUTHOR ACKNOWLEDGES/HIS INDEBTEDNESS TO SHRI MADHUKAR KAMBLE, MEMBER OF LEGISLATIVE ASSEMBLY, MAHARASHTRA STATE, AT/POST — SHEGAV, TAL. JAT, DISTRICT SANGLI FOR GRANT-IN-AID RECEIVED BY HIM TOWARDS THE COST OF PUBLICATION OF HIS BOOK.

Typeset at
APD Computer Graphics, Delhi

Printed in India at
Mehra Offset Press, Delhi

DEDICATED TO

SUGARCANE GROWERS,

WHO ALWAYS HAVE A HABIT OF PATIENCE,
ADVERSITIES AND AUSTERITIES

FOREWORD

Sugarcane Pricing is a very sensitive and subjective applied economic paradigm with incidental effects on the canegrowers *vis-a-vis* sugar manufacturers, Government, and such other institutions and agencies in the society. The issue of agricultural pricing becomes more paradoxical when the agricultural produce is used for industrial purposes as a raw-material. Sugarcane is the main raw-material used to produce sugar. Co-operative sugar factories in Maharashtra have made major strides in socio-economic upliftment and revolutionary organisations of collective action to enhance the well-being of agriculturists in the cane growing belt of Western Maharashtra. Pricing becomes dichotomised, when sugarcane is supplied to private sugar enterprises. While pricing in co-operative sector is hormonised, because cane growers are the equity shareholders of the co-operative sugar factories.

Sugarcane and sugar are centrally regulated commodities. Their prices are fixed statutorily by the Government, but could not compel the farmers to undertake cane plantation. The issue of the sugarcane pricing becomes more contradictory when the opera has been governed by the State Governments. The policies in concern to sugar and sugarcane are centrally regulated, whereas the procedures and operations have been simultaneously followed by the State Governments and sugar mills.

The issue of Sugarcane Pricing became more decisive with deep-rooted effects on the cane farming and sugar production in the year 1995-96, when the state administered sugarcane prices were reduced. Since then the 'lead industry' along with its forward and backward linkages exhaustively experiencing a peculiar obstructive stagnation in the overall economic activities in Western Maharashtra. The lead industry since its inception was state-patronised, whenever it was found in trouble. But now such rescues cannot be expected from the State due to liberalisation process. The co-operative movement in general and the sugar co-operatives in particular are experiencing various shocks rather than stimulants as earlier. A challenge has been put before the sector.

Dr. V.B. Jugale's contribution through this book is a timely addition to the knowledge of pricing. I personally, and on behalf of the whole industrial community congratulate Dr. Jugale for his painful efforts to explore the mechanism of sugarcane pricing (Policy, Procedure and Operations). The book is very helpful to the policy makers, industrialists, agriculturists and the academicians involved in exposing the important aspects of sugar industry in Maharashtra. I wish the best to this valuable effort of Dr. V.B. Jugale.

Jayantrao Patil
President, Maharashtra State
Co-operative Sugar Factories'
Federation (Sakhar Sangh),
Mumbai.

ACKNOWLEDGEMENT

This work has been assisted by various agencies and organisations, who have directly and indirectly strengthened my will power to examine the issue of pricing by availing the necessary data information and important references. I am glad to express my deep gratitude to them.

I am very thankful to the office bearers of the Directorate of Sugar, Sakhar Sangh, Commissioner of Sugar, Vasantdada Sugar Institute and Indian Sugar Mills Association for the help and cooperation they have extended by providing necessary data information and supplying valuable references.

The work remains incomplete unless I thank the UGC, Department of Economics and the Shivaji University for their assistance under SAP-DRS for this project.

I must thank Shri Madhukar Kamble, MLA of Jat (Dist. Sangli) for his inspiration and insight towards an academic and applied issue of pricing by providing the publication grant for this project work.

While busy in the field work and writing the manuscript, I have really encroached upon the time and joy of my adorable children, Pramod and Pallavi and beloved wife Mrs. Yojana. I must also thank them for their sacrifice.

DR. V.B. JUGALE

CONTENTS

LIST OF TABLES

1

INTRODUCTION

The beginning of the sugar season; 1995-96 was most decisive and deep-rooted effects on the sugarcane cultivation in particular and the sugar industry in general. Since 1980s the sugar industry is frequently facing number of obstructive issues. The 'lead industry' is caught in a transition after a long period of time. The cane harvesters and bullockcart workers (hence referred as farm sector work force) were on indefinite strike demanding their wage revision pending after the Dadasaheb Rupwate Award. The earlier tripartite award lapsed due to its date of expire. All honourable agreement had been signed by the tripartite members in November, 1995. Similarly the tripartite agreement between Government, industry and sugar workers (factory workers) comes to close by December 1997. On the advent of Fifth Pay Commission, sugar workers are belligerent on their demands, fundamentally concentrated on their wage revision. The issue is still alive. The trade union leaders have lost the faith on Wage Boards as it was farce and irritant to the sugar workers after the Third Wage Board. The issue of low sugarcane prices had been raised by the cane growers during the season of 1995 in Western Maharashtra. The '*bundh*' of cane harvesting had been announced by the cane growers at village levels. The 'lead industry' along with forward and backward organizations was exhaustively experiencing a peculiar obstructive stagnation in the overall economic transactions of the Western Maharashtra region since then. The financial agencies were in doldrums due to the stringency of funds, which was because of the inability of the farmers to repay their loans. Simultaneously, the political economy of the State Government begun to abuse the co-operative movement since it is in the hands of 'Sakhar Samrats'; the sugar barons or co-operative barons, most of them are congressmen. Thus the political war between the past rulers and the present rulers once again has to stir up to protect co-operative movement in Maharashtra. The situation is still belligerent.

However, the problem of sugarcane pricing had been led, when the first Sugarcane Act, 1934 was passed. The cane growers are the members of the co-operative sugar factories. Ultimately the surplus earned by way of processing the sugarcane and manufacturing the sugar goes directly to the cane growers. Consequently, there is no problem of controversy in distributing the surpluses. But the nature of stagnation caused by various issues was disturbing because the cane growers were pressed to accept low prices for their sugarcane as compared to earlier sugar season in 1995.

The present trend will trouble the overall functioning of the sugar industry in future. As a result of low sugarcane prices, the sugar factories during the season; 1996-97 have to close down early due to lack of supply of sugarcane. Around 27 lakh tonnes of sugar is being produced less as compared to the previous season. The uncertainty is left for the corresponding seasons. Around 27 sugar factories in Maharashtra were set down during the season; 1997-98 and 50 per cent are sick. So, this will spoil the crushing schedule of the sugar factories. Similarly the issue of zoning rose its head during the season. The controversy now is cooled down after the verdict of the Supreme Court. The aftermath results are yet to come forward.

By virtue of its procedure, the Govt. of Maharashtra has to announce advance sugarcane prices much earlier before the sugar season starts. At the beginning of the crushing season of 1995-96, the Government officials including concerned Ministry had begun to support and profound the case of low sugarcane prices, which was because of large amount of production of sugar during the year 1994-95. The sugar prices of buffer stock after realizing the corresponding sugar prices after a crushing season have been brought down from Rs. 1,250 to Rs.1,000 per tonne by the Government of Maharashtra. As a result, the sugarcane prices have to fall down. The prices of sugar in buffer stock have a direct implication on the procedure of fixing the advance sugarcane prices.

The prices of buffer stock sugar are fixed in anticipation that the prices of sugar may go up during the corresponding period. The Ministerial Committee chaired by Chief Minister determines the prices of buffer stock sugar. The Bhargav Commission while reviewing the problems of sugarcane pricing observed that, the prospective prices of buffer stock sugar should be taken into account while fixing the sugarcane prices in pursuance of the inflationary trend during the off crushing season. When sugar prices hike, the extra realization that after deducting all types of conversion cost of sugar, the excess income earned by a co-operative sugar factory by selling its sugar stock has to be equally distributed among the cane suppliers as per their quantity of sugarcane they have supplied to the factory. Additional rise or fall of sugar prices during the corresponding season enforce the Govt. to raise or to reduce buffer stock sugar prices. In anticipation to this the Ministerial Committee fixes the sugar prices and are included in the procedure of determining the sugarcane prices. More detailed analysis is explored in the ongoing explanations.

The entire gamut of sugarcane pricing system (*i.e.*, policy, procedure and operations) has been exhibited in this book. Chapter 2 of the book manifests the significance and functions of agricultural pricing. Historical background and some fundamental obstructions in agricultural pricing has been illustrated in Chapter 3. Besides it exposes, how agricultural prices are being determined including the norms of Commission on Agricultural Costs and Prices (CACP). Sugarcane policy with historical background is described in Chapter 4 and the cost of conversion is elaborated in Chapter 5. The process and operation of sugarcane pricing is explained in Chapter 6 and sugarcane pricing in Maharashtra is demonstrated in Chapter 7. Chapter 8 illustrates the trend of sugarcane prices since 1950. Chapter 9 explores the sugarcane pricing in Indian States and some foreign countries. Chapter 10 accounts for the different types of deductions from sugarcane prices. And Chapter 11 discloses the position of terms of trade and parity prices of sugar and sugarcane. Chapter 12 introduces the cost of cultivation of sugarcane production. Chapter 13 illustrates the significance of economics of sugar recovery in sugarcane prices. Chapter 14 discloses the consequences of delicensing and decontrol of sugar industry in Maharashtra. The last part concludes the overall analysis with some major recommendations to improve the policy, procedure and operation of sugarcane pricing in Maharashtra.

2

FUNCTIONS AND SIGNIFICANCE OF AGRICULTURAL PRICING

There are three economic reasons of capricious agricultural prices, which remain fluctuating within a agricultural season and even seasons together, *viz.*, (a) the price elasticity of agricultural produce comparatively remains less. The subsistence needs are being provided by agricultural sector, (b) the nature of agriculture is biological which naturally fall under the circumstances of risk and uncertainty. The irregularities due to geo-climatic conditions, spread of diseases and responses of the farmers are some of the routine occurrences in the agricultural sector, and (c) the seasonal nature of agricultural production eventuate to fluctuate the supply of agricultural produce. Whereas the demand subsists throughout the year. Consequently, the prices of agricultural produce may hike without any limit.

All above characteristics reorient the inevitable state intervention in fixing up the agricultural prices so as to keep them within the control of the Government. In less developed countries an instability in agricultural sector is more irritative. This purports the Government intervention in the fixation of minimum prices or administered prices of agricultural produce.

Normally there are three main functions of price determination (Kahlon and Tyagi, 1993), which in fact are being accomplished through Government intervention, (i) use of resources to the fullest extent is possible through administered prices, (ii) distributive justice can be obtained, (iii) capital accumulation is the pre-requisite to sustainable and steady economic growth. Which can be made it possible to obtain through Government intervention by determining the prices of agricultural produce. Simultaneously, to direct the circular flow so as to bring a distributive justice and dynamism in macro-economic variables in the economy is conceivable. General price line also comes under the control of Government with an equilibrium in terms of trade between agriculture and industry. The agricultural pricing is significant because of its forward and backward linkages with rest of the economy.

AGRICULTURE-INDUSTRY LINKAGES

Agriculture-industry relationship is a matter of interest particularly when two sectors acquaint dual growth performance in some common macro-economic parameters like, production, income, employment and their share in overall growth performance. Various arguments are made particularly when industrial growth slows down either through backward linkages or through forward linkages or when agriculture prices spur even when there is no shortage in the market. Varieties of such occasions can be traced, where certain discrepancies in the performance of macro variables in the context of these two sector occurs.

We must agree the fact that, agricultural performance has a considerable impact on non-agricultural growth. Such non-agricultural growth is urban biased vis-a-vis economic development again is industry biased. Giving least significance to agriculture sector in determining macro-policies, particularly in LDCs, is a normal practice in most of the countries of the world. Arida and Taylor (1958) comprehensively surveyed the fact that, the recent literature on short-run macro-economic policy issues facing low income economies generally fails to appreciate agriculture's importance for macro-economic policy. More or less same is the case with the India.

In the theoretical frameworks in economic literature, general equilibrium methodologies are being used for measuring the effects of agriculture price intervention, particularly when the agricultural procedure is used for industrial uses.

Scandizo and Bruce (1980) developed partial equilibrium methodologies for measuring the effects of agricultural price intervention. Whereas Timber (1986) examined the scope and limitations to agricultural price policy in a partial equilibrium framework.

Inter-relationships can be developed in the context of agriculture and rest of the economy, agriculture and industry, balance imbalance between agriculture and non-agricultural policies, applying economic variables to measure performance and role of particular sector in the economy.

Similar other inter-relationships can be developed in the context of :

1. Final demand linkages relating to agriculturist's final demand for non-agricultural goods and to non-agriculturist's demand for agriculture goods.
2. Intermediate demand linkages including the demand of agro-producers for non-agricultural inputs and *vice versa.*
3. Wage goods linkages, whereby changes in agricultural prices affect through nominal wage indexation, non-agricultural wages, production costs and (mark up) prices.
4. Saving and investment linkages.
5. Fiscal linkages involving public expenditure allotted to agriculture sector in UDCs as public revenue from agriculture.
6. Balance of payment linkage through agricultural exports and agriculture's direct and indirect import requirement.

D.M. Nachane *et al.,* (1989) examined the exchange of products between agricultural and non-agricultural sectors of the Indian economy. They concentrated on the supply or the forward linkages of agricultural sector and the demand or backward linkages of agriculture in particular or of the rural sector in general with other sectors.

Agarwal (1992) tries to explore the linkages in the context of a state.

Bhattacharya and Mitra (1989) examined the nature and causes of industrial growth in place of slow agricultural growth.

They hypothesised that the nature of the agriculture-industry relationship would depend crucially on the relative growth of income and employment in not only the industrial sector but also in tertiary sector. If income grows faster than employment, then it tends to generate more demand for industrial goods *vis-a-vis* agricultural goods, and consequently the disparity between industrial and agricultural growth widens. Fast development of industry and tertiary sector in India has brought employment opportunities in supply and demand linkages and *vice versa.*

In India priority is given to agriculture in public sector investment. Agriculture being a core sector and dominates in most of the parameters generates less employment opportunities. Whereas industry and tertiary sector generates more employment opportunities as compared to agriculture sector. This results to demand the industrial goods more as compared to agricultural goods.

Agriculture first *Vs.* industry first was the much debated subject in agriculture-industry linkages (Chakraborthy, 1987). Theoretically the inter-relationship has been categorically explored by physiocrats first in 17th century. The issue of surplus (agricultural surplus first and industrial surplus after industrial revolution) was discussed by the physiocrats. During the 19th century, classical approach explored agriculture-industry linkages, wherein the role of agriculture in relaxing the saving constraints is signified. Saving act as a constraint in the process of capital formation, because distribution of income is weighted in favour of classes with low propensities to save. Profits are saved and invested. Then two sector model was developed by illustrating wider significance to cautions reinvestment of the capital sector's profit or surplus. Fei-Ranis then systematically developed the issue in a theoretical framework. Keynes (1936), Rodan (1943), Murkes (1953), Richard Kahn (1972), Kaleki (1953) explored the issue of full employment as that level of activity at which the effective demand elasticity of output and employment is zero. Kaldor (1976) stressed an urge of forced saving for required relationship between agriculture and industry (terms of trade). Wage good constraint where capital is less and labour is underused is the central idea of Kaldor's analysis.

Neo-classical approach [Jorgenion (1961), J.M. Homby (1968) and Kelhey *et al.*, (1973)] has signified full employment efficiency and price distortions.

An issue of terms of trade between agriculture and industry encounters a range of mixed evidences. Incidentally the relationship becomes more complicated in this process. There is a wide range of exhaustive literature so far explored in this section since 1970s. Task Force on Terms of Trade (1995) has reviewed various methods of calculating terms of trade. It recognised the positive role of terms of trade for increasing agricultural production and income. It also recognises the technological upgradation, infrastructure and institutional arrangements etc. The critical role of terms of trade cannot be ignored.

Agriculture-industry linkages particularly in LDCs has been a long debated issue with renewed and applied relevance in the context of India's economy particularly since 1960s *i.e.*, after Green Revolution. Specifically the issue comes in focus when non-acceleration of growth and concurrent stagnation in the industrial front occurs. Industrial front can be categorised into SSI, LSI, capital intensive, consumer's basic goods, consumer durable etc. The historical literature on inter-sectoral linkages in the growth process generally emphasises the significance of agriculture as a prime supplier of wage goods and raw-materials to industry which is termed as 'supply linkages'. And as a provider of major output for industrial goods which is termed as 'demand linkages'. In both side linkages, the tertiary sector plays an important role in inter-sectoral linkages in the growth process. In fact agriculture-industry linkages becomes more complicated in growth process.

Bhattacharya (1982) classified industries as : (i) Resources based; (ii) Demand based; (iii) Skill based; (iv) Ancillary based. Resources based industries subsequently are linked to agriculture and subsidiary sectors in the economy. They are grouped into : (a) Agro based; (b) Forest based; (c) Animal Husbandry and Poultry based; (d) Mineral based and Marine based. Agro-based industries directly establishes the link with agriculture sector. Agro-based industries are generally classified into

(1) Agro-produce manufacturing industries; (2) Agro-produce processing industries; (3) Agro-input producing industries and (4) Agro-service industries.

Agro-industries can further be classified on the basis of size, structure and factors favouring and non-favouring in determining their size. Sandip Sarkar (1995) has analysed a different view in respect of classification of agro-industries. Austin (1987) categorised agro-industries into three stages on the basis of degree of processing. Higher degree of processing is accompanied with capital investment, technological complexities and management requirement and is characterised by higher value added. Shrivastava (1989) divided Indian agro-industries into manual-mechanical, mechanical, mechanical-chemical and chemical signifying higher degree of processing in that order. He observed some movement of agro-industries from mechanical-based to chemical based processing but still mechanical-based processing dominates. Singh and Vyasulu (1990) observed the domination of primary processing in Indian agro-industries. Panchamukhi (1975) categorised the industries into direct backward linkages and total linkages.

Agriculture-industry linkages raises number of economic issues such as (i) Pricing of agricultural produce *i.e.,* raw-material, which is used by the industrial sector; (ii) Conversion cost of the industrial groups; (iii) Parity prices (comparative input prices and output prices) and terms of trade, pricing of substitute items, estimation of sectoral shares in national product etc. While analysing terms of trade between industrial and agricultural sector, we conveniently classify the issue into three groups : (a) Prices of competing crops; (b) Prices of competing industrial products and (c) Input and output prices. This issue requires separate thinking to explore the fact behind the gamut.

In a country like India, Government intervention in fixing SMP for agricultural produce is inevitable because of peculiar characteristics of agricultural sector. Social and economic justice are the twin objectives of socialistic pattern of society. Besides the issue of pricing becomes more significant when one sector is supplying the raw-material to another sector. Nearly 65 to 70 per cent of industrial conversion cost of sugar is shared by sugarcane. Pricing of foodgrains is a different issue as its nature of requirement is basic. Normally sugar may not be an essential commodity like that of foodgrains. Sugar has different sweetening alternatives, most competing is jaggery.

Sugarcane is a commercial crop. Even a subsistence (MF and SF) size holders, now-a-days cultivate sugarcane as their means of life. So, the traditional concept of subsistence farming (*i.e.*, undertaking only foodgrains cultivation) is changing. Under the traditional subsistence farming system, only marketable surplus of foodgrains were sold out in nearby local markets. Now the assured markets for processing sugarcane is made available by establishing sugar co-operatives by the cane growers themselves. Automatically cane growers have a collective ownership on sugar co-operatives. Actually cane growers are collectively processing their sugarcane by setting the co-operative sugar factories. Farmers, by constitution, have a right to process their crops. In this process, in fact, there arises no problem SMP of sugarcane etc. In case of privately owned or managed sugar factories, the industrialists have to purchase sugarcane as an important raw-material for production of sugar. Private industrialists have to depend on (1) farmer's will to cultivate sugarcane, (2) his will to sell his produce to a particular industrialist. In this regard, there is an effective link between two sectors. SMP is essential in this system.

Now-a-days an entrepreneur of agro-based industrial undertaking feel essential to have his own farms for cultivating the required crops as a source of raw-material supply to his factory. This system is normally observed in case of tea and coffee industry. Even in early 1950s, in the erstwhile Bombay province, the efforts were made by private industries to undertake the contract farmings for sugarcane cultivation and processing the same by erecting the sugar factories in the nearby sugarcane farms so as to keep the recovery high. This tendency had been interrupted by a triumph of co-operative sugar factory in Pravaranagar (District Ahmednagar) during late 1940s. The co-operative sector has linked both the sectors effectively. In this case actually there is no need to have SMP.

New terms like contract farming and corporate farming

are generally advocated by the industrialists so as to have their hold in the supply of raw-material from agriculture sector for producing a agro-based manufacturing products. In this system also there arises no problem of setting SMP. Thus SMP becomes essential only when the owners of the raw-material and its processors or manufacturers differ.

3

HOW PRICES ARE FIXED?

The British Government after World War-I had obliged to give a guarantee to the cereal prices. Even during the depression of 1929s, U.S.A. Government had coacted to enact legislation to bestow guarantee to agricultural produce prices. Since then a convention of assuring minimum prices to agricultural produce continued.

During the World War-II, minimum prices were fixed for wheat, jowar, maize with a view to increase their production. The price policy particularly for foodgrains was an outcome of the World War, which was dealt with the problems of inflation and acute food shortages. The policy was introduced so as to keep down the cost of living and to stabilize the prices.

The Committee on Food Policy-1947 was assigned to deal with sufficient food production in India. Whereas the Committee of 1950s, was dealt with food procurement and recommended to institute rationing scheme in India. In response to the approbation of these two Committees, the foodgrains was decontrolled. Due to which the foodgrain prices begun to hike. This naturally bulldozed the Government to impose a partial control on foodgrains. Consequently, Government had appointed the Food Inquiry Committee in 1957 to study the issues related to foodgrains production. The Committee strongly recommended to had a complete control on foodgrains prices. Thus the policy was consumer oriented, which included, (a) Procurement of foodgrains at a lower rate by the Government; (b) Import of foodgrains and (c) Equitable distribution of foodgrains to non-producing consumers through rationing. After that the policy of gradual relaxation of controls was introduced. Free trade of foodgrains was decided upon. It was in early 1950s, that the process of minimum support prices had been contemplated. However, Foodgrains Policy Committee (1947, interim report) reiterated to increase the production of foodgrains within the earliest possible time instead of permanent control of foodgrains and imports.

In the later part of 1955, the prices of foodgrains started to rise. As a result, Government tend to protect the consumers. Scientific procedures of price determination had been made practicable only after appointment of the Foodgrains Prices Committee (Jha Committee), 1964. The committee highlighted the difficulties in determining the agricultural prices. To protect the interests of both agriculturists and consumers was a task before the Committee. The Committee therefore, recommended to establish the Agricultural Price Commission (APC). Which was expected to look into the optimum use of land resources and work as an incentive to increase agricultural produce and equilibrate the demand and supply of agricultural produce. There is no provision of establishing separate APC for each crop since its beginning. However, the policy aimed to (a) Announce minimum price for major foodgrains (paddy, jowar, wheat, gram, maize and sugarcane) well in advance of a sowing season; (b) Fixing the procurement price normally less than market price for purchasing the marketable surplus; (c) To operate the public distribution system for low income groups; (d) To develop the buffer-stock for emergencies and to protect the extreme price fluctuations. But the APC had to face number of problems to deal with the crucial issues of agricultural prices. V.M. Dandekar (December 1965, Arthvignan) had explicitly developed the guidelines for the policy and programmes.

The APC latterly renamed as CACP had fixed some norms in determining the agricultural prices. They were : (i) Cost of production; (ii) Risk factor; (iii) Input prices; (iv) Market prices; (v) Demand and supply; (vi) Effects on industrial structure; (vii) Expenses on standard of living; (viii) Effects on general prices; (ix) Parity approach and (x) Motivations etc.

Standing Technical Committee (1967) administered the

scientific estimation of indices of input costs of cultivation adopting the farm management studies. This had been accepted by the Statistical and Economic Bureau in 1968 to launch a comprehensive scheme for studying the cost of cultivation of principal crops. In its procedure it collects representative data on inputs and outputs per hectare from the individual size classes selected from cluster area. The comprehensive scheme ensured to collect the cost according to a certain uniform concepts *viz.* A, B, C etc. Same method had been followed to estimate the cost of cultivation of some selected crops since 1970-71. Meanwhile Special Expert Committee on Cost and Production Estimate (Sen Committee) 1979 had been appointed to study how to account and estimate the cost incurred due to farm management activities (time, skill and decision). Some important views were expressed by the Special Expert Committee in connection with transport cost and farm management cost etc.

The cost concepts used in as cost A1, A2, B and C are as under :

Cost A1 :
(i) Value of hired human labour,
(ii) Value of hired bullock labour,
(iii) Value of owned bullock labour,
(iv) Hired machinery charges,
(v) Value of owned machine labour,
(vi) Value of seed (both farm produced and purchased),
(vii) Value of insecticides and pesticides,
(viii) Value of manure (owned and purchased),
(ix) Value of fertilizers,
(x) Depreciation on implements and farm buildings,
(xi) Irrigation charges,
(xii) Land revenue, cesses, and other taxes,

(xiii) Interest on working capital,

(xiv) Miscellaneous expenses (artisans etc.)

Cost A2 : Cost A1 + rent for leased-in-land

Cost B : Cost A2 + imputed rental value of owned land (less land revenue paid thereon) + imputed interest on owned fixed capital (excluding land)

Cost C : Cost B + imputed value of family labour.

However, vital efforts were made in the Third Five Year Plan to focus on the issues of determining the agricultural prices. "The producer of foodgrains must get a reasonable return. The farmer, in other words, should be assured that, the prices of foodgrains and the other commodities that he produces will not be allowed to fall below a reasonable minimum." The idea of support prices was introduced to protect the producer's interest, whereas a limit to fusing prices protect the consumers.

The establishment of APC had however, created a confidence among the producers. This was an incentive to them. Simultaneously a precaution was took to account that, cost of living and cost of industrial activities should not hike. Besides a care was also taken for the first time to equate the terms of trade of agriculture sector to that of rest of the sectors in India since 1977. The scope and intensity of CACP has been vitalized in 1978. Input prices and output prices have been correlated and considered while determining the agricultural prices.

Every country has its own strategy to fix the agricultural prices *e.g.*, minimum price guarantee, support prices, fixed prices, incentive prices, price range guarantee, procurement prices, statutory minimum prices, etc. However, the principle is near about the same. By the way to determine the agricultural prices is a difficult task. The decision to cultivate a crop depends on individual decisions, whereas the price of agricultural produce has been determined through market mechanism, the market mostly remains imperfect. As a result support prices are essential. Fixation of price depends upon different conditions and norms. Minimum support prices is a kind of insurance to agriculture sector. On the contrary maximum prices are allowed to grow according to this category. In other norms, the price range has been fixed within which the price can fluctuate.

After the World War-II an idea of fixed prices was introduced, but during the corresponding period this idea has been converted into incentive scheme. The intention behind this was that, agricultural prices are normally fixed on two systems (a) Minimum prices which are fixed every year; (b) Procurement prices declared during khariff and rabbi season by the Government. Both these types of prices are important as a Government's policy.

Normally industrial prices are hedged to a maximum limit, whereas, agricultural prices are hedged to minimum limit. It is obvious that, agriculture is different from that of industrial sector. The intention behind the administered prices in LDCs is to stabilize price and income with that of the pace of growth and development in India.

Thus the fundamental objectives of administered prices in LDCs are : (a) To increase the credibility of the farmers in farming by way of increasing investment, production and the use of modern technology; (b) To attain the target of food production; (c) To increase the marketable surplus and (d) To protect the consumers of agricultural products.

Generally agricultural prices are fixed on the principal norm of the purpose behind the pricing. For example, whether Government wants to insure against the damage of agricultural produce or to increase the agricultural yield or to increase the income of the farmers, etc. However, commonly, following norms are contemplated while fixing the administered prices *viz*., (i) Cost of cultivation; (ii) Food policy; (iii) General price level; (iv) Demand and supply forecasting; (v) Earning of foreign money; (vi) Alternative crops; (vii) Effects of agricultural labourers; (viii) Wage structure of industrial workers and changes in standard of living etc.

Economics of agricultural pricing ponders, four methods of fixing the pricing *viz*., production cost, agricultural income, parity and multi-factor analysis (Kahlon and Tyagi, 1983).

Cost of production method counts each item of cost of production in arbitrating the agricultural produce. Sometime cost indices are accounted. But it lacks in counting the varying individual cost estimation and the barriers in estimation of return on capital investment and depreciation etc. Farmers only account the current cost of cultivation rather than issues covered in the costing pattern.

Under the scheme of agricultural income, farmers have been given a guarantee of net income, based on the size of farm or the type of crop. But this scheme lacks in fixing the norms of size of farms depending on the quality of soil and group of farmers holding such sizes.

Parity norm entrusts two factors, historical average prices and actual price paid to the farmers. This helps to equalize the agricultural prices for a long period, also keeps purchasing prices equal. Particularly, this method lacks in its scientificness and experiments.

Multi-factor norm cogitate number of factors *e.g.,* changes in demand are estimated on the basis of averages of international prices, future opportunities, cost of cultivation, wage structure and general prices, etc. But unexpectedly the foregoing prices are taken into account. While fixing the corresponding prices rather than judging the above factors.

Accounting the share of input costs in the total volume of cost structure is one of the cogitation while inculcating the agricultural prices. It has been reckoned that 22.87 per cent of the total cost of paddy in Andhra Pradesh is associated to purchase input costs in 1978-79. In Punjab 34 per cent of total cost relate to the purchased input cost of wheat cultivation in 1978-79. And in Maharashtra around 26.8 per cent of total cost was associated to purchase input costs of sugarcane cultivation in 1977-78. The share of input cost in the total cost basically depends upon the prices of input items.

Under the scheme of parity index, prices of various crops are juxtaposed on the background of the different regional variations. While ascertaining the administered prices, the general price level is taken into account. But this norm was discarded by the APC in its first report. However, the ensuing scheme has been justified by Dr. Rajkrishna and others commencing that, demand and supply forces in the market must be accounted while agreeing with the agricultural prices, because market prices are accounted while concluding the minimum agricultural prices. Since then this norm has been accepted. Thus the scheme of parity index identifies the rational and efficient use of farm unit and farm technology.

Number of studies have been carried out to measure the price elasticity of supply and demand of agricultural produce. This gave off number of approaches and analyses. Which are in fact the guidelines to the CACP. Both sugar and sugarcane are the price elastic commodities, as a result Government control is inevitable. Particularly price elasticity of sugarcane is always less than one. Rajkrishna and Chandrashekhar Kumar have explored the shortrun and longrun sugarcane price elasticity in U.P. and Meerut. Which was ranging 0.60 and 0.34 in U.P. and 0.44600 and 0.2166 in Meerut respectively.

4

SUGARCANE POLICY

Ordinarily, in the recent context of agricultural prices, the prices of final industrial products *vis-a-vis* its cost structure are influential if raw-material is originating from agricultural sector.

There are two procedures of computing the cost of sugar (a) Forward working approach and (b) Backward working approach. In the first proposition, the cost of production is computed beginning from the price of raw-material to that of cost incurred to produce the final product. In this process the price of raw-material is fixed earlier. In case of latter proposition, the cost of production excluding the cost of raw-material has been subtracted from the market price of the final product. Residual is the price of agricultural produce (*i.e.*, sugarcane), which can be distributed to its producers. In this case, there is a possibility of showing extravagant expenses as its cost of conversion. Besides, the factory management has no role to show its managerial skills in this respect. Sugar is controlled by the Central Government. Both the levy price and market prices of sugar is taken into account while determining the sugarcane price. Under the scheme of parity approach the prices of various other crops alternative to sugarcane are also considered. Similarly input-output prices are taken note of. Such type of parity indices are computed to attain to a certain scientific level of minimum support prices.

It was before 1932, the possibility of producing white crystallized sugar from sugarcane in Maharashtra was potentially identified. But the industrialists had no confidence in getting sufficient supply of sugarcane. So, the idea was left behind.

However, an opportunity of sugarcane cultivation was conceived alongwith the Nira Canals in Bombay presidency through Government efforts creating an increasing attachment to the crop. The sugarcane block system[1] (IIC, 1902; Viswesvaraya, 1901, 1903) was introduced as an effective irrigation policy.

Even after independence (upto 1960), the main centre of sugar industry was located in northern India (U.P., Bihar, Haryana, Punjab). In 1920, U.P. and Bihar produced 60 per cent of sugarcane in India, and had 13 out of 18 sugar factories.

There were only 3 sugar factories in Bombay Province when the sugar prices had hiked in 1920s. However, two out of three were closed soon, because of (i) growing cost of cultivation of sugarcane as compared to U.P. The costs per acre were 70 per cent lower in North than in Deccan (Rs. 6.65 per tonne in North and Rs. 8.75 in Bombay). Indian Tariff Board in 1930 estimated the cost at Rs. 7.50 per tonne in North as against Rs. 17.75 in Bombay. The cost of cultivation in Bombay Deccan in 1920 was around Rs. 80 — 85 per acre and yield rate was 26 tonnes per acre (I.S.C., 1921). (ii) There was a tradition of paying sugarcane prices through middlemen in U.P. which could not reach Maharashtra, (iii) The price of jaggery was higher than sugar. The sugar prices had begun to fell down since 1924.

Indian Sugar Committee (ISC) 1921 reiterated the fact that, Indian sugar factories are small and inefficient, also found difficult to obtain adequate supply of cane. For efficient utilization of the factory's capacity it was thought essential to schedule factory field co-ordination. So, the private factory owners started to lease-in the sugarcane fields for cultivation and development. This also helps to keep the recovery at the maximum level, because cane should be harvested at peak maturity, when sucrose is at a maximum.

Thus, the initial growth of sugar industry in Bombay was due to semi-arid environment. When the Deccan canals came into operation in 1880s, the enterprising cultivators begun to discover the profits in sugarcane. Before, that sugarcane was a garden crop, which was used to prepare jaggery (Attwood, 1993).

Sugar Industry (Protection) Act, 1932 was a landmark in the history of sugar industry. But without sugarcane no sugar industry can operate. Consequently, Government of India was compelled to pass Sugarcane Act in 1934. Meanwhile the industry's management had started to cultivate sugarcane by leasing-in the land pieces from the farmers even when a large group of farmers was reluctant to lease-out their land areas. The Bombay Government had considered, helping the factories by compulsory leasing along the new canals (Deccan Canal Financial Improvement Committee, 1932). But it was not operated because of the fear that, the farmers would not support this, there would be a strong opposition. This was diagnosed by the eminent scholars like S.T. Tambavekar, and he cautioned his leader Vithalrao Vikhe Patil; Chairman of the 40 Village Bagaitdar Sanghtana (Laud 1986). However, Government was in favour of factories. So, what it did was that, perennial canal irrigation was guaranteed to the sugar factory's area. Factory areas were demarcated and declared (Vartak 1966). This was the first step to establish operational zones for sugar factories in Maharashtra. Canal irrigation was an incentive to cultivate sugarcane. The sugarcane was being cultivated by factories and simultaneously by farmers (*i.e.*, Malis) for producing jaggery. "Irrigation frontier" (Attwood 1993) was motivated by migrant Malis of Sasvad in Nira Canal area. The sugarcane farms were leased-in at the rate of Rs. 25 (5 per cent of the total cost) in 1914 for cultivation of sugarcane (*Ibid.*). The rate of return of this crop was high. This technique was followed by the local tenants. As a result the demand for leasing-in was rising. The number of Canals had gone to 6 in 1936, with irrigation area of 2,42,000 acres including 40,000 acres of sugarcane in Bombay region. In 1890 only, 300 acres of sugarcane was grown along the Nira canal which rose to 5500 acres at the beginning of 20th century.

The War time demand for sugar was a boon to develop the sugar industry with great hopes. In 1930-40 decade, the private sugar factories in U.P. and Bihar were dominating in sugar affairs. This made the dominating mills to form a cartel : the Indian Sugar Syndicate (ISS) in 1937. Indian Sugar Syndicate strive to reduce overproduction and competition. The canegrowers in U.P. had formed the co-operative unions. After independence, the canegrowers started to demand high pric• to their canes. During the period, when gur prices rose relative to cane prices, the farmers used their cane to manufacture gur. This disrupted cane supplies to the sugar factories. In 1947, ISS posed a resolution to prohibit the gur production particularly in the operational areas of the sugar factories. This resolution was vigorously opposed by the growers. Meanwhile, the Pravaranagar experience in co-operative enterprising was proved successful.

ISS policy to reduce overproduction and competition was opposed by Bombay factory owners *viz.*, Deccan Sugar Manufacturers Association. Though the industry got off to a slow start in Bombay, it was clearly ready to expand by late 1930s and early 1940s, because of all above situation in the region. The Maharashtrian stalwarts and scholars like Y.B. Chavan, Annasaheb Shinde and D.R. Gadgil motivated the Govt. to set a more favourable regulatory measures to co-operative sugar enterprises.

After independence, Government has set up a regulatory system to promote and expand this 'lead industry'. The first major step was to restrict all new licenses to co-operative enterprises. This was opposed by the private factory owners. The domination of private mill owners had slowly worsened to a few in Maharashtra.

The second regulatory measure was introduced to protect the interest of cane growers in 1955, which was revised in 1966. Prior to the emergence of Maharashtra State, the State Government committed to buy the shares of Pravara Co-operative Sugar Factory and to guarantee to its debt (Gadgil, 1955). In 1954, Government of Maharashtra recommended the Central Government that, the licenses to new sugar factories be given preferentially to co-operative enterprises. At the same time, the State Government drew up the Central Government's attention towards the list of twelve sites, where the supply of sugarcane would be sufficient for new factories and where co-operative would be encouraged (Baviskar, 1990). The role of then Finance Minister, Vaikunthabhai Mehta was pivotal in making these decisions. The Central Co-operative Bank (Maharashtra State Co-op. Bank) has played a great significant role in mobilizing and supplying financial resources to new sugar factories in the State.

Since then there is a phenomenal growth of sugarcane area, production and yield of sugarcane in Maharashtra (See Table 1). The establishment of co-operative credit agencies in rural area and central initiatives in land reforms motivated the farmers to undertake sugarcane crop. Within the vicinity of the sugar factories, commercial peasantry has grown up, as there is a assured market for their sugarcane crop. Co-operative Sugar factories are active in promoting other kinds of co-operative enterprises since their establishments.

POLITICS OF CANE PRICES

Co-operative sugar factories in Western Maharashtra have occupied a prominent place in State's politics. The best performance are rife with political competition and fractionalism. So, the economic efficiency and political competition seems paradoxical. No factory works efficiently which serves an arena for fractional politics. Corruption and mismanagement restrains the economic efficiency. Factory's economic efficiency rests in paying remunerative cane prices to its share members. High cane prices are likely to carry political weight in the region.

Each sugar factory has several sides of competition.

(a) Competition in supplies of sugarcane;

(b) Competition in technical efficiency;

(c) Competition in cane prices and

(d) Competition in establishing co-operative complexes.

Sugar factories compete to expand sugarcane area, if sugarcane supply is scarce. Co-operative sugar factories are very cautious in allotting a new membership to a particular person or to a group. Rivals of ruling group could not be accepted as a member of particular co-operative sugar factory with the intention that, they may trouble and hinder the management of the factory. Sugar factories will give stress on to increase the sugarcane area by its existing members rather than accepting new members.

TABLE 1

Area, Production and Yield of Sugarcane in Maharashtra

(Area - 000 hectares
Production - 000 tonnes
Yield - kg. per hectare)

Years	Area	Production	Yield
1952-53	85	559	6,576
1953-54	75	538	7,173
1954-55	85	633	7,447
1955-56	91	682	7,495
1956-57	103	789	7,660
1957-58	113	877	7,761
1958-59	118	903	7,653
1959-60	133	978	7,353
1960-61	156	1,156	7,410
1961-62	154	1,152	7,481
1962-63	135	1,020	7,556
1963-64	140	1,130	8,093
1964-65	148	1,002	6,770
1965-66	161	1,054	6,561
1966-67	161	1,114	6,940
1967-68	165	1,189	7,206
1968-69	170	1,428	7,501
1969-70	222	1,625	7,317
1970-71	217	1,679	7,729
1971-72	182	1,298	7,137
1972-73	146	1,311	8,982
1973-74	165	1,414	8,592
1974-75	185	1,853	10,006
1975-76	212	18,870	8,909
1976-77	241	21,499	8,924
1977-78	246	23,320	9,479
1978-79	244	22,482	9,210
1979-80	222	19,819	8,927
1980-81	256	23,591	9,089
1981-82	298	28,731	9,640
1982-83	325	31,320	9,610
1983-84	294	26,549	9,030
1984-85	292	26,367	9,010
1985-86	264	23,706	8,970

(Contd.)

Years	Area	Production	Yield
1986-87	280	24,091	8,610
1987-88	292	24,983	8,560
1988-89	314	25,500	8,110
1989-90	383	34,009	8,870
1990-91	444	38,426	8,650
1991-92	456	38,758	8,500
1992-93	453	30,850	4,213
1993-94	344	27,892	8,110
1994-95	518	44,260	8,550
1995-96	580	46,656	8,040
1996-97	475	40,375	8,500

Fixing of zones or their operational area to each sugar factory is a task before the Government. Particularly, the task becomes vigorous when there arises a shortage of sugarcane. Some villages in Western Maharashtra comes under the operational areas of two-three sugar factories in their vicinity. Two nearby sugar factories are political allies, ultimately they always remain economic competitors more or less openly for the supplies of sugarcane, in showing mark up technical efficiencies and in paying remunerative sugarcane prices.

Most ultimate force behind the competition is the sugarcane price and establishing varieties of co-operative units. Co-operatives are paying the additional cane prices after deducting the cost of production of sugar. The popularity of the management lies directly in cane price. A co-operative, which belongs to the political leader, is expected to pay more remunerative cane prices. Such factories perform more social costs due to area development activities. The intense competition in elections of management board translates into intense competition to offer higher sugarcane prices. To avoid such competitions, the State Government appointed a Cane Price Committee headed by Chief Minister. The committee consists of several Cabinet Ministers, Director of Sugar, Chairman of 'Sakhar Sangh'; the Federation of Co-operative Sugar Factories. This Committee inspect the accounts of each sugar factory after the close of the crushing season and renders a decision on the highest cane prices, which it may pay, such prices are termed as State Administered

Prices (SAP). The SAPs are generally fixed on the basis of some norms *e.g.*, financial obligations for future, maintenance and replacement of equipments, cane prices of nearby factories, cost of production of sugar, etc. In Maharashtra, there is no uniformity of sugarcane prices paid by the sugar factories (See Table 6). Price differentials affect the cane supply, particularly from non-members outside the area of operation. This becomes more vigorous at the time of cane shortages. Sugar factories at such instances initiate to acquire the gate-cane purchasing, because member's sugarcane is an assured cane supply, which can be crushed any time during the season. However, at the time of cane supply abundancy, sugar factories have to prefer the member's sugarcane and who have made an agreement of cane supply much earlier before the beginning of the sugar season.

Political rivalry is a spur to economic performance while the demands of economic competition serve to keep political misbehaviour within reasonable limits (Attwood, 1993). But only well-managed sugar factories can pay better prices. In most cases, innovations and expansion of productive capacities are also determined on the line of the nearby factories. Expansion of crushing capacities means expansion of the constituencies of the directors (Attwood, 1993).

Another political aspect of the sugar industry in Maharashtra is that, each fraction of the political parties tried to acquire licenses for operating the sugar factories in Maharashtra with state support, even ignoring the technical factors and feasibilities of their locations and economies of scale. The factories were given sanction even in dry areas also, where sugarcane is grown very sporadically. The present sickness of the industry originates in such licensing policy, economies of scale and the locational aspects of the sugar factories.

Directly or indirectly, the next generation of the founder leaders of the co-operative sugar factories is managing the sugar factories and continued to dominate in the regional politics as an ancestral inheritance. This has been criticized by the people. The party or a group who possess a power of managing co-operative. Lift irrigation scheme can obtain the power to rule the Grampanchayat and Co-operative Credit Society in a village. The domination of a group or party is being judged on the basis of how many co-operative societies and institutions, the group is handling and has retained them under its power.

There is a politics based on the economics of the region. Managing the agricultural inputs and outputs are the main institutional sources of power politics *e.g.*, credit, markets, irrigation etc. On this background the rural leadership has emerged and spread with an effective chain of leadership from the Centre to the Grampanchayats.

NOTE

1. The basic features of the system were as under : (See Attwood, 1993)

(a) The cultivators from certain area (which constitute the block) can apply for canal water for six years, and Government would guarantee to supply the water. The cultivators ultimately would be more willing to invest in the preparation of their fields to use irrigation water for several years. The temptation of sugarcane profits was the best inducement for getting peasants to demand irrigation on a regular basis. Once irrigation had been guaranteed for several years, rich farmers would date to invest in sugarcane (expensive) crop.

(b) Block irrigation would be charged at fixed rate per acre regardless of the crops growth.

(c) Perennial irrigation suitable for cane cultivation would be provided on 1/3 of each block and other 2/3 would receive irrigation for eight months, suitable for double cropping in the monsoon and winter seasons. And no irrigation to this proportion of the block during hot season. This would help to establish the crop rotation.

(d) In the cluster of 30 villages under the block system, the total block area would be about 21 per cent of the cultivable area under command of the canal, and the area of perennial irrigation would thus be only 7 per cent (1/3 or 21 per cent) in these villages. The total block area would be 18000 acres with 6000 acres of cane planted each year. Distributing the blocks among all 30 villages would encourage local cultivators to take up sugarcane and correct the imbalance caused by immigrant, entrepreneurs, clustered near the market towns, who were using a large share of the water.

(e) The distribution of perennial irrigation water on this basis could not be guaranteed below the first 65 miles of the canal. Preference would be given on the last 40 miles, serving 33 villages for seasonal irrigation. The stored water available for rabbi crops would irrigate from 23000 to 33000 acres, on the amount of rainfall collected in the previous monsoon season.

5

COST OF CONVERSION

We have peculiar type of varieties of conversion costs of sugarcane processing and sugar manufacturing in various sugar co-operatives in Maharashtra. The BICP has developed nine point norms of cost calculations in sugar factories. While arriving at the levy sugar prices and fixation of sugar prices under P.D.S., the cost of harvesting and transport of sugarcane is not considered by the BICP. The National Federation of Co-operative Factories had communicated the BICP in 1986 to take into account the cost of harvest and transport of sugarcane as the co-operative sugar factories are managing it in Maharashtra.

According to the Report of the Sugar Industry Enquiry Commission (1974), after deducting all types of taxes, the sugar industry earned a profit of 5.4 per cent per year. The public sector factories were earning 5.3 per cent profit and the public limited factories were earning 8.4 per cent of profit. The rate of profit by private factories was to the tune of 2.8 per cent and co-operative sector factories were earning the profit rate around one per cent. Since 1980s the rate of profit of co-operatives is further declining because of the increased input prices. During 1980-81 season, sugar factories in Maharashtra have earned the profit of Rs. 417 lakhs, whereas the loss was Rs. 3,011 lakhs. This trend has continued since then. In 1983-84 season too, the total loss borne by sugar co-operatives was Rs. 32,128 lakhs. While the profit was only Rs. 368 lakhs. Only 4 sugar co-operatives were in profit in 1985.

The accumulated losses of 75 co-operatives sugar factories as at the end of 1984-85 season are of the order of Rs. 195.77

crores, out of which an amount of Rs. 64.62 crores was the business loss. Even the four units, which have made profit, have altogether made a meagre profit of Rs. 5.03 lakhs only. This results into capital erosion and reflected in the position of payment or default position. An average amount of Rs. 24.31 crores as principal and Rs. 10.38 crores as interest thereon totalling Rs. 34.69 crores was the default committed by 36 co-operative sugar factories in 1985 (See Table 2). The accumulated losses of 57 co-operative sugar factories has gone up to Rs. 34,063.63 lakhs by the end of 1995-96 season (See Table 6). The accumulated losses of Co-operative Sugar Factories on 31st March, 1998 went up to Rs. 698.18 crores (Godbole Committee Report, 1999, p. 73). As on 30 September, 1998, the overdues of IDBI alone amounted to Rs. 117.34 crore. IDBI believes that, some of the factories are wilful defaulters. The sickness of this core sector will have large consequences for the State budget in future.

TABLE 2

Statement Showing Total Accumulated Losses of Co-operative Sugar Factories as per Published Balance Sheet as on 30th September, 1985

Sl. No.	Name of the Factory	Total Losses	Business Cash Losses	Profit
1	2	3	4	5
1.	Bhogawati (Kolhapur)	*17.75	—	—
2.	Chha. Shahu	*7.52	—	—
3.	Datta (Shiroli)	306.65	191.57	—
4.	Daulat	*87.62	—	—
5.	Dudhganga Vedganga	118.10	9.08	—
6.	Datta (Asurle)	52.19	NA	—
7.	Gadhinglaj	107.90	21.50	—
8.	Kumbhi-Kasari	131.78	—	—
9.	Panchaganga	95.36	—	—
10.	Warana	360.97	167.31	—
11.	Hutatma Kisan Ahir	140.03	2.36	—
12.	Mahakali	—	—	0.16

—Contd.

1	2	3	4	5
13.	Manganga	—	—	1.99
14.	Shetkari (Sangli)	88.58	35.09	—
15.	Vishwas	485.52	161.10	—
16.	Rajarambapu Patil	23.21	—	—
17.	Balasaheb Desai	67.00	4.63	—
18.	Krishna	332.21	—	—
19.	Sahyadri	99.68	—	—
20.	Ajikyatara	130.05	—	—
21.	Satara	205.24	127.52	—
22.	Shriram	*53.38	15.37	—
23.	Bhima (Patas)	*145.29	—	—
24.	Chhatrapati (Pune)	15.21	1.87	—
25.	Malegaon	16.00	—	—
26.	Someshwar	41.94	2.99	—
27.	Vighnahar	*240.32	122.09	—
28.	Yeshwant (Theur)	* 94.51	—	—
29.	Bhima (Solapur)	920.28	136.67	—
30.	Bhogawati (Solapur)	663.16	150.91	—
31.	Shankar	68.95	32.04	—
32.	Siddeswar (Kumthe)	6.51	—	—
33.	Vitthal	91.68	—	—
34.	Yashwant (Akluj)	41.49	—	—
35.	Girna	74.61	71.12	—
36.	Kadwa	545.10	96.21	—
37.	Karmveer Kakasaheb Wagh	201.44	—	—
38.	Nasik	646.18	210.09	—
39.	Niphad	75.04	68.85	—
40.	Vasantdada Patil	350.81	9.95	—
41.	Ashok	146.90	53.11	—
42.	Dnyaneswar	90.97	—	—
43.	Ganesh	232.29	107.27	—
44.	Jagdamba	348.89	195.05	—
45.	Kopergaon	27.83	—	—
46.	Mula	42.36	—	—
47.	Pravara	—	—	1.01
48.	Parner	*269.29	NA	—
49.	Rahuri	12.91	—	—

—*Contd.*

1	2	3	4	5
50.	Sangmner Bhag	—	—	1.87
51.	Sanjivani	73.40	—	—
52.	Shirgonda	59.43	—	—
53.	Vridheshwar	370.78	228.06	—
54.	Panzarakan	309.65	*224.84	—
55.	Satpuda Tapi	195.74	68.63	—
56.	Sanjay	424.40	NA	—
57.	Shirpur	273.24	4.50	—
58.	Belganga	450.88	76.05	—
59.	Madhukar	463.40	218.34	—
60.	Vasant (Kasoda)	543.24	241.38	—
61.	Gangapur	351.35	318.40	—
62.	Kannad	*367.94	213.53	—
63.	Sant Eknath	268.01	—	—
64.	Siddheshwar (Sillod)	73.49	116.64	—
65.	Vinayak	181.09	164.87	—
66.	Samarth	279.13	1.84	—
67.	Ambejogai	.482.10	178.54	—
68.	Jai Bhavani	445.07	114.13	—
69.	Kada	387.69	81.79	—
70.	Gajanan	102.45	NA	—
71.	Terna	111.73	96.20	—
72.	Shetkari (Killari)	307.94	154.58	—
73.	Godavari (Manar)	479.70	74.54	—
74.	Kalambar	661.13	374.18	—
75.	Godavari Dudhna	497.71	111.28	—
76.	Marathwada	986.50	445.68	—
77.	Purna	675.97	**183.21	—
78.	Jijamata	1038.81	**185.42	—
	TOTAL	19577.13	6461.91	5.03

* = Provisional ** = Business Loss

Source : Director of Sugar, Maharashtra, Quoted in Memorandum to Third Wage Board, Maharashtra.

Rajya Sakhar Sangh, February, 1987, Annexure-II.

According to the study conducted by RBI in the context of the finances of medium and large public and private limited companies shows that, the wages and cost elements as percentage of value of output is increasing since 1982-83 (See Table 3). Particularly, the rate of interest, cost of wages and salaries and other costs are increasing. While the cost of inputs are declining during the same period. Sugarcane is an important input (raw-material). The profitability of sugar factories had come down since 1960s (See Table 4). The financial performance of this industry as found was uneven over the years. Besides the industry was showing decreasing returns to scale as the cost of production and as per cent of value of output showed a rising trend.

TABLE 3

Wages and Other Cost Elements as Percentage of Value of Output

Sugar Year	Cost of Input	Costs of Wages and Salaries	Others	Depreciation	Interest	Total
1	2	3	4	5	6	7
1960-61	70.8	9.8	7.7	2.7	2.2	93.2
1961-62	71.1	10.2	8.2	2.9	3.0	95.4
1962-63	68.9	10.6	9.4	3.6	3.7	96.2
1963-64	67.0	10.5	8.9	3.7	2.8	93.4
1964-65	71.2	9.7	6.8	3.5	2.2	93.4
1965-66	72.8	10.4	6.3	3.2	2.5	95.2
1966-67	73.4	10.2	6.5	3.1	3.4	96.6
1967-68	68.5	12.9	8.1	4.1	4.8	98.4
1968-69	71.9	9.0	6.4	2.8	3.3	93.4
1969-70	75.9	8.9	6.1	2.7	2.8	96.4
1970-71	76.8	9.4	6.7	3.5	4.2	100.6
1971-72	70.6	10.1	7.4	3.4	5.7	97.2
1972-73	65.7	9.9	8.3	3.2	4.2	91.5
1973-74	76.1	8.7	7.1	2.4	3.0	97.3
1974-75	74.1	9.1	7.9	2.4	3.3	96.8
1975-76	77.4	10.0	7.9	2.1	4.4	101.8

—Contd.

1	2	3	4	5	6	7
1976-77	70.7	11.1	8.8	2.4	5.0	98.0
1977-78	74.7	10.5	8.3	2.1	5.2	100.8
1978-79	78.7	10.4	7.5	2.2	5.7	104.5
1979-80	70.1	11.1	11.5	2.0	7.2	101.9
1980-81	68.0	11.0	8.0	3.0	5.0	95.0
1981-82	71.0	10.0	8.0	3.0	5.0	97.0
1982-83	76.0	9.0	7.0	3.0	5.0	100.0
1983-84	74.8	10.5	7.9	3.5	7.7	104.4
1984-85	70.3	12.1	9.8	3.8	9.2	105.2

Source : Sugar : Rising Costs, Squeezing Profits, M.Y. Khan, Commerce, May 28, June 3, 1988, p. 14 (Originally compiled by the author, on the basis of data from R.B.I. Studies on Finance of Medium and Large Public Ltd. Com. Published in *R.B.I. Bulletins*.

TABLE 4

Profitability Ratio of Sugar Industry

Years	Gross profit as per cent of sales		Gross profit as per cent of total net assets		Profits after tax as per cent of net worth	
1	2		3		4	
1960-61	10.6	12.4	10.0	8.5	11.0	11.3
1961-62	10.5	9.7	10.0	7.0	10.0	07.3
1962-63	10.6	7.5	10.1	7.1	8.7	2.1
1963-64	10.8	9.5	10.7	10.6	9.5	7.8
1964-65	10.6	10.5	10.4	9.3	9.3	8.7
1965-66	10.7	12.1	10.1	10.2	8.9	6.0
1966-67	10.5	9.8	9.8	8.2	9.1	6.0
1967-68	9.2	6.6	8.6	6.8	7.3	1.7
1968-69	8.8	12.4	8.5	13.0	7.0	13.2
1969-70	9.6	9.3	9.6	8.4	9.5	7.5
1970-71	9.9	6.4	10.4	4.8	10.1	3.6
1971-72	10.3	9.4	10.7	8.9	10.8	9.5
1972-73	9.7	12.2	10.5	15.5	10.4	16.9

—*Contd.*

1	2		3		4	
1973-74	10.7	9.5	11.2	9.7	11.6	11.3
1974-75	11.4	8.8	12.8	9.6	13.7	9.6
1975-76	9.2	5.4	10.6	6.1	8.2	N.A.
1976-77	9.0	8.0	11.0	10.6	7.9	9.0
1977-78	9.0	7.1	11.0	7.3	8.8	0.7
1978-79	9.5	3.2	11.7	2.7	11.5	N.A.
1979-80	10.1	7.3	12.6	7.8	14.5	3.4
1980-81	9.6	9.2	12.0	13.0	14.9	26.0
1981-82	10.2	8.8	11.2	10.5	13.4	15.0
1982-83	8.9	8.5	9.9	7.7	12.1	6.0
1983-84	7.9	7.1	8.4	6.1	6.8	N.A.
1984-85	8.1	6.2	8.6	7.8	7.0	N.A.

Note : 1960-61 to 1980-81 are from Studies of R.B.I.

Source : As per Table 4. Originally compiled by the Author from various issues of *R.B.I. Bulletins* and *Financial Statistics of Joint Stock Companies in India* 1960-61 to 1970-71.

The cost of sugarcane obviously differs which is because of climate, soil and farm size. The average cost of production of sugar, normally should be nearby equal to all sugar factories. But this has not been observed in Maharashtra. Table 5 exhibits the range of cost of sugar production in different regions of Maharashtra, Kolhapur region (which includes Sangli, Kolhapur districts and southern part of Satara district) performs better in economising the cost of production of sugar. However, there exist again a wide range of differences in intra-region cost of production of sugar and the final prices paid by the sugar factories.

Table 6 discloses the item-wise cost of production of sugar by sugar factories in Maharashtra for the seasons 1993-94 to 1995-96, where we find wide range of differences in costs. The difference is because of the wide range of differences in the cost items *viz.*, cane harvesting and transport of sugarcane. Same has been brought up for crushing from different distances. So, the cost differs. Besides BICP is not considering this cost because of the system prevailing in U.P. In U.P. cane is being

TABLE 5

Maximum and Minimum Cost of Sugar Production 1988-89 (Per M.T.)

Region	Cane Harvest & Trans	Salary and Wages	Store	Other Misc.	Interest	Depreciation	Cost of Prod. (per M.T.)	Cost of Prod. (per Bag)	Sugarcane price
Pune Division									
Min.	49.62	12.86	27.04	7.86	5.84	7.83	184.50	163.00	252
Max.	88.19	52.92	42.73	33.91	96.31	33.20	297.80	298.35	414
Kolhapur									
Min.	42.61	13.69	25.05	17.26	2.89	7.21	192.00	141.98	350
Max.	87.86	45.73	46.27	71.55	54.71	48.12	298.52	256.41	475
Ahmednagar									
Min.	51.02	18.27	22.61	11.91	16.31	9.26	225.16	200.00	242
Max.	129.43	109.54	52.54	117.39	149.27	87.56	674.19	637.21	375
Aurangabad									
Min.	50.88	17.87	20.56	18.69	15.54	7.17	211.51	216.51	242
Max.	110.55	189.45	62.77	64.18	176.81	119.80	563.90	554.38	363
Nanded									
Min.	56.50	14.83	24.17	13.69	26.16	7.75	245.87	234.16	242
Max.	90.20	99.45	67.06	44.33	155.97	64.38	405.82	387.49	320
Nagpur									
Min.	51.59	17.25	30.80	2.15	14.75	15.53	296.03	280.21	242
Max.	137.27	59.34	96.94	243.28	204.69	175.22	372.36	934.14	283

Sources : Economic and Technical Efficiency of Cooperative Sugar Factories, R.M. Kharche, First Conference of Sugar Factories, 24-25 Sept. 1990, Shri Datta, C.S.F., Shirol.

supplied at the cane collection centres or directly to the factories. There is a chain of middleman in collecting the canes and passing it to the sugar factories. In Maharashtra cane harvesting and transporting is the work to be operated by the co-operative sugar factories as per their bye-laws. However, now-a-days the industrial relations have changed due to the judicial confirmation, that the cane harvest and transport workers are the employees of the sugar industry (Jugale, 1997). A few sugar factories in Maharashtra have established the trusts, labour societies and other institutions to undertake the work of cane harvesting and transport of cane through them. Even some sugar factories have changed their bye-laws stating that, "cane harvesting and transport of cane is exclusively concerned to the cane growers and it is not the duty of sugar factories. However, sugar factories will help in this regard."

The share of sugarcane cost normally stands around 75 per cent to 80 per cent in the total cost of sugar production. The issue became controversial when the claim was made that, the additional sugarcane price should retain with the sugar factories instead of paying it to the cane growers. Obviously, more than 80 per cent of overall cost of sugar is shared by a single raw-material *i.e.*, sugarcane.

In Table 6, the cost items are indicated for each sugar factory for the year 1993-94 to 1995-96, which also indicate varying range of difference in cost items. Particularly, the cost of harvesting differs from factory to factory and season to season. This has been followed by interest costs. Only a few sugar factories have paid *Khodaki* (ratoon) prices.

Sugar recovery, duration of crushing and capacity utilisation of sugar factories are important parameters for determining conversion cost. These parameters although based on zonal conditions have been evolved by number of reports on the basis of past experience prevailing in the industry. Bhargav Commission (1974) suggested RME, RBHE, ROE and TL as the technical norms to determine the technical efficiency of a sugar factory. Expert Committee (1987) which was set by the Ministry of Food and Civil Supplies referred to five norms of efficiency to be adhered to by sugar factories *viz.*, RME, RBHE, total sugar loss, steam consumption and downtime. BICP undertook a study of sugar industry for recommending conversion cost schedules for the purpose of fixation of levy sugar price for the season 1993-94 to 1995-96. The report was submitted in October 1996. The BICP recommended the following norms to determine the conversion cost of sugar :

1. The pol percentage bagasse at 2.3 per cent for mills with machineries as per the 1987 specification (2000 TCD and above) and 2.6 per cent for mills with the 1973 specifications (1250-2000 TCD). Normative loss

in bagasse can be calculated on pol percentage bagasse and fibre percentage cane.

2. The purity of final molasses at 30 per cent.
3. Loss in press mud at 0.07 per cent cane and undermined loss at 0.10 per cent.
4. Total normative loss is the sum of loss of bagasse, molasses, loss in press mud and undermined loss.
5. Normative sugar recovery calculated on actual pol percentage cane and normative total loss of sugar.
6. Quality and quantity of cane.
7. Norms can be applied mill-wise or aggregated at zonal level.
8. 100 per cent capacity utilization.
9. Total downtime at the rate of 10 per cent.
10. Duration of crushing (based on cane availability, capacity utilisation and downtime).
11. Steam consumption based on fuel/bagasse consumption at 25 per cent cane for mills with 1987 specification and 27.5 per cent for mills with 1973 specification.
12. No norms have been suggested for mills with capacity below 1250 TCD. Their performance is generally termed as poor.

TABLE 6

Conversion Cost and Sugarcane Prices (Per M.T.)

KOLHAPUR DISTRICT

(Rs. in Lakhs)

Sl. No.	ITEMS	BHOGAWATI			CHATRAPATI RAJARAM		CHATRAPATI SHAHU		
		1993-94	1994-95	1995-96	1993-94	1994-95	1993-94	1994-95	1995-96
			(1)			(2)		(3)	
1.	Cost of Harvesting	481.20	484.61	709.03	263.59	605.52	331.42	455.18	435.47
2.	Sugarcane Purchase Tax	121.96	115.94	132.98	56.55	90.81	65.94	77.63	93.27
3.	Cane Feeding	5.00	4.95	6.28	11.25	17.90	1.40	1.88	1.87
4.	Store	329.00	347.05	464.58	218.47	270.31	167.18	246.52	313.09
5.	Wages & Salaries	391.75	424.75	533.33	257.13	306.12	260.87	323.49	378.09
6.	Overheads	278.85	300.60	368.12	82.97	88.83	150.78	146.52	179.66
7.	Interest	626.75	629.10	853.06	178.34	202.47	241.23	402.90	546.63
8.	Depreciation	193.75	825.32	190.71	88.45	88.33	37.71	210.69	394.45
9.	Khodki	123.44	109.63	113.90	—	84.26	77.95	64.68	74.65
10.	Bonus	130.00	90.00	118.00	43.91	31.51	51.58	59.21	73.13
11.	Education Fund	0.75	0.75	0.75	0.75	0.75	0.63	0.75	0.75
12.	Sakhar Karkhana Sangh	3.69	2.74	3.68	1.66	1.75	1.69	2.17	2.12
13.	Audit Fee	—	4.75	5.85	1.18	5.33	—	5.23	1.80
14.	VSI Contribution	6.92	6.34	7.51	3.06	5.00	3.79	5.00	4.78
15.	Total Cost of Production	3324.73	2546.62	249.69	1239.47	1798.71	1476.41	2001.84	2499.76
16.	Rate Per Tonne (Rs.)	594.02	494.90	40.94	469.70	405.79	445.00	489.87	638.07
17.	Rate Per Bag (Rs.)	480.78	401.59	24.12	405.67	457.73	355.10	400.22	443.17
18.	Accumulated Losses	—	—	198.62	257.06	247.12	—	1.99	—
19.	Surplus	3885.23	3744.06	3989.76	2090.56	3210.99	2329.74	2980.36	2643.02
20.	Deduction	0.15	11.00	18.50	6.00	10.00	6.00	10.00	6.00
21.	Deposits	12.50	13.50	22.50	10.00	15.00	25.00	15.00	32.50
22.	Sugarcane Price Per M.T.	831.00	690.00	686.00	856.00	717.00	910.00	776.00	730.00

(*Contd.*)

TABLE 6 (*Contd.*)

Sl. No.	DATTA ASURLE			DATTA SHIROL			DAULAT			DUDHGANGA VEDGANGA		
	1993-94	1994-95	1995-96	1993-94	1994-95	1995-96	1993-94	1994-95	1995-96	1993-94	1994-95	1995-96
		(4)			(5)			(6)			(7)	
1.	183.14	315.95	438.84	610.07	831.93	1052.00	383.31	380.40	553.40	460.50	570.54	627.31
2.	34.11	48.13	44.73	94.97	132.80	138.35	73.18	69.86	90.14	91.37	125.96	152.75
3.	0.39	0.71	0.58	2.49	4.13	4.71	1.19	1.18	1.99	0.81	1.02	2.13
4.	141.48	234.92	273.99	469.01	616.47	803.45	302.01	264.57	429.54	404.40	394.81	682.07
5.	160.36	241.97	278.39	387.80	480.81	640.21	248.63	262.32	367.15	379.79	429.69	639.66
6.	130.64	160.36	161.25	315.49	347.50	485.46	180.33	153.78	182.80	220.92	195.22	311.41
7.	194.29	207.03	574.15	755.68	785.36	1294.04	280.06	328.65	759.77	409.67	353.09	623.20
8.	118.64	124.39	155.83	276.72	255.35	1587.30	72.77	69.78	100.94	98.38	99.82	133.57
9.	48.91	49.58	59.90	—	—	—	61.07	—	—	60.63	124.08	149.85
10.	—	—	—	52.32	65.19	42.48	40.57	49.75	74.89	77.59	87.17	189.78
11.	0.32	0.57	0.62	—	0.75	2.58	0.17	0.65	0.15	0.75	0.75	0.75
12.	0.76	1.25	1.47	2.95	3.89	4.21	1.54	1.58	2.20	2.52	2.19	2.77
13.	0.66	3.08	1.91	—	—	5.26	1.45	5.10	2.09	1.58	7.90	4.30
14.	1.89	3.13	3.67	7.36	9.73	10.51	4.40	3.94	5.50	5.96	6.92	7.75
15.	15.57	1418.02	1995.33	2713.19	3504.72	5068.45	1603.55	1599.17	2507.56	2264.16	2452.16	3564.09
16.	625.66	500.78	647.64	447.03	440.17	572.62	455.55	486.06	560.03	517.85	433.39	565.20
17.	536.68	453.52	549.67	368.42	1223.45	462.81	364.43	405.87	1592.07	426.80	354.25	459.63
18.	245.32	29.95	—	500.29	61.81	52.14	7.40	55.81	47.25	287.55	414.75	46.13
19.	348.44	2032.92	1723.96	7742.73	5879.76	1197.02	2709.47	2473.64	2747.25	3506.87	4189.32	4022.46
20.	8.00	0.50	5.00	16.00	15.00	1.00	21.00	14.00	14.00	11.00	10.00	10.00
21.	10.00	10.00	20.00	10.00	10.00	10.00	10.00	—	60.00	10.00	10.00	20.00
22.	858.00	678.00	652.00	901.00	730.00	701.00	921.00	752.00	705.00	842.00	740.00	701.00

TABLE 6 (*Contd.*)

Sl. No.	GADHINGLAJ			JAWAHAR			KUMBHI-KASARI			WARNA		
	1993-94	1994-95	1995-96	1993-94	1994-95	1995-96	1993-94	1994-95	1995-96	1993-94	1994-95	1995-96
		(8)			(9)			(10)			(11)	
1.	236.95	359.34	511.97	470.50	238.02	656.33	498.24	583.66	592.27	677.33	662.66	838.55
2.	55.24	71.52	71.64	106.19	52.78	102.11	116.13	137.84	141.09	167.91	172.89	230.52
3.	1.20	1.22	3.66	1.76	1.00	2.10	1.69	1.77	1.82	—	0.09	—
4.	226.83	257.57	399.49	376.88	200.48	537.51	425.00	462.28	545.30	533.97	567.46	721.48
5.	205.21	216.44	441.81	155.00	89.12	241.02	360.69	446.17	458.39	552.06	608.52	669.95
6.	135.58	150.40	171.57	254.38	171.90	276.65	254.10	258.05	313.92	416.29	493.41	331.97
7.	237.44	297.88	446.89	590.64	324.80	745.21	402.87	266.03	657.39	500.54	445.00	674.97
8.	94.26	87.94	90.90	386.48	354.80	394.01	117.45	120.04	110.77	171.92	170.47	186.15
9.	57.25	68.00	84.62	111.52	55.68	129.17	133.36	140.70	138.14	194.67	176.52	213.85
10.	39.08	29.74	55.73	23.61	11.00	39.08	80.09	79.06	114.07	50.55	149.85	165.74
11.	0.75	0.58	0.75	0.75	0.46	0.10	0.75	0.75	0.75	0.75	0.75	0.75
12.	0.80	1.52	1.78	2.24	1.10	2.60	—	2.70	2.79	3.34	3.98	3.62
13.	1.00	1.15	6.45		0.98	0.40	2.63	5.13	4.84	2.63	10.12	3.77
				11.09								
14.	3.79	4.44	5.40		2.74	6.50	5.96	7.10	9.07	9.94	9.06	10.74
15.	1296.38	1547.74	154.73	2549.74	1175.06	3143.44	2404.44	2519.50	3090.56	3271.90	1370.78	584.62
16.	407.68	421.22	34.57	549.40	498.69	570.38	450.73	447.56	559.32	419.75	491.54	75.84
17.	341.72	407.50	23.93	639.60	429.00	484.15	356.67	361.06	446.20	445.33	422.79	108.01
18.	—	—	—	268.33	—	258.33	32.66	26.88	18.65	524.48	—	—
19.	2597.15	2760.24	2782.00	3543.84	—	3123.12	4271.48	4305.58	4189.10	6203.52	5664.40	5977.94
20.	11.00	10.00	10.00	15.00	16.00	15.00	10.00	7.00	7.00	6.00	11.00	13.50
21.	10.00	10.00	20.00	10.00	10.00	10.00	71.00	10.00	24.00	12.50	33.00	50.00
22.	901.00	751.00	751.00	786.00	976.00	700.00	905.00	765.00	766.00	675.00	805.00	826.00

(*Contd.*)

Table 6 (*Contd.*)

Sangli District

Sl. No.	HUTATMA			MAHAKALI			MANGANGA	R.B. PATIL			TASGAON		
	1993-94	1994-95	1995-96	1993-94	1994-95	1995-96	1993-94	1993-94	1994-95	1995-96	1993-94	1994-95	1995-96
		(1)			(2)		(3)		(4)			(5)	
1.	356.04	356.04	394.10	225.66	353.96	484.69	189.93	795.44	685.41	896.19	168.94	359.27	395.78
2.	72.32	72.33	94.37	7.58	31.25	48.66	16.16	180.67	182.25	244.28	35.82	65.34	—
3.	1.72	1.72	1.86	0.30	0.48	0.27	—	2.94	2.69	3.08	0.91	1.38	1.63
4.	213.23	233.23	265.60	143.06	205.35	317.57	102.31	472.37	430.11	624.92	54.82	123.8	155.42
5.	201.61	201.61	277.18	185.73	222.00	305.01	167.37	355.12	412.64	474.04	125.48	152.72	251.38
6.	271.69	271.69	241.66	151.59	183.96	205.27	136.73	384.19	344.70	453.37	212.07	173.04	326.40
7.	370.24	370.23	489.26	144.84	156.05	280.06	230.26	368.96	551.49	734.43	376.88	305.63	468.29
8.	90.00	90.00	101.55	90.53	157.94	86.63	113.24	253.55	233.55	280.89	157.54	510.31	71.21
9.	88.52	88.52	97.17	2.71	20.78	9.87	4.23	163.86	183.81	171.34	39.35	62.67	66.09
10.	68.40	68.47	80.90	28.00	37.64	52.72	27.41	72.29	103.32	125.23	36.72	32.98	19.75
11.	0.71	0.71	0.75	0.37	0.56	0.67	0.18	0.75	0.75	0.75	0.34	0.64	0.65
12.	1.80	1.80	1.98	—	—	—	0.34	—	—	—	0.67	1.24	1.41
13.	1.25	1.25	—	0.82	3.37	1.50	0.42	—	7.28	4.77	—	2.48	2.48
14.	4.50	4.50	4.96	1.78	3.39	4.13	0.95	10.21	9.27	10.64	1.90	3.56	3.60
15.	1742.10	1762.10	194.76	9097.03	1376.33	1797.05	873.29	3507.41	3318.93	4166.27	782.22	1569.50	93.98
16.	491.80	539.75	58.60	611.87	490.00	534.61	931.75	535.11	451.41	607.89	463.08	493.41	28.99
17.	422.29	1632.72	50.11	511.59	610.84	490.00	1378.59	442.29	364.48	510.27	409.67	442.36	—
18.	170.20	21.08	215.58	—	—	—	172.65	34.34	24.81	2.54	322.93	480.89	600.79
19.	2604.41	—	2743.39	1064.26	2039.83	2015.86	46.10	4850.81	6508.69	5798.12	421.41	1780.40	1884.56
20.	6.00	5.00	45.00	6.00	5.00	12.00	10.00	10.00	46.00	16.00	10.00	8.00	—
21.	10.00	10.00	10.00	10.00	10.00	20.00	10.00	75.00	10.00	54.00	10.00	10.00	—
22.	915.00	776.00	825.00	751.00	726.00	730.0	655.00	976.00	885.00	775.00	845.00	717.00	—

TABLE 6 (*Contd.*)

SATARA DISTRICT

Sl. No.	VASANTDADA PATIL			VISHVASRAO NAIK			YASHWANT		B. DESAI			KRISHNA		
	1993-94	1994-95	1995-96	1993-94	1994-95	1995-96	1993-94	1994-95	1993-94	1994-95	1995-96	1993-94	1994-95	1995-96
	(1)			(2)			(3)		(4)			(5)		
1.	906.66	1075.05	1124.37	160.88	356.52	384.80	227.71	240.49	199.67	215.65	249.97	973.99	840.35	1087.42
2.	193.73	214.25	235.50	36.77	56.21	62.81	22.51	33.44	38.11	43.76	57.35	224.16	227.32	312.62
3.	—	—	67.05	131	1.73	2.59	0.97	1.37	0.71	0.82	0.90	2.51	2.55	3.02
4.	573.17	608.33	749.98	88.92	196.36	225.63	70.21	116.08	109.89	127.64	156.83	747.09	752.01	1016.20
5.	694.02	736.30	911.63	151.85	171.85	270.68	186.45	202.74	148.24	173.53	218.73	643.50	807.08	941.50
6.	407.77	579.22	597.42	189.34	308.50	301.85	114.64	127.61	120.72	115.86	144.14	443.04	493.49	565.23
7.	704.40	627.74	1298.89	163.81	167.39	361.89	168.39	106.92	735.00	85.63	156.73	820.19	864.69	1073.23
8.	183.50	180.10	183.06	78.72	79.25	74.58	79.72	80.98	346.13	14.93	13.84	147.30	164.45	179.05
9.	176.37	218.44	265.78	36.18	36.18	57.56	—	21.36	38.19	41.28	52.42	261.23	230.07	279.94
10.	152.64	175.68	202.70	11.18	13.60	16.47	49.29	41.51	50.33	58.00	57.71	1158.07	183.67	290.14
11.	0.75	0.75	0.75	0.34	0.52	0.61	0.36	0.49	0.36	0.41	0.45	0.75	0.75	0.75
12.	4.90	5.14	4.67	121	0.83	1.50	0.95	2.84	0.85	0.96	1.05	4.13	5.13	4.82
13.	3.30	8.19	8.19	0.54	1.42	3.16	—	0.96	0.53	1.68	1.00	—	8.04	13.24
14.	10.56	11.01	12.04	2.07	3.18	3.75	1.81	2.75	2.13	2.41	2.62	10.34	14.58	13.68
15.	4011.77	4435.20	494.83	923.12	1355.01	1857.38	1040.25	981.06	843.54	890.12	126.12	4539.92	4594.46	5780.84
16.	435.12	467.29	46.18	587.03	518.98	610.87	575.22	400.50	473.89	433.11	56.19	436.20	486.06	516.21
17.	366.55	447.93	44.37	482.05	426.76	495.12	508.50	356.23	371.12	474.33	50.17	351.52	426.06	486.07
18.	—	—	—	60.27	79.03	715.44	527.00	962.54	—	—	—	—	—	—
19.	6283.14	6482.20	4.88	1209.27	1384.48	2101.50	1286.61	1448.62	1281.13	1542.65	1615.27	7959.10	8164.15	7596.47
20.	10.00	14.00	9.00	6.00	11.00	20.00	10.00	10.00	22.00	20.00	20.00	20.00	19.00	19.00
21.	10.00	10.00	15.00	10.00	—	20.00	10.00	10.00	5.00	5.00	35.00	10.00	40.00	71.00
22.	845.00	700.00	625.00	855.00	728.00	750.00	830.00	610.00	832.00	768.00	741.00	965.00	880.00	840.00

(*Contd.*)

TABLE 6 (*Contd.*)

PUNE DISTRICT

Sl. No.	SAHYADRI			AJINKYATARA			KISHANVEER SATARA			SHRIRAM		BHIMA PATAS		
	1993-94	1994-95	1995-96	1993-94	1994-95	1995-96	1993-94	1994-95	1993-94	1994-95	1995-96	1993-94	1994-95	1995-96
		(1)			(2)			(3)			(4)		(5)	
1.	782.12	934.28	1258.42	463.63	626.39	797.13	508.37	385.57	593.30	273.62	354.61	458.86	623.17	605.08
2.	148.04	179.75	0.64	87.96	106.39	83.83	107.28	92.06	114.87	48.38	77.77	89.41	138.79	100.21
3.	4.29	5.50	8.16	2.35	2.71	3.56	1.46	1.70	2.21	2.04	6.84	1.83	2.35	2.25
4.	454.69	547.75	698.29	329.37	315.07	492.44	338.24	309.24	406.34	144.28	168.82	142.62	417.97	412.36
5.	349.23	416.07	554.15	223.31	215.87	303.96	276.50	270.02	363.68	214.19	234.18	336.76	406.18	558.67
6.	282.90	342.36	381.07	266.27	263.86	338.19	288.71	296.53	287.74	188.61	163.43	405.09	280.25	241.99
7.	494.95	1024.15	1541.28	2099.24	668.97	1068.55	292.34	303.13	293.43	151.46	229.94	251.28	230.96	628.64
8.	105.13	79.44	662.37	120.01	39.87	306.95	148.87	160.47	278.01	74.07	71.04	84.43	187.84	178.54
9.	169.99	183.47	240.82	33.18	53.96	68.30	—	—	—	53.91	77.82	8.69	31.27	—
10.	54.94	66.28	88.82	27.75	25.87	25.87	37.18	18.05	53.03	14.65	17.59	45.25	50.00	64.29
11.	0.75	0.75	0.75	0.75	0.75	0.75	37.18	0.75	0.75*	—	0.63	0.75	0.75	0.75
12.	2.28	3.48	4.47	1.45	2.18	9.20*	0.75	1.68	2.20	10.88	1.39		1.84	2.88
												1.52		
13.	1.95	2.77	8.87	1.04	3.81	3.64	2.14	2.14	4.59*	1.08	0.20		2.40	7.55
14.	6.51	8.74	11.17	4.15	5.45	—*	5.34	4.21	5.50	2.51	3.47	4.59	6.30	4.78
15.	2900.68	3702.13	5128.36	2254.39	2346.14	3517.20	2008.61	1846.35	2705.65	1374.98	1402.04	1831.08	2378.23	2307.99
16.	426.61	504.46	532.26	527.53	477.23	602.63	437.48	491.24	531.43	607.70	443.99	445.99	420.63	587.32
17.	358.38	423.60	204.46	432.49	430.87	535.36	402.24	378.66	492.08	447.80	403.87	432.55	377.15	532.30
18.	—	—	—	—	NIL	NIL	—	—	NIL	—	85.11	199.68	167.31	164.65
19.	4887.20	5146.42	5904.74	3072.49	3171.89	2773.57	3177.86	2654.65	2506.02	1410.35	2540.01	3073.76	3482.10	2172.26
20.	11.00	10.00	10.00	26.00	25.00	15.00	9.00	7.00	7.00	12.53	5.00	11.00	10.00	—
21.	10.00	8.74	75.00	10.00	46.00	25.00	10.00	60.00	50.00	33.40	70.00	10.00	60.00	—
22.	891.00	700.00	715.00	900.00	690.00	585.00	901.00	701.00	625.00	675.00	800.00	575.00	762.00	536.00
					*Combine			*Combine						

TABLE 6 (*Contd.*)

Sl. No.	INDAPUR			RAJGAD			SHRI CHATTRAPATI			SHRI SOMESHWAR		
	1993-94	1994-95	1995-96	1993-94	1994-95	1995-96	1993-94	1994-95	1995-96	1993-94	1994-95	1995-96
		(6)			(7)			(8)			(9)	
1.	244.96	374.77	435.13	122.63	352.93	455.99	360.26	486.25	541.85	380.19	586.40	750.10
2.	48.60	87.12	84.18	15.07	47.58	52.54	67.80	101.45	100.46	77.50	98.93	87.29
3.	0.46	0.85	1.17	2.62	4.01	7.05	0.69	1.09	0.95	0.87	1.58	1.63
4.	210.37	309.72	325.47	133.98	135.32	268.10	301.69	421.24	478.40	212.32	309.25	409.51
5.	167.50	213.75	259.24	74.91	78.64	148.34	227.80	291.86	337.08	212.83	283.71	303.92
6.	69.41	96.90	141.78	82.13	136.48	242.09	91.37	118.65	139.08	162.82	195.04	298.91
7.	157.01	161.38	284.35	756.09	329.15	458.18	1248.65	191.50	401.26	246.22	223.30	381.84
8.	121.84	118.11	129.28	288.98	29.79	194.67	50.38	59.07	62.23	131.05	138.05	138.34
9.	55.50	86.75	93.22	—	—	28.52	64.94	82.12	0.94	43.17	60.23	81.69
10.	9.44	11.43	21.28	—	24.71	25.71	56.00	63.50	70.00	35.00	64.61	65.05
11.	0.45	0.21	0.75	0.16	0.39	0.52	0.75	0.61	0.75	0.63	0.57	0.75
12.	0.87	1.66	0.54	0.26	0.82	1.12	1.57	1.40	1.84	—	1.27	1.94
13.	0.93	—	2.29	0.20	0.52	2.36	1.50	3.00	4.58	—	3.55	4.61
14.	2.49	3.84	3.86	0.77	2.06	2.81	3.51	4.60	4.88	3.17	4.86	5.48
15.	1094.62	1577.53	1783.52	1046.46	1350.94	1688.00	1511.69	1735.89	2249.30	1517.02	2017.59	2229.12
16.	485.36	426.65	475.93	3352.91	692.14	703.60	480.70	419.20	485.26	534.54	475.31	506.11
17.	413.35	395.05	432.23	659.64	655.22	690.92	431.14	377.20	421.24	477.92	415.53	408.97
18.	7.95	82.46	35.59	692.50	1318.26	—	—	30.05	26.18	1514.78	446.34	162.43
19.	1630.29	2011.21	1887.32	-513.89	465.08	845.67	2519.90	3213.73	2625.08	571.09	4208.50	2259.29
20.	8.00	17.00	7.00	6.00	—	—	9.00	8.00	11.00	6.00	5.00	15.00
21.	10.00	—	30.00	10.00	10.00	10.00	1.00	10.00	10.00	10.00	40.00	50.00
22.	785.00	725.00	630.00	625.00	700.00	525.00	875.00	751.00	676.00	700.00	810.00	815.00

(*Contd.*)

Table 6 (*Contd.*)

Sholapur District

Sl. No.	SHRI VIGHNAHAR			MALEGAON			YASHWANT			ADINATH		
	1993-94	1994-95	1995-96	1993-94	1994-95	1995-96	1993-94	1994-95	1995-96	1993-94	1994-95	1995-96
		(1)			(2)			(3)			(4)	
1.	483.19	468.84	584.91	467.94	488.66	529.88	498.01	463.52	578.20	164.55	415.86	684.50
2.	76.70	89.46	75.58	90.17	126.61	141.53	103.02	117.54	118.88	27.71	77.19	110.05
3.	1.23	1.35	2.02	—	58.80	—	1.13	1.29	11.48	0.65	—	2.24
4.	318.08	268.34	543.54	393.05	457.29	497.03	311.63	303.25	396.62	73.43	235.77	427.21
5.	166.05	186.12	271.82	377.71	384.46	453.35	355.01	454.93	470.62	35.70	97.63	178.78
6.	167.83	174.12	197.87	94.91	94.35	121.81	256.77	262.91	276.52	36.71	121.44	178.21
7.	1399.99	120.84	409.92	234.994	240.55	424.47	232.34	235.70	438.48	174.50	1538.16	784.20
8.	135.46	137.66	168.56	74.93	97.37	89.90	97.49	109.52	110.86	302.28	284.61	266.51
9.	90.50	75.12	136.28	83.82	92.84	95.48	26.67	108.25	127.60	—	—	—
10.	57.34	28.28	34.87	71.25	—	106.28	103.47	127.60	112.61	5.45	10.10	24.00
11.	0.88	0.75	0.75	0.75	0.75	0.75	1.50	0.75	0.75	0.26	0.50	0.88
12.	0.81	1.00	1.76	1.57	4.45	2.69	1.84	2.16	2.26	0.37	1.31	1.89
13.	1.42	1.50	7.22	2.26	—	2.14	—	1.10	6.74	—	2.28	2.60
14.	5.11	4.24	7.45	3.37	4.95	6.72	5.05	5.40	5.64	1.16	3.29	4.72
15.	2397.48	2901.02	4385.02	1915.69	2210.75	2499.11	2063.62	2236.71	1842.32	1840.15	672.30	2662.79
16.	680.17	794.42	957.26	455.53	408.40	442.79	432.84	466.45	358.45	584.07	523.11	554.17
17.	578.80	658.69	770.98	406.05	461.89	426.09	417.30	413.47	333.42	641.91	577.55	493.74
18.	168.74	126.41	1222.65	6.40	24.97	12.57	30.11	65.14	19.06	—	135.80	245.35
19.	2085.79	2270.43	2915.15	2804.21	4084.96	3302.64	3074.75	3074.30	771.30	68.70	1480.11	1886.30
20.	10.00	15.00	25.00	16.00	15.00	15.00	6.00	10.00	10.00	6.00	5.00	15.00
21.	10.00	10.00	20.00	5.00	5.00	65.00	10.00	10.00	10.00	12.50	12.50	69.50
22.	986.00	786.00	756.00	900.00	875.00	815.00	821.00	710.00	670.00	675.00	521.00	590.00

TABLE 6 (*Contd.*)

Sl. No.	BHIMA TAKLAI			BHOGAVATI		PANDURANG			SANT DAMAJ			SHRI SHANKAR		
	1993-94	1994-95	1995-96	1994-95	1995-96	1993-94	1994-95	1995-96	1993-94	1994-95	1995-96	1993-94	1994-95	1995-96
	(5)			(6)		(7)			(8)			(9)		
1.	223.49	375.11	483.45	241.88	364.29	263.45	314.68	430.48	161.46	329.29	481.08	436.48	546.45	760.66
2.	56.70	89.06	82.03	43.61	49.29	47.93	60.23	69.71	15.76	53.24	75.78	64.21	102.76	112.74
3.	0.84	1.37	1.81	1.08	1.63	0.28	—	0.47	0.68	1.61	2.13	1.56	2.01	2.95
4.	179.64	244.71	306.86	122.01	219.54	185.21	191.95	257.23	60.73	162.30	284.13	269.78	330.30	618.92
5.	203.07	241.33	317.97	169.60	295.05	151.07	175.85	263.37	57.68	84.62	136.65	188.23	220.86	301.90
6.	151.57	144.82	164.21	58.97	80.89	97.18	100.91	123.99	43.93	109.32	130.56	148.37	170.77	202.87
7.	156.46	148.08	375.98	86.77	241.54	179.06	152.75	263.21	171.45	548.01	646.992	493.24	445.70	826.75
8.	54.60	64.17	76.20	33.28	33.41	28.45	27.16	21.72	287.43	4.02	274.34	226.32	195.89	201.35
9.	65.11	90.86	108.21	—	—	—	—	—	NIL	—	—	55.55	79.74	128.71
10.	14.00	16.16	22.00	14.00	18.60	11.42	19.84	31.17	3.94	12.34	3.16	32.65	17.95	43.25
11.	0.53	0.73	0.75	0.35	0.51	0.05	0.50	0.62	0.18	0.50	0.75	0.75	0.75	0.75
12.	1.00	1.39	1.62	0.69	0.98	—	—	—	0.30	0.94	1.43	1.78	9.53	1.92
13.	0.91	2.28	2.32	1.21	1.29	0.58	2.76	1.08	0.22	3.28	2.68	0.73	1.35	1.89
14.	2.15	3.96	4.64	1.73	1.84	2.07	2.61	3.53	0.87	2.69	0.15	3.46	—	5.70
15.	1110.07	1424.03	1356.33	774.73	1308.87	972.55	1049.69	1390.45	524.66	1308.43	2043.55	1696.79	2123.96	3210.36
16.	420.46	391.74	313.38	448.50	512.42	437.45	423.24	449.87	583.26	487.21	538.80	539.07	498.47	587.74
17.	357.13	359.33	301.11	447.54	448.51	418.45	429.03	445.44	605.28	470.05	494.68	490.42	538.03	470.56
18.	548.50	1319.74	1101.60	1377.23	1437.39	44.70	39.36	45.3	NIL	19.77	12.08	—	167.43	237.00
19.	1883.93	2174.16	1903.27	741.05	611.65	1440.46	1459.47	1270.14	676.10	1428.76	921.24	1844.13	2984.43	2005.19
20.	6.00	5.00	5.00	5.00	—	6.00	5.00	5.00	6.00	5.00	2.00	6.00	6.00	—
21.	10.00	10.00	25.00	10.00	10.00	10.00	10.00	50.00	10.00	17.50	22.50	10.00	10.00	10.00
22.	756.00	665.00	610.00	590.00	460.00	741.00	665.00	585.00	600.00	681.00	500.00	663.00	700.00	—

(*Contd.*)

TABLE 6 (*Contd.*)

AHMEDNAGAR DISTRICT

Sl. No.	SHRI SIDDESHAWAR (1)			SHRI VITTAL (2)			S.M. MOHITE PATIL (3)			AGASTI (4)		ASHOK (5)		
	1993-94	1994-95	1995-96	1993-94	1995-96	1993-94	1994-95	1995-96	1993-94	1994-95	1995-96	1993-94	1994-95	1995-96
1.	375.46	494.04	853.75	612.03	876.93	733.47	918.04	1095.36	127.05	557.26	831.30	221.99	377.16	672.55
2.	46.45	93.22	139.34	117.84	156.79	147.60	201.65	178.77	27.12	81.98	89.65	42.81	84.94	75.35
3.	0.94	1.17	1.48	1.10	1.54	3.24	4.25	4.64	0.42	1.20	1.40	0.46	1.06	1.55
4.	174.05	279.35	426.05	283.69	421.08	4.29	530.16	666.57	79.10	140.23	253.09	130.85	238.76	296.79
5.	193.59	245.30	321.64	305.13	295.52	214.83	357.20	486.80	73.07	85.41	167.03	203.60	319.51	382.62
6.	125.68	169.77	192.45	153.89	198.85	439.11	484.82	399.86	106.81	141.31	176.32	176.42	218.19	278.28
7.	241.58	236.83	489.15	341.45	409.12	867.52	891.80	1313.06	489.00	491.45	620.80	188.40	203.00	439.25
8.	96.20	99.98	115.15	187.07	256.03	241.88	336.33	289.81	344.00	364.76	366.71	48.74	55.97	68.33
9.	52.99	96.98	142.97	136.64	179.44	161.45	205.70	236.46	24.50	37.45	57.03	31.69	59.87	78.37
10.	35.82	47.21	68.83	42.70	35.85	55.00	83.00	72.33	—	—	39.53	20.70	31.47	32.03
11.	0.53	0.75	0.75	0.75	0.75	0.75	0.75	0.75	0.26	0.62	0.75	0.38	0.69	0.75
12.	1,27	1.07	2.48	2.14	2.91	2.91	2.26	—	0.44	1.45	1.85	0.77	1.50	1.84
13.	—	4.47	2.43	1.51	8.37	2.29	3.53	5.65	—	2.77	3.24	1.88	0.93	2.31
14.	2.62	4.31	6.20	5.85		7.36	8.87	9.61	1.24	3.62	4.63	1.94	3.74	4.61
15.	1346.16	1786.87	2775.23	2093.95	2866.30	3448.98	4027.08	4908.67	4301.50	565.16	2613.33	1135.39	1710.85	2418.30
16.	506.71	440.10	442.12	383.12	399.10	—	488.00	575.56	34.57	472.50	610.84	599.30	493.50	531.48
17.	433.85	414.45	440.10	357.75	393.55	—	490.00	510.62	33.49	432.09	461.17	586.31	457.54	524.30
18.	9.74	70.00	44.44	—	23.94	31.55	—	—	147.00	203.96	207.88	366.87	383.90	337.55
19.	1420.02	—	2273.80	841.15	3344.28	4064.25	5688.21	4305.12	411.91	662.33	1457.31	680.92	1452.32	1676.76
20.	6.00	5.00	5.00	11.00	25.00	9.00	20.00	8.00	61.00	20.00	5.00	5.00	10.00	10.00
21.	10.00	10.00	25.00	10.00	10.00	30.00	10.00	10.00	12.50	12.50	32.50	12.50	12.50	22.50
22.	681.00	683.00	565.00	841.00	647.00	720.00	723.00	566.00	827.00	627.00	630.00	605.00	610.00	575.00

TABLE 6 (*Contd.*)

Sl. No.	DR. VIKHE PATIL			SHRI GANESH			KOPARGAON			MULA		
	1993-94	1994-95	1995-96	1993-94	1994-95	1995-96	1993-94	1994-95	1995-96	1993-94	1994-95	1995-96
		(6)			(7)			(8)			(9)	
1.	821.31	1091.30	1966.76	137.45	394.33	673.8	690.65	653.72	951.95	330.97	389.71	703.76
2.	118.20	173.30	197.13	24.41	68.60	80.68	72.90	109.90	128.25	70.60	99.32	140.33
3.	4.00	6.64	8.61	1.37	1.87	0.01	—	1.66	2.36	1.28	1.29	2.12
4.	237.90	437.39	482.31	118.69	255.74	293.14	248.18	257.96	370.67	311.91	389.45	597.86
5.	420.82	349.51	582.06	164.19	203.31	287.90	295.97	331.73	434.45	226.78	311.22	385.85
6.	294.42	310.47	353.80	125.06	230.38	194.76	280.64	326.57	374.94	131.02	140.20	146.15
7.	689.08	620.85	960.57	89.53	173.00	300.72	484.44	544.86	837.55	344.21	1735.89	646.06
8.	288.67	117.07	168.84	37.82	40.40	35.19	67.22	70.38	78.36	115.07	149.18	166.25
9.	79.36	121.78	141.03	7.11	31.39	47.63	37.10	53.08	121.19	8.57	—	—
10.	62.75	62.75	131.75	25.00	2.50	20.64	49.77	59.07	76.08	36.44	41.05	56.35
11.	0.75	0.75	0.75	0.23	0.56	0.75	0.75	0.75	0.75	0.65	0.75	0.75
12.	3.02	3.02	3.12	0.45	1.12	1.61	—	—	—	1.45	1.80	2.58
13.	—	2.09	8.61	1.14	1.19	2.39	3.35	3.35	5.00	0.91	4.76	2.51
14.	6.15	6.15	9.66	1.12	2.98	4.04	3.92	4.78	6.28	3.65	4.51	6.44
15.	2973.33	3610.50	478.87	733.57	1485.90	1955.70	2300.18	2496.09	3501.29	1715.61	1938.09	2857.01
16.	528.95	503.73	48.73	647.85	530.42	476.42	620.37	571.89	566.92	570.26	478.49	463.38
17.	483.55	459.97	60.75	400.00	497.99	530.42	586.06	521.85	557.75	460.53	429.70	378.70
18.	.42.54	—	74.16	198.48	350.00	449.55	—	—	418.95	—	380.63	319.35
19.	2178.71	—	2570.27	101.55	374.39	861.36	675.25	1362.89	1349.41	2151.05	2774.04	3090.27
20.	10.00	—	20.00	22.00	21.00	5.00	8.00	8.00	10.00	11.00	11.50	11.50
21.	10.00	—	20.00	10.00	10.00	10.00	20.00	10.00	30.00	42.00	31.00	20.00
22.	686.00	635.00	600.00	654.00	600.00	575.00	675.00	645.00	635.00	715.00	675.00	635.00

(*Contd.*)

TABLE 6 (*Contd.*)

Sl. No.	PAMER			SANGAMNERS			SHRI GYANESHWAR			JAGDAMBA		
	1993-94	1994-95	1995-96	1993-94	1994-95	1995-96	1993-94	1994-95	1995-96	1993-94	1994-95	1995-96
		(10)			(11)			(12)			(13)	
1.	64.47	297.89	351.32	528.16	810.89	1306.32	415.73	635.12	944.07	47.90	159.98	
2.	6.82	54.84	45.12	77.03	145.22	180.85	75.63	146.75	177.96	12.22	40.56	
3.	0.21	1.22	0.48	0.80	1.61	2.17	1.25	2.22	2.73	0.08	1.00	
4.	39.10	107.18	157.53	235.32	433.83	478.00	270.66	507.57	625.51	52.40	155.85	
5.	35.40	199.32	336.46	327.44	323.92	494.29	289.32	369.78	534.36	107.03	187.72	
6.	05.94	139.98	160.42	205.09	231.83	242.86	300.15	298.53	394.14	43.84	101.58	
7.	493.08	151.74	318.42	408.85	506.81	732.93	314.33	382.13	709.00	61.91	237.28	
8.	48.27	48.80	46.33	54.73	239.48	153.20	128.23	1396.02	164.76	41.39	42.28	
9.	—	—	—	68.99	68.99	117.72	—	—	NIL	—	—	
10.	10.07	13.69	22.91	16.91	16.91	25.97	60.80	67.03	82.57	10.92	10.00*	
11.	0.06	0.45	0.54	0.75	0.75	0.75	0.70	0.75	0.75	0.15	0.42	
12.	180.00	0.13	0.82	3.00	1.76	2.79	1.47	2.60	3.20	0.21	0.62	
13.	—	1.87	2.10	3.02	2.23	4.21	1.42	4.86	3.17	0.66	0.15	
14.	0.29	2.05	1.91	7.85	3.98	8.21	3.67	.6.51	8.01	0.62	1.78	
15.	558.38	1020.52	1446.30	1937.08	2951.89	4174.07	1863.36	2652.57	3659.87	492.80	841.75	
16.	1765.80	455.33	538.23	541.49	492.75	542.85	536.20	442.58	475.85	869.17	505.66	
17.	900.73	497.33	579.45	426.07	432.12	492.75	507.09	410.65	457.03	804.37	472.63	
18.	562.32	779.06	997.04	—	—	—	78.64	50.85	3291.00	—	895.85	
19.	-370.99	942.26	509.01	826.51	—	2655.90	1944.24	4218.63	3815.03	328.60	869.09	
20.	16.00	15.00	15.00	26.00	5.00	17.00	14.00	13.25	13.00	6.00	5.00	
21.	10.00	10.00	10.00	30.00	10.00	20.00	27.50	20.00	27.50	10.00	10.00	
22.	566.00	561.00	460.00	826.00	675.00	589.00	740.00	700.00	655.00	600.00	600.00	

TABLE 6 (*Contd.*)

Sl. No.	VRIDHESHWAR			RAHURI		SANJIWANI			SHRI GANDO		
	1993-94	1994-95	1995-96	1993-94	1995-96	1993-94	1994-95	1995-96	1993-94	1994-95	1995-96
		(14)			(15)			(16)		(17)	
1.	24.56	164.07	618.13	532.61	898.74	645.34	735.64	1055.26	408.86	365.41	590.98
2.	4.14	35.42	71.06	106.22	127.38	85.11	103.42	125.94	85.53	93.04	126.49
3.	0.18	0.66	1.30	2.57	4.76	2.62	2.75	3.34	0.01	—	—
4.	59.16	103.74	264.03	480.97	685.84	370.03	471.54	626.79	281.11	264.85	393.63
5.	57.30	160.04	227.54	629.94	772.93	351.08	399.03	473.81	270.79	360.29	407.54
6.	41.91	64.30	147.47	291.75	344.11	294.77	357.63	211.33	204.68	189.19	295.30
7.	100.87	148.50	508.18	401.95	953.94	350.24	472.90	600.96	181.06	191.70	468.83
8.	25.77	185.65	208.37	70.06	85.09	117.66	111.51	118.60	150.22	90.96	120.62
9.	—	—	15.44	123.12	180.03	44.34	95.50	114.64	—	—	—
10.	6.12	9.07	15.20	43.01	65.85	25.81	31.70	41.60	63.68	63.76	70.00
11.	0.04	0.29	0.63	0.75	0.75	0.75	0.75	0.75	2.00	0.75	0.75
12.	0.07	0.58	1.24	2.19	2.51	2.00	1.85	1.91	1.45	—	—
13.	0.24	1.10	1.63	—	2.62	2.15	3.68	3.50	1.24	3.35	3.90
14.	0.14	1.45	3.13	5.48	7.71	4.36	4.79	6.40	6.88	4.16	5.55
15.	375.80	874.96	2083.38	2778.68	4228.99	555.22	2792.69	3557.76	1658.09	1632.18	2492.00
16.	1957.50	605.24	664.78	538.06	587.35	532.19	661.14	579.16	430.67	431.25	456.50
17.	836.97	600.00	599.50	484.04	549.93	139.28	583.46	661.14	367.80	392.34	449.12
18.	535.24	95.00	1106.76	—	146.42	13.34	—	NIL	121.46	35.83	44.33
19.	-266.45	407.52	-120.95	2883.64	3178.75	1201.83	2590.65	1905.24	2646.48	3565.54	3189.47
20.	11.00	10.00	10.00	19.25	18.00	8.00	7.00	20.00	6.00	7.00	7.00
21.	10.00	12.50	15.00	20.00	10.00	20.00	10.00	20.00	7.50	7.50	20.00
22.	200.00	660.00	525.00	675.00	575.00	690.00	645.00	635.00	800.00	705.00	640.00

(*Contd.*)

TABLE 6 (*Contd.*)

NASHIK DISTRICT

Sl. No.	NASHIK		K.K.WAGH		GIRNA		KADWA		
	1994-95	1995-96	1993-94	1994-95	1995-96	1994-95	1993-94	1994-95	1995-96
	(1)		(2)		(3)		(4)		
1.	261.16	318.13	142.78	256.65	438.50	185.61	172.80	194.10	344.65
2.	40.66	28.19	25.84	43.58	54.11	25.64	34.82	44.75	70.23
3.	0.85	0.81	—	—	16.80	1.42	0.44	0.72	1.23
4.	120.87	79.38	86.52	131.89	205.19	52.37	139.30	139.59	230.30
5.	184.31	242.90	182.13	207.45	310.55	312.62	117.95	140.47	184.92
6.	83.89	175.19	32.94	37.10	59.41	234.91	140.88	199.96	174.87
7.	124.43	242.43	65.91	76.92	158.88	144.92	140.92	66.06	121.51
8.	18.59	526.94	45.42	26.59	22.64	66.71	37.57	745.25	47.55
9.	—	—	15.17	—	—	—	39.32	45.75	62.17
10.	35.00	46.55	15.09	15.00	18.31	15.85	35.00	15.97	54.92
11.	0.41	0.40	0.25	0.37	0.50	0.75	0.40	0.37	0.55
12.	0.22	0.68	0.50	0.78	1.19	0.34	0.91	0.83	0.73
13.	0.43	1.12	0.46	1.02	1.00	0.24	1.00	1.55	2.15
14.	1.73	2.22	1.17	1.96	3.12	0.98	1.39	2.00	2.40
15.	1866.94	1204.14	635.28	904.69	1291.06	891.49	848.50	899.08	1319.50
16.	1085.51	605.15	531.80	405.07	412.97	855.64	862.70	489.93	471.35
17.	1135.41	605.15	531.80	405.07	412.97	855.64	862.70	489.93	471.35
18.	1387.23	1338.39	—	653.05	702.46	—	—	209.63	232.88
19.	529.74	797.16	322.06	535.72	654.93	—	1029.61	1192.21	1902.57
20.	—	—	25.00	5.00	1.00	10.00	15.00	10.50	15.00
21.	10.00	48.84	10.00	10.00	20.00	—	63.00	10.00	25.00
22.	561.00	603.00	766.00	605.00	557.00	600.00	756.00	725.00	758.00

TABLE 6 (*Contd.*)

Sl. No.	NASHIK DISTRICT: NIFAD 1993-94	1994-95	1995-96	VASANTADADA PATIL 1993-94	1994-95	1995-96	DHULE DISTRICT: SHIRPUR 1993-94	1994-95	1995-96	PANZARKAN 1993-94	1994-95	SATPUDA TAPI 1993-94	1994-95
		(5)			(6)			(1)		(2)		(3)	
1.	632.92	632.38	919.71	267.41	376.83	684.54	253.96	473.08	861.18	106.48	166.48	752.17	914.98
2.	124.19	147.64	192.70	51.52	78.83	113.77	48.53	72.35	88.63	21.09	50.62	128.11	162.40
3.	9.00	9.61	15.53	10.07	0.82	2.12	1.06	1.72	2.11	1.90	3.66	3.10	4.25
4.	186.15	220.84	325.54	257.67	268.99	421.43	119.41	218.13	307.06	40.38	70.97	230.51	280.82
5.	550.83	595.39	769.68	247.10	275.39	505.15	179.92	209.50	318.40	268.93	301.79	404.37	430.68
6.	352.52	379.70	468.35	64.35	70.42	91.55	188.27	252.79	262.33	128.71	77.76	693.07	586.58
7.	405.70	428.22	888.20	248.55	173.93	567.11	302.11	227.90	363.85	145.84	116.91	646.32	676.58
8.	136.80	147.22	156.46	96.71	80.00	181.35	199.78	97.80	101.68	17.43	17.00	270.00	212.63
9.	110.82	149.95	—	—	—	—	—	—	89.69	—	—	—	—
10.	76.15	87.25	105.59	15.78	20.00	27.23	41.22	48.89	84.98	21.50	16.54	70.04	33.00
11.	0.75	0.75	0.75	0.47	0.65	0.75	45.00	0.65	0.75	0.20	0.42	0.75	0.75
12.	2.45	3.00	2.68	0.66	0.98	1.55	0.80	1.18	1.89	0.32	0.89	2.84	3.27
13.	—	8.76	3.74	0.90	1.14	5.04	0.57	3.59	2.16	0.23	1.86	2.01	2.63
14.	5.13	7.25	6.88	2.55	3.42	5.16	2.91	3.44	4.32	0.92	2.06	6.90	7.52
15.	2713.50	3072.14	4022.29	1228.72	1228.72	2606.75	1338.36	1611.02	2289.42	761.97	1161.96	3208.39	349.27
16.	469.62	509.63	505.59	516.37	516.37	518.79	592.11	497.04	526.79	771.02	556.76	465.15	450.14
17.	389.45	423.60	449.96	479.32	479.32	429.25	584.47	479.61	497.43	551.16	561.85	436.60	427.80
18.	—	64.89	—	314.32	311.64	337.36	63.90	543.08	852.53	1170.90	1181.96	1.00	6.99
19.	366.82	4598.88	1526.03	1036.00	1919.83	2466.11	883.31	1980.28	2357.54	98.15	1229.56	4150.58	1911.66
20.	11.00	10.00	1.00	13.00	7.00	5.00	7.00	6.00	6.00	—	16.00	40.00	10.00
21.	30.00	5.00	11.00	10.00	10.00	20.00	10.00	10.00	10.00	10.00	10.00	10.00	10.00
22.	823.00	761.00	727.00	723.00	647.00	640.00	562.00	611.00	585.00	600.00	561.00	691.00	650.00

(*Contd.*)

TABLE 6 (*Contd.*)

Sl. No.	JALGAON DISTRICT												AURANGABAD		
	BELGANGA			MADHUKAR			VASANT		CHOPDA			DEVGIRI		
	1993-94	1994-95	1995-96	1993-94	1994-95	1995-96	1994-95	1995-96	1993-94	1994-95	1995-96	1993-94	1994-95	1995-96
		(1)			(2)		(3)			(4)			(1)	
1.	307.94	308.77	421.63	380.07	366.47	595.70	265.12	349.88	4.68	82.69	558.35	265.67	420.11	647.40
2.	59.05	70.13	61.91	71.83	80.91	91.79	49.12	38.62	—	28.01	64.19	46.665	78.31	78.57
3.	2.27	1.19	2.60	6.68	7.35	13.69	1.24	1.96	—	56.87	2.29	1.10	1.11	1.77
4.	123.13	116.32	159.55	190.04	246.80	337.80	84.48	138.89	66.21	96.70	110.35	64.73	282.76	150.95
5.	292.00	303.69	323.85	259.26	300.81	423.91	220.91	277.00	5.26	51.66	227.42	83.64	139.47	297.05
6.	277.93	220.64	303.39	193.06	232.89	241.66	131.20	82.84	17.88	43.65	312.27	198.01	375.78	153.92
7.	1295.46	264.35	470.04	190.72	227.33	586.02	22.82	489.32	29.72	456.21	833.23	430.61	615.34	342.33
8.	107.77	75.51	82.83	81.59	95.00	869.78	39.80	36.94	26.24	25.10	344.43	339.60	328.92	300.07
9.	—	—	NIL	—	—	—	—	—	—	—	—	—	—	—
10.	2.50	22.14	22.00	70.00	6.36	27.37	—	—	—	7.00	0.16	—	—	—
11.	0.47	0.85	0.75	0.75	0.67	0.75	0.39	—	—	0.25	0.75	0.43	—	—
12.	0.86	1.00	1.01	—	0.89	1.34	0.79	—	—	0.02	1.34	0.69	1.11	1.11
13.	—	0.75	2.06	1.00	—	2.34	1.63	—	0.22	0.89	0.57	—	0.79	—
14.	2.15	2.27	2.75	3.50	—	4.84	1.97	—	—	0.11	3.36	1.98	3.16	—
15.	1483.60	1418.08	28.57	1711.49	1727.81	2404.22	1009.70	1504.36	188.77	4050.50	35.49	2773.04	4032.91	4846.29
16.	636.75	490.31	7.49	586.20	521.19	454.64	498.51	537.40	9101.69	1012.22	10.15	1281.61	1269.21	1072.49
17.	610.22	472.80	—	606.54	519.94	482.54	512.93	588.70	10143.75	9.63	—	1316.73	1267.34	1196.00
18.	81.35	728.90	1107.27	—	155.71	150.40	1639.74	—	—	—	804.79	—	—	—
19.	693.99	1853.91	1518.72	2046.65	1720.40	2015.44	916.26	—	—	—	1609.86	664.37	636.88	—
20.	6.00	—	—	6.00	1.00	2.00	5.00	—	—	5.00	—	6.00	17.00	—
21.	10.00	1.00	—	10.00	10.00	10.00	—	—	—	10.00	12.50	12.50	12.50	—
22.	701.00	641.00	536.00	701.00	641.00	515.00	700.00	460.00	701.00	760.00	510.00	673.00	250.00	460.00

Table 6 (*Contd.*)

Jalna District

Sl. No.	GANGAPUR 1993-94	GANGAPUR 1994-95	KANND 1993-94	KANND 1994-95	KANND 1995-96	SHRI EKANATH 1994-95	SHRI EKANATH 1995-96	SIDDHESHWAR 1993-94	SIDDHESHWAR 1994-95	SIDDHESHWAR 1995-96	VINAYAK 1994-95	JALNA 1994-95	JALNA 1995-96
	(1)			(2)		(3)			(4)		(5)	(6)	
1.	168.22	320.04	321.99	246.27	509.93	209.83	220.29	247.97	352.80	570.96	179.02	290.80	419.33
2.	33.64	70.10	59.38	66.19	66.49	48.11	23.28	52.28	74.74	84.92	40.80	57.91	58.05
3.	3.47	6.09	1.50	1.52	2.78	0.92	0.98	0.55	0.65	0.32	0.69	0.50	1.26
4.	116.99	246.21	206.30	381.20	305.98	138.49	104.97	171.34	231.39	307.03	96.11	268.48	220.09
5.	221.33	243.63	271.33	198.88	446.28	245.36	302.62	227.80	297.92	346.06	173.56	211.82	209.33
6.	87.42	106.04	98.75	113.66	124.85	106.67	139.69	91.48	96.09	124.90	70.09	125.62	135.04
7.	869.43	193.04	199.24	178.35	262.44	174.40	514.12	133.65	189.39	400.43	165.21	114.06	97.02
8.	105.80	93.88	53.87	56.19	192.09	45.32	45.16	90.36	73.95	72.54	36.30	137.20	116.16
9.	—	—	36.73	56.24	—	—	—	60.63	30.96	43.40	—	—	—
10.	0.41	16.80	55.10	—	85.18	0.41	16.49	47.00	64.29	75.46	16.71	44.27	30.00
11.	0.35	0.57	0.55	0.59	0.81	0.39	0.33	0.49	0.62	0.75	0.43	0.47	0.53
12.	0.65	1.24	2.11	1.37	1.79	0.84	0.18	0.97	1.31	1.70	0.69	0.82	0.95
13.	0.54	16.80	2.01	3.58	1.72	0.82	1.16	1.73	3.83	2.38	0.60	3.03	0.68
14.	1.66	3.11		2.82	2.82	2.07	1.69	1.81	3.29	4.26	3.33	2.34	2.72
15.	1019.39	1301.32	1306.76	1335.41	2032.48	2097.36	1172.47	1136.36	1440.02	2035.91	1717.06	1276.16	1291.79
16.	653.26	—	475.52	490.20	498.26	1068.01	705.08	468.60	403.50	480.50	1030.85	538.05	483.93
17.	446.82	—	450.26	473.00	533.98	1014.21	508.00	469.67	438.16	456.08	989.00	544.35	475.30
18.	60.54	59.53	186.76	—	635.80	1194.51	1194.51	66.31	58.60	28.14	975.73	77.54	—
19.	1215.09	1827.86	7188.23	—	1185.72	932.31	469.66	1797.83	1915.28	1736.44	896.37	1104.69	2223.01
20.	17.00	15.00	8.00	—	—	5.00	—	6.00	5.00	5.00	6.00	5.00	20.00
21.	50.00	22.00	10.00	10.00	10.00	10.00	10.00	10.00	10.00	10.00	10.00	10.00	10.00
22.	690.00	639.00	673.00	667.00	460.00	565.00	460.00	740.00	665.00	618.00	611.00	561.00	701.00

(*Contd.*)

TABLE 6 (*Contd.*)

Sl. No.	BEED DISTRICT SAMARTH			AMBE JOGAI	JAI BHAVANI		KADA	MAJALGAON			SHRI GAJANAN		PARBHANI DISTRICT GODAVARI DUDHNA	
	1993-94	1994-95	1995-96	1993-94	1994-95	1995-96	1994-95	1993-94	1994-95	1995-96	1994-95	1995-96	1993-94	1994-95
		(1)		(2)	(3)		(4)		(5)		(6)		(1)	
1.	137.14	329.75	547.44	85.85	382.37	456.87	224.74	183.06	306.71	545.34	172.92	213.85	171.98	238.56
2.	22.51	64.99	76.97	20.53	76.70	50.61	40.38	33.54	68.92	78.05	35.95	15.08	28.90	58.13
3.	0.70	1.49	2.26	0.90	1.73	1.81	0.80	1.06	2.30	2.77	0.84	0.17	1.10	2.00
4.	66.18	212.31	499.04	97.96	185.68	336.05	133.40	119.90	201.49	389.13	158.61	235.46	97.19	228.71
5.	165.61	180.80	255.79	138.00	169.32	225.93	107.51	520.80	80.87	153.54	97.47	145.12	207.70	226.21
6.	67.60	82.83	91.20	47.79	78.44	101.07	85.61	38.75	81.43	138.25	58.54	57.77	75.89	81.19
7.	142.67	152.80	619.01	380.03	171.76	411.86	181.61	841.08	921.39	709.31	164.50	234.52	186.01	192.45
8.	93.15	—	255.23	160.00	151.16	139.65	33.82	301.68	295.00	282.12	38.88	57.83	43.00	40.00
9.	—	—	—	—	—	—	—	—	—	—	—	—	—	—
10.	14.60	15.45	18.45	—	11.45	16.98	7.44	—	5.44	9.35	—	—	49.39	48.74
11.	0.21	0.53	0.75	0.19	0.63	0.66	0.33	0.20	0.56	0.75	0.30	0.29	0.27	0.51
12.	0.39	1.10	1.85	3.03	1.16	1.26	0.02	0.55	1.14	1.62	0.52	0.33	—	0.90
13.	—	1.93	3.23		1.10	1.84	0.64	—	—	2.03	0.37	0.62	—	0.56
				0.22										
14.	0.94	2.76	4.62		3.25	3.14	1.72	1.31	2.86	4.05	1.48	0.97	0.86	2.56
15.	850.85	174.38	2375.84	401.59	1233.94	1746.95	815.86	1957.89	3124.70	2316.31	729.31	962.01	862.29	1070.37
16.	813.15	65.28	551.50	15.05	393.73	531.88	494.58	1398.81	1100.04	551.56	497.28	663.76	643.27	451.08
17.	772.47	63.17	514.34	592.66	378.65	555.95	474.72	1407.22	1092.08	649.01	492.02	524.14	583.58	417.50
18.	262.71	—	1142.23	1728.72	710.40	531.82	1452.35	—	—	484.17	950.82	1129.05	52.39	552.63
19.	407.13	1424.34	2125.99	-201.50	2090.02	1105.60	709.46	538.37	—	1562.42	608.28	120.05	155.02	1372.62
20.	6.00	5.00	—	—	8.00	—	2.00	6.00	6.00	5.00	15.00	—	6.00	5.00
21.	12.50	12.50	—	10.00	12.50	10.00	—	10.00	12.00	20.00	10.00	10.00	10.00	10.00
22.	536.00	672.00	595.00	590.00	667.00	460.00	561.00	600.00	629.00	510.00	590.00	460.00	600.00	624.00

TABLE 6 (*Contd.*)

NANDED DISTRICT

Sl. No.	MARATHWADA			PURNA		GODAVARI MANAR			KALAMBAR		SHANKAR	
	1993-94	1994-95	1995-96	1993-94	1994-95	1993-94	1994-95	1995-96	1993-94	1994-95	1993-94	1994-95
		(1)			(2)		(3)			(4)		(5)
1.	14.61	137.48	130.20	322.64	368.63	301.78	463.71	542.62	84.75	127.86	204.88	283.90
2.	1.84	27.59	27.59	67.18	86.52	42.21	78.17	80.58	18.09	31.35	31.65	49.84
3.	—	0.79	0.79	1.093	1.90	0.77	1.20	1.55	0.21	0.53	0.99	1.34
4.	27.35	83.57	83.57	245.74	238.18	138.93	217.99	413.16	127.41	168.73	114.78	111.30
5.	167.14	235.95	235.95	192.35	298.62	203.92	254.95	395.02	72.72	94.45	130.66	134.01
6.	36.54	41.21	41.21	226.98	139.30	105.97	127.45	154.85	36.94	41.68	135.16	120.48
7.	236.12	267.10	267.10	281.10	237.77	379.35	466.29	716.02	99.38	73.89	718.99	94.49
8.	23.55	20.24	20.24	124.53	100.50	52.74	721.98	205.07	26.93	23.91	95.92	80.65
9.	—	—	—	—	—	—	—	—	NIL	—	66.32	—
10.	14.00	12.41	—	57.82	64.58	38.99	46.60	—	10.00	5.00	21.51	22.95
11.	0.02	0.22	—	—	0.70	0.41	0.65	0.77	0.21	0.32	0.29	0.40
12.	0.02	0.44	—	1.40	1.50		1.31	1.43	0.23	0.46	0.59	0.80
						1.33						
13.	0.13	0.39	—	—	2.64		3.34	1.12	0.19	0.81	6.00	1.44
14.	0.10	1.09	—	3.39	3.78	2.16	3.28	3.58	0.77	1.16	1.47	2.00
15.	508.76	814.06	814.06	1535.04	1480.05	2067.71	2490.82	—	477.83	570.15	892.53	892.56
16.	5992.47	723.13	723.13	484.21	419.11	848.68	1222.62	—	575.32	449.96	607.18	607.18
17.	9917.35	747.06	747.06	453.06	390.96	843.86	1152.23	—	622,.94	492.51	603.08	603.08
18.	—	2557.31	—	932.19	974.61	606.26	659.51	1166.71	870.41	872.12	—	155.93
19.	691.98	-152.21	—	1191.29	235.89	1242.51	1162.15	468.58	114.10	629.70	950.19	1174.31
20.	6.00	—	—	11.00	15.00	7.00	10.00	—	6.00	5.00	6.00	10.00
21.	—	10.00	—	10.00	—	10.00	10.00	—	10.00	10.00	10.00	10.00
22.	360.00	460.00	460.00	700.00	700.00	600.00	561.00	460.00	606.00	561.00	646.38	622.00

(*Contd.*)

TABLE 6 (Contd.)

Sl. No.	Usmanabad District: TULJABHAVANI 1993-94	1994-95	1995-96	TERANA 1993-94	1994-95	1995-96	Latur District: JAI JAWAN JAI KISAN 1993-94	1994-95	1995-96	MANJARA 1993-94	1994-95	1995-96	SHETAKARI KILLARI 1993-94	1994-95	1995-96
		(1)			(2)			(1)			(2)			(3)	
1.	87.61	226.51	379.85	189.19	396.78	639.67	130.69	226.22	303.97	390.36	412.39	518.57	144.66	412.39	360.30
2.	10.82	48.48	42.93	32.12	105.03	115.53	24.29	51.57	60.41	59.89	95.01	94.20	28.66	95.01	61.26
3.	0.51	0.85	1.27	0.92	1.62	4.37	0.43	0.50	1.07	0.79	1.35	1.70	0.68	1.35	1.81
4.	73.26	201.07	136.85	170.43	409.32	579.14	97.02	127.20	202.79	230.92	305.75	390.44	66.08	305.75	109.0
5.	96.53	111.82	263.93	231.15	283.46	387.93	152.19	167.67	224.23	194.78	279.25	319.60	182.62	279.25	340.14
6.	32.55	90.45	166.97	146.31	160.63	281.86	100.56	117.14	161.79	93.64	124.92	182.04	46.29	124.92	200.66
7.	396.58	193.62	341.95	198.23	205.87	551.10	108.15	90.42	199.70	183.17	127.19	314.73	120.88	127.19	249.24
8.	64.11	117.78	865.35	78.80	68.87	2728.56	47.52	45.22	45.90	74.21	60.88	67.83	17.55	60.88	24.43
9.	—	43.10	17.02	—	—	—	—	—	—	69.91	9.43	—	—	9.43	—
10.	9.50	9.50	17.99	16.50	20.90	20.90	10.61	10.57	8.82	40.66	—	9.58	25.00	—	88.23
11.	NIL	0.50	0.65	—	0.75	0.75	0.23	0.42	0.57	0.56	0.75	0.75	0.27	0.75	0.63
12.	NIL	0.75	0.98	0.55	1.87	1.87	0.40	0.90	1.13	1.13	1.47	2.09	0.50	1.47	1.33
13.	NIL	0.19	—	0.34	1.23	1.23	—	1.83	1.90	1.03	0.17	2.61	0.41	0.17	2.57
14.	0.60	1.62	2.44	1.37	4.67	4.67	1.15	2.25	2.84	3.24	4.53	5.23	1.44	4.53	3.24
15.	406.68	1050.36	1527.05	995.13	1660.99	2728.56	687.47	841.91	1214.42	1259.89	1412.53	1909.37	668.60	1412.53	1462.89
16.	655.86	486.83	620.46	675.63	384.40	471.14	610.97	400.01	428.83	453.19	361.26	415.68	482.66	361.26	464.06
17.	659.74	482.63	—	724.78	355.10	475.39	534.01	374.81	400.01	337.01	312.50	365.83	459.70	312.50	427.32
18.	NIL	375.33	451.52	309.04	320.99	—	30.16	267.27	227.54	NIL	96.95	88.18	95.98	96.00	182.25
19.	279.89	1098.72	135.93	916.44	3541.69	—	651.07	1396.00	1130.26	2339.32	2975.85	2407.58	1455.38	—	1358.04
20.	6.00	5.00	8.00	10.00	5.00	5.00	7.50	6.50	5.00	16.00	15.00	15.00	6.00		5.00
21.	10.00	10.00	10.00	10.00	10.00	10.00	10.00	10.00	27.00	10.00	10.00	10.00	10.00		10.00
22.	610.00	565.00	565.00	600.00	819.00	460.00	625.00	676.00	580.00	876.00	842.00	805.00	706.00		721.00

TABLE 6 (*Contd.*)

SL. No.	YAVATMAL DIST.						AKOLA DIST.		WARDHA DIST.		BHANDARA DIST.	
	YAVATMAL	VASANI (PUSAD)			SHANKAR SHETAKARI		BALAJI		MAHATMA		VAINGANGA	
	1994-95	1993-94	1994-95	1995-96	1994-95	1995-96	1994-95	1995-96	1993-94	1994-95	1995-96	1993-94
	(1)	(2)			(3)		(1)		(1)		(1)	
1.	227.05	336.46	443.32	530.37	195.20	56.45	244.55	230.55	358.00	179.18	391.77	75.04
2.	23.18	60.98	80.96	60.38	22.30	8.04	30.31	23.92	19.01	16.70	19.09	11.95
3.	1.11	1.22	1.51	1.66	0.78	0.83	1.00	1.41	0.52	0.88	1.48	—
4.	67.15	224.41	245.59	306.93	69.56	34.46	119.77	52.42	46.96	45.44	104.09	46.16
5.	71.93	304.15	324.21	375.63	75.73	141.10	189.44	197.65	169.31	186.93	248.67	90.56
6.	123.85	113.37	148.06	147.84	96.88	77.45	98.62	233.67	146.01	51.48	43.02	46.46
7.	442.32	322.98	430.76	474.07	475.96	419.80	142.25	311.89	85.32	57.85	85.02	127.25
8.	309.14	99.94	98.20	675.59	259.79	96.13	90.55	145.75	58.21	942.83	43.41	112.39
9.	—	—	—	—	—	—	—	—	—	—	—	—
10.	6.00	18.66	18.00	10.85	—	11.75	13.73	15.12	12.00	13.00	14.65	7.74
11.	0.27	0.54	0.75	0.67	0.18	0.07	0.25	0.30	0.17	0.14	0.28	0.11
12.	0.42	1.17	3.90	2.29	0.33	0.12	0.46	0.55	0.34	0.29	0.59	0.22
13.	0.29	—	0.85	0.68	0.20	0.09	0.25	0.71	—	0.49	0.74	0.14
14.	1.17	2.35	—	4.64	—	0.26	1.16	1.39	0.97	0.72	1.48	0.57
15.	1276.58	1486.23	1775.21	2036.31	1196.96	528.13	934.08	1896.41	975.38	883.22	17.74	518.57
16.	—	547.44	—	605.30	—	1415.70	—	1281.48	1106.15	1295.87	12.57	926.64
17.	—	524.23	—	—	—	698.49	—	1367.79	1008.50	1231.48	21.48	—
18.	242.83	60.10	356.11	714.45	—	266.27	565.32	—	328.48	483.96	6222.48	748.10
19.	—	1450.91	1753.03	1043.21	—	- 27.36	231.85	142.01	—	725.69	505.80	133.15
20.	9.00	5.00	5.00	5.00	5.00	6.00	—	—	6.00	—	—	6.00
21.	5.11	12.50	12.50	22 50	12.50	10.00	10.00	—	—	—	10.00	10.00
22.	460.00	610.00	585.00	491. 00	460.00	410.00	460.00	460.00	410.00	460.00	460.00	410.00

(*Contd.*)

TABLE 6 (*Concld.*)

Note : The data of the following sugar cooperatives is not available for the respective years :

1. 1993-94 : (1) Bhogawati
   (2) Nashik
   (3) Vasant
   (4) Shri Eknath
   (5) Jaina
   (6) Jai Bhavani
   (7) Shri Gajanan

2. 1993-94/95-96 : (1) Girna
   (2) Vinayaik
   (3) Kada
   (4) Jai Kisan
   (5) Shankar Shetakari

3. 1994-95 : (1) Shree Vitthal
   (2) Rahuri.

4. 1994-95/95-96 : (1) Manganga
   (2) Ambejogai
   (3) Vainganga

5. 1995-96 : (1) Chattrapati Rajaram
   (2) Yashwant
   (3) Shriram
   (4) Jagdamba
   (5) Panzarkan
   (6) Satpuda Tapi
   (7) Gangapur
   (8) Godawari Dudhna
   (9) Purna

6. 1993-94/94-95 : (1) Panchganga
   (2) Sanjay
   (3) Sindkoda 95-96
   (4) Jijamata
   (5) Amravati

6

SUGARCANE PRICE POLICY

Sugar prices have direct link with the cultivation of sugarcane. The demand for sugar is being estimated every year. The prices of sugar and its demand may fluctuate with the availability of sugarcane. To keep the balance in all macro variables, buffer stock of sugar has been made. Thus sugar prices, buffer stock sugar prices and export prices of sugar etc., impinge upon the prices of sugarcane. Buffer stock sugar prices and open market sugar prices, since 1960's, has been accepted as an important norm of fixing sugarcane price.

Sugarcane pricing policy has a long history. After passing up of 1932's Sugar Industry Protection Act, proper management of sugarcane supply was thought essential. Initially it was thought that, this Act will protect both industry and cane growers. But the industrialists were gigantically benefited by this. Due to which Sugarcane Act (1934) was enacted to protect the interests of the cane growers. Accordingly, fixation of sugarcane prices came under the discretion of provincial government. U.P. and Bihar Governments had led a foundation to dispose off the sugarcane prices on scientific lines. At the end of 1950-51, majority of provincial governments had enacted Sugarcane Acts. And a process of sugarcane pricing had been led. Anomalous norms and principles were embedded to determine the sugarcane prices.

Two Acts qualified to attain high degree of sugarcane cultivation with an improvement in the quality of sugarcane. As a result the sugar prices begun to fall down and the need to attain a fair price was felt. The conflict between sugar factories and cane growers sporadically came up. This conflict gave a way out to undertake production of jaggery which was a harm to the sugar industry. As the sugar was being a controlled commodity by Central Government, the industry got muzzled. Since then Government's policy is vacillating. Control, decontrol, partial control, etc. became the regular features of this industry. The levy prices of sugar were fixed on the regional and cost of production basis. The production cost of sugar factories in Northern India was less. The sugar factories in U.P. were benefited by this procedure gigantically. They had been protected from the Southern aggression in this industry. Even today, the Northern interests are protected in determining the central sugarcane policy.

Tariff Board was in favour of the agriculturists. It was rather the main objective of the Board. This responded to increase the area under cultivation from 2.9 million acres to 3.4 million acres in 1932-33. This was also one of the causes of fall of the sugarcane prices during the period. Tariff Board fixed the factory gate price of sugarcane at 8 annas per mound in 1935. At that time sugarcane prices in U.P., Bihar, Orissa were at the range of 3 to 3.5 annas per mound (Shah 1940). The cost of cultivation of sugarcane in U.P. was 4 to 5 annas, in Bihar it was 5 annas and 6 paise per mound. I.T.B. in 1938 had registered the cost of cultivation of sugarcane at 3 annas and 7 paise in U.P. and 5 annas in Bihar. This obviously explored the fact that the farmers had been exploited (Randhava, 1969). The issue of cane price was debating in Northern India during the period. The 'Gate Cane' and 'Rail Cane' were the controversial issues in U.P. (Amin, 1984). Gate cane was the shorthand adopted in the literature of the period for cane brought to the factory gates by the peasantry at their own cost. Correspondingly, rail cane referred to the cane brought by the factory's agents at the mufussil railway stations and sent in special wagons to the factory. Until the passing of the 1938 Sugar Factory Control Act, which formally attacked the problem of middlemen and made it obligatory for the mills to purchase cane through co-operative societies.

The I.S.M.A. Standing Committee in 1934-35 highlighted the problem of 'rate war' *i.e.,* the competition for sugarcane price. The competition in U.P. was natural enough, because the sugar factories were situated in close proximity to each other. The competition seems to have forged the alliance between sugar capitalists and landlord-moneylender-contractors to the detriment of the peasantry (Amin, 1984). Sugar factories had been employing middlemen to eliminate competition. The problem of sugarcane supply was a crucial issue before the sugar factories. I.T.B. (1931) had specially noted that 'we desire to emphasize that, the strongest aspect of the case of protection is that based upon the national importance of promoting the cultivation of sugarcane'.

The Report of the Indian Sugar Committee, 1920 (Para 317-26) had recommended a scheme of statutory minimum price for sugarcane to the peasants. On the background of the protection to the sugar mills, it was stated that protection alone would not serve the purpose. It was stipulated that, the industry should pay at least statutory minimum prices to the cane growers. But I.T.B. (1931) ruled out even the regional price schedule on the grounds of practicability. An adequate payment to the cane growers was left to the 'good sense of the factory owners'. Better prices for sugarcane would bring fourth a high yielding better quality cane to the sugar factories. The sugar capitalists were not willing to pay guaranteed minimum prices to the cane growers voluntarily (Amin, 1984). Payment of minimum prices to sugarcane was termed as hurdle to the onward march of the sugar industry.

Simala Sugar Conference (1933) had resolved to give minimum prices to sugarcane which was once again opposed by the industrialists. Govt., though afforded to protect the sugar industry in the name of cane growers, had made no provision to protect the peasant class against the revenges of the sugar capitalists. However, the detailed note of U.P. Govt. castigated the sugar industrialists in no uncertain terms. It was quoted :

> ".... The main objective of the tariff which was to enable the cultivator....to get a suitable price for his sugarcane and so to avert the danger of economic unrest has not been fulfilled. In some cases factories

> are giving absurdly low prices for the sugarcane... and making large profits. In the majority of cases however, the price paid by a factory does not reach the growers; the contractor makes big profits (Memorandum to U.P. Govt. quoted in Amin 1984). In fact they were firm determining the sugarcane prices on the demand and supply forces. However, U.P. Govt. guaranteed the minimum prices and protected the farmers."

In order to link the minimum price of sugarcane to the ruling price of sugar and thus secure for the peasant a 'fair share' of the sugar profits, a sliding scale sugarcane pricing based on the following formula was introduced. In November 1933, the U.P. Govt. explored a formula of sugarcane pricing as under :

$$C_t = (S_{t-1} + P_t)/200$$

Where

C_t = Factory gate price of sugarcane expressed in annas for the time t.

S_{t-1} = Percentage of recovery t-1 (An Average extraction of sugarcane).

P_t = Price of sugar per mound during t time.

If S is the percentage of extraction to have a production of one mound of sugar then it requires 100/S amount of sugarcane. If the cost on sugarcane is 50 per cent, the price of 100/S sugarcane will be p/2. P is the price of sugar. Then $C = S \times P/200$ will be the price of sugarcane (Shah, 1969). It is assumed here that the cost incurred on sugarcane is 50 per cent. This was against the farmers. In Bombay province, at that time, the cost of sugarcane was assumed to 60 per cent. Whereas the Tariff Board had arrived the same cost percentage at 66 per cent for Bombay Province. Some independent work shows that the cost incurred on sugarcane in the process of sugar production was 75 to 80 per cent. The minimum price schedule in U.P. between November, 1934 to March, 1937 was between the range of Rs. 6 to 6-8 to Rs. 9 to 10 per mound. The share of peasants in the price of sugar percentage ranged between 43 to 52. During the corresponding days, number of changes took place in this formula.

Sugar prices during the World War-II were hiked. As a result sugar factories and the sugar growers benefited enormously. Later on, the sugar prices started to fall, which had disappointed the innovators of Pravara Co-operative Sugar Factory. The sugar industry during the period had faced number of distresses and hardships while competing with gur and khandasari production. Besides there was no uniformity in payment of sugarcane prices. Cane growers were disappointed to undertake sugarcane cultivation. However, the sugar factories somehow managing their economics of sugar production even by paying remunerative prices to the cane growers. Farmer's demand was rational, that is at least the cost of cultivation should be matched with the payment of sugarcane prices.

According to the formula given above, sugarcane price was paid at the rate of 5 annas per mound (40 kg.) of sugarcane weight. Whereas the sugar price was 8 annas and 5 paise per mound having a sugar recovery at the rate of 9 per cent. On this background sugarcane prices were demanded to be paid on sliding scale. Sugarcane prices were demanded at higher prices. Every half rupee (8 annas) increase or decrease in the prices of sugar was entitled to receive 3 paise higher or lower sugarcane prices. P is fixed even when it differs actually. As a result the cane growers were receiving less prices to their sugarcane. So, this formula was given up in 1937-38. The algebraic formulae had a marginal impact on the price received by the region. Cane Grower's Union (Ikh Sangh) led a instrumental role to highlight the grievances on this aspect and other aspect like payment, weightments, delaying carts etc., and to keep the Govt. informed of the prices and agitations. Simultaneously, the passage of the 1934 Sugarcane Act at the centre had empowered, the U.P. Govt. to go ahead with its own minimum legislation. The basic idea behind this was to give a fair proportion of the sugar prices realised by the sugar factories as distinguished from a fair price for cane.

An idea of minimum price was justifiable on the ground that, the cane growers in India were small and marginal farmers, who were pitted against the monopolistic combine of the sugar mills. The minimum prices for sugarcane in U.P. were announced every fortnight depending on the fluctuations in the ruling prices of the ten highest factory quotations (Amin, 1984). Thus an idea of minimum price was introduced and implemented. It was also pointed out that if sugar prices are rising, the cane prices should also get raised on the sliding scale basis. This policy had been accepted in the states of U.P. and Bihar. Since then payment of additional sugarcane price came out. Between 1942 to 1947 the decision to fix sugarcane prices was took by the respective State Governments. Due to which there were variations in the level of sugarcane prices. But Tariff Board had strictly warned that, there should be a uniformity in the rates, and the authority to fix the sugarcane rate should come under the jurisdiction of Central Government. This caused to enact the Sugar and Gur Control Order in 1950. Since then minimum sugarcane prices were begun to be fixed on the basis of weight of sugarcane by the Central Government (Baru, 1990).

Unfortunately, even after an enactment of 1950's Sugar and Gur Control Order, the sugarcane prices were not uniformly fixed. Some State Governments have developed their own formulae to fix the sugarcane prices. The current sugar prices were linked as a norm to determine sugarcane price. Farmers demanded to consider the respective season's actual sugar prices (sold prices) rather than sugar prices at the time of sugarcane supply, because there might be a possibility of increasing sugar prices during the off sugar season. So, it was consented that, additional sugarcane prices be paid to the cane growers, if the sugar prices hike after the supply of sugarcane to the factory. The expected rise in sugar prices in near future was taken note off while fixing the sugarcane prices.

Meanwhile in 1952-53, the Madras Government accepted SISMA (South-Indian Sugar Mill Association) formula to fix the additional sugarcane prices. The formula was as under :

$$C = (X . P) / Y$$

Where,

C = Additional cane price (ACP)

X = Net share of cane suppliers realised after the sale of one tonne of sugar.

P = Sugar price per tonne

Y = Sugar recovery

When the sugar factories earn excess income by selling the sugar at higher prices, it was demanded that, the remunerative share should be given to the cane growers. This was compelled on the U.P. and Bihar Governments by the farmers, but the industrialists could not afford this. At last, government intervention was inevitable. The revised formula had been accorded by the industrialists, which is given below :

$$C = X/100.\ P - (\ t \pm d + 0.015\ )\ /\ Y$$

Where,

C = Additional cane price

X = Grower's percentage share of the net amount raised by the factory from the sale of one tonne of sugar.

Y = Sugar recovery from cane

P = Average price of sugar per mound realised by a mill and adjusted to ISS grade E 27.

t = Taxes paid by the mill

d = The difference between the cost of manufacture of sugar of a factory and the region as a whole, on account of the differences in duration of season and recovery.

0.01= One per cent of the sales commission by the mill.

This formula was fitted for the entire nation. The variable was separately determined on the basis of the region. The grower's share (X) for Bombay region was 60 per cent. The cane growers were happy over this formula, because they were receiving more than minimum prices. However, a problem was raised, how much advance be paid to the cane growers immediately after the (15 days) supply of sugarcane to the factory.

The Government was thwarted over much formulae. The political economy of sugar industry was very active during the period. As a result Sugarcane Control Order, 1955 was passed. Accordingly SMP and ACP were required to be paid by the sugar mills. Following norms were enumerated while determining the Statutory Minimum Price (SMP) for sugarcane; (a) Cost of sugarcane production, (b) Fair sugar prices to the consumers (c) Producer's sale price of the sugar.

Since, 1955 both SMPs and ACPs to be paid to the canegrowers have been brought under practice regularly. It was principally accepted in the Sugarcane Control Order of 1955, that, additional sugarcane prices be paid to the cane growers if a factory is getting higher prices by selling its sugar. A modified Sugar Control Order (1955) stipulated the SMP for sugarcane payable by white sugar factories. The norms of fixing the SMP were,

(i) the cost of sugarcane production,

(ii) the return to the grower from alternative crop and the general trend of price of other agricultural commodities,

(iii) a fair price of sugar for consumers,

(iv) the price at which sugar is sold by the producers of sugar.

The quality of sugarcane and cost of cultivations were not taken into account while fixing the SMP before 1960. In lieu of these two factors, prices of alternative crops and gur prices were judged. Whereas fixing of ACP was depending on the sugar prices. As sugar is a controlled commodity alternatively ACP depends on levy prices of sugar and sugar policy of the Government.

Though the sugarcane weight is linked to sugar recovery of a particular sugar factory, the minimum price of sugarcane was being fixed purely on weight basis except Gujarat and Maharashtra upto 1960-61 season. As a result once again interregional variations in the prices continued. Some State Governments, during the period have developed the special formulae to link sugarcane prices to that of sugar. So, the Sugarcane Control Order, 1955 had been replaced by Sugarcane Control Order, 1966 requiring the G.O.I. to fix the minimum prices of sugarcane.

The Central Government fixes SMP factorywise in terms of Clause 3 of the Sugarcane Control Order, 1966 (as amended upto 1983) for each sugar season with consideration of having regard to the following points on the basis of the study conducted by CACP :

(i) cost of production of sugarcane,

(ii) returns to the growers from alternative crops and the general trend of prices of agricultural commodities,

(iii) availability of sugar to the consumers at a fair price,

(iv) price at which sugar produced from sugarcane is sold by sugar producers,

(v) recovery of sugar from sugarcane.

Generally the GOI announces the price recommended by CACP. However, the Government deviated from the recommendations of CACP only on four occasions. In 1990-91 and 1993-94 Government announced SMP lower by Re. 1 and Rs. 2 respectively, in 1992-93 and 1994-95, Government announced SMP higher by Rs. 4 and 60 paise respectively.

From 1952-53 to 1961-62 no perceivable changes were made in SMP even when there was an increase in the cost of sugarcane production. In 1966-67, a scheme of premium was introduced to pay for increase in recovery (See Table 11). The rate of premium has undergone a continuous increase since then. This caused to differ the SMP of each sugar factory. Good quality of sugarcane and an efficient sugar factory can get more SMP. So both the cane growers and the factory owners get benefited by this scheme.

But this scheme lacks in, if anybody weaken his performance. There may be a possibility of getting less SMP due to the inefficient management of the sugar factories. Normally the efficiency of the sugar factory depends upon rate of mill extraction (RME), rate of boiling house efficiency (RBHE) and reduced overall efficiency (ROE). This had been brought to the notice of CACP and Sugar Inquiry Committee (1965). This is one of the causes of different SMP in different sugar mills. To remove such distortions, the Central Government led down some principles in determining SMP for sugarcane through Sugarcane Control Order, 1966. They were as under (Misra, 1985) :

(a) Linking of cane prices to prevailing (current) sugar prices.

(b) Fixing minimum cane prices/unrelated to sugar price for the whole or part of the season.

(c) Fixing the 'consolidated price' related to percentage of sugar recovery.

(d) Linking of price to extra realisation from the sale of sugar.

An intention behind this was to remove the distortions in the sugarcane prices. Under this scheme a provision has been made to give considerations to the recommendations of CACP, which is specially established for the purpose. The CACP has been asked to consider the views of the State Governments, sugar industry, sugarcane growers and other concerned interests in this respect.

Since the establishment of CACP, the problem of setting up of the agricultural prices has been systematically and scientifically done keeping in mind the producer's and consumer's interests involved in it. While recommending price policy and the relative price structure, the CACP is required to keep in mind the following considerations in views :

(a) the need to provide incentive to the producer for adopting improved technology (to maximise production) and fair developing production pattern broadly in accordance with national requirements,

(b) the need to ensure rational utilisation of land, water and other production resources,

(c) the likely impact of price policy in rest of the economy and specially on cost of living and level of wages, and

(d) the likely impact of price policy on terms of trade between agricultural and non-agricultural sectors.

During the period of complete control on sugar, the sugar manufacturers were unsatisfactory due to the G.O.I's relunctancy to impose any control on Gur and Khandasari.

This is a weak point of the Government's policy. The Sugar Enquiry Committee recommended to bring down the rate of recovery from 10.4 per cent to 9.4 per cent. This was opposed by some State Governments. Correspondingly with the joint consensus of CACP and Sugar Enquiry Committee, the rate of recovery has been fixed at 8.5 per cent and this has continued till today. The rate of recovery depends on number of factors like, water, climate, soil, efficiency of sugar mill, etc.

A CONTROVERSY

A controversy has been raised during the period (1974) between Indian Sugar Mills Association (ISMA) and Indian Federation of Co-operative Sugar Factories (IFCSF) regarding the issue of recovery. Sugar recovery is an integrated work of all sections of the sugar factory and combined efforts of the cane growers including the feasible response of the climate and geo-physical conditions which helps to improve the quality of the sugarcane. It has been earmarked by ISMA that, it is because of overall mill efficiency that the sugar recovery remains more, so, the share in the additional income (excess income after deducting all costs) of sugar factories must be retained with them and not to be paid to the cane growers. Whereas IFCSF justified the case that the recovery of sugar is wholly depends upon the quality of sugarcane and its maturity and not on the overall efficiency of the sugar factories.

While representing before the Talwar Committee (1970) the ISMA claimed that, at least 50 per cent of ACP share of this nature should be given to factory owners. But no problem

A Case of ISMA	A Case of IFCSF
1. Recovery is related to sugar and the rate of waste of sugar.	1. Recovery is being created in sugarcane farms. The quality of sugarcane is more important for good recovery.
2. Sugarcane growers are mainly centered in growing the crop and not the improvements in the quality of sugarcane.	2. Additional prices is a premium paid for the quality of sugarcane.
3. Recovery is not only related to the quality of sugarcane but the overall efficiency of the sugar factories is also a significant factor of good sugar recovery. The share of sugar factories in better recovery rate constitute to 84 per cent. There are some example of less recovery even when good quality of sugarcane is supplied to the sugar factories.	3. This demand of ISMA is unscientific and impracticable.
4. The expenses of each sugar factories on raw materials varies, which is because of the efficiencies that differ in them.	4. Sugar factories must reduce their conversion cost. To produce more sugar on the available supply of sugarcane is the exclusive responsibility of sugar factories.

arises in respect of co-operative undertaking, because the cane growers are the owners of the sugar factories.

Table 7 accounts for the technical efficiency of the sugar factories in Maharashtra. In most cases the technical efficiency of sugar factories in Maharashtra is satisfactory. ISMA claimed

TABLE 7

Technical Efficiency of Sugar Industry in Maharashtra

Sl. No.	Items	Standard norms	Position in the State			
			1989-90	1990-91	1992-93	1993-94
1.	Crushing period	160-180	210	240	148	124
2.	Productive capacity	100	91.62	89.61	91.64	85.79
3.	RME (%) (Mittal)	94	94.54	94.50	94.94	94.96
4.	RBHE (%) (G. Rao)	90	90.25	90.32	90.47	90.47
5.	ROE (%) (Mittal & Rao)	84	85.33	84.35	85.89	85.91
6.	Waste Hours (%)	10	15.59	17.30	15.20	18.18
7.	Waste Sugar (%)	2	2.27	2.28	2.12	2.05

Source : Working Results of Sugar Factories in Maharashtra, VSI.

that, mill extraction efficiency is 80 per cent responsible for better recovery. But actually difficult to arrive at the percentage share of each section in the sugar factory. Good sugar recovery is due to the integrated efforts of all sections in the sugar factories. However, the share of quality sugarcane in the sugar recovery is noteworthy. The technical efficiency of the mill sector is normally given. Every technical section in the sugar factories is expected to work upto its maximum capacity. Whereas sugarcane quality, harvesting and its transport does not require any such capacities. Capacity is quantitative phenomenon whereas quality is not. Therefore, most part of good recovery goes to the sugarcane farms, and crushing time and the period of high and low recoveries.

Table 8 (a and b) illustrates the overall technical efficiency of all sugar factories operating in Maharashtra for the crushing season 1993-94.

Most of the technical parameters are reflecting good results in the Kolhapur Zone. Mill extraction is a very good indicator of the efficiency of a milling section. The performance of mill depends upon fibre content in cane. Higher fibre content increases difficulties in getting a good mill extraction. So, RME is more useful in comparing the performance of milling section, which may crush cane with different fibre contents (See GOI Report, 1996). RME indicates the mill extraction of a factory that would be obtained if fibre content was 12.5 per cent on cane. The RME of about 94 per cent is considered as standard efficiency norm. The average RME in the State was 94.60 per cent in 1990-91 season (VSI 1990-91). Thus, it is clear from above analysis that quality of sugarcane is more significant to perform good RME.

Boiling house efficiency can be had from boiling house recovery and also on final molasses purity. The boiling house recovery indicates the percentage extraction of sugar that is available. It is dependent on purity of mixed juice. So the R.B.H.R. (which is calculated for mixed juice purity equivalent to 85 per cent) is more useful for comparing the performance of the boiling house of two different sugar factories having different juice purities. In this respect too, the quality of cane plays significant role in determining the technical efficiency of sugar factories.

Reduced overall efficiency includes the overall technical efficiencies of the sugar factories. This includes other than RME and RBHE like energy management, bagasse consumption and saving, chemical consumption, percentage of molasses, purity of juice, cane quality, pol and fibre percentages in cane, brix of primary juice etc.

In all above respect it is obvious that, ISMA claim, that the share of mill section efficiency in total average sugar recovery *i.e.*, 80 per cent is futile, because almost all technical efficiencies depends upon the quality of the sugarcane. So, the AIFSF Ltd.'s claim in determining sugar recovery is worthwhile.

Table 8 (A and B) illustrates the position of operational efficiency of the sugar factories in Maharashtra for the sugar season 1993-94. In almost all norms of technical efficiencies, the performance of sugar factories in Maharashtra reflects good as compared to Table 7.

BHARGAV FORMULA

The Second Commission on Sugar Inquiry was set-up in 1974 under the Chairmanship of Ex-Supreme Court Judge, Justice V. Bhargav. The Commission has submitted its Report in 1974. It considered the problem of erratic supply of sugarcane to the sugar factories and came to conclusion that, it could be greatly established if cane growers could be held to their agreements for supply of cane in the years of shortages. An incentive was recommended to give the growers, a share of profits which is coming out of the Commission arising out of excess realisation from the sale of free sugar. This scheme is known as Bhargav Formula. Accordingly under Statutes (Clause 5A, Sugarcane Control Order, 1966) the sugar factories are required to pay an additional cane price to the growers computed in accordance with the following formula :

$$X = (R - L + 2A + B) / 2C$$

Where,

X = is the additional price in rupees per quintal of sugarcane payable by the producer of sugar to sugarcane grower.

R = is the amount in rupees of sugar produced during the sugar year excluding the excise duty paid or payable to the factory by the purchaser.

L = is the value in rupees of sugar produced during the sugar year, as calculated on the basis of the unit cost per quintal, ex-factory, exclusive of excise duty determined with reference to the minimum sugarcane price fixed under Clause 3, the final working results of the year and the cost schedule and return recommended by such authority as the Central Government may specify from time to time.

A = is the amount found payable for the previous year but not actually paid.

B = is the excess or shortfall in realisation from actual sales of the unsold stocks of sugar produced during the sugar year as on 30th days of September, which is carried forward and adjusted in the sale realisation of the following year.

C = is the quantity in quintals of sugarcane purchased by the producer of sugar during the sugar year.

Under this formula farmers and the mills share the excess realisation broadly in the ratio 50:50. The Government of India determine the Zonewise L factor, and factorywise ADP is determined by the State Governments. Time taken in notification of 'L' factor by the Department of Food for different sugar seasons is given below (Co-op. Sugar, November 1997, Vol. 29) :

Sugar Season	Date on which 'L' factor was communicated	Time taken after end of the season
1990-91	17-11-1992	14 Months
1991-92	04-02-1994	17 Months
1992-93	15-12-1994	14 Months
1993-94	19-09-1995	12 Months
1994-95	18-11-1996	14 Months
1995-96	06-10-1997	13 Months

The High Power Committee (Mahajan Committee) recommended the cane price in each Zone by the following formula :

$$\text{Cane price per tonne} = \frac{\text{Average price of sugar per quintal in Zone during the year} \times \text{Growers percentage share} \times \text{Average recovery in the Zone during the year}}{\text{All India average recovery during the year}}$$

Grower's percentage share in cane price is assumed uniform throughout the country. However, some weightage is thought off based on recovery in the Zone. Setting up of Sugarcane Pricing Board is suggested by the HPC.

The Government of India has accepted the formula from 1974-75. The Planning Commission appointed a Working Group in 1983 to set the targets of sugar production on the basis of the estimate of requirements. This Group, with number of other recommendations instructed that, the cane price to be paid to the farmers should be based on cost of production of sugarcane and the practice of declaring more cane price by some State Governments more than what is fixed by Government of India should be stopped (Kharche, 1989). It is statutory obligation on the sugar factories to pay the minimum price of sugarcane as declared by the Government of India to the sugarcane supplied to them. However, the State Governments have been advising the sugar factories to pay higher price than the prices fixed by the Central Government. For instance, the Uttar Pradesh Government had decided a price of Rs. 13.50 per quintal and the Bihar, Punjab and Haryana Governments have fixed Rs. 12.50 per quintal in 1979 (Kharche, 1989). It was decided by the State Governments that, the difference between the statutory minimum sugarcane price fixed by the Central Government and the higher sugarcane price fixed by the State Governments will be disbursed to the grower by the State Government concerned. (Kharche, 1989).

STATE ADMINISTERED PRICES

Since early 1970 onwards, the State Advised Price (SAP) came into existence. The SAP can be viewed as a 'mark up' over the SMP, and reflects the power of the sugarcane growers lobby in any given State, since it is the State Government which advise the sugar factories to pay a price for sugarcane over and above the SMP. Such prices in some States are not linked to the sugar recovery. In fixing these prices, the State Governments are mainly guided by prices being paid in adjoining States and prices paid by co-operative sugar factories during the previous season. For obvious reasons, the prices of sugarcane are likely to be on the higher side (Baru, 1990). In India out of 16 Sugar Zones, 11 Zones have paid the prices, as advised by State Governments. It is statutory obligation on the sugar factories to pay minimum sugarcane price as declared by the Central Government. Very recently the Allahabad High Court delivered the judgement that, the SAP are not statutory. The SAP should be immediately stopped. The GOI is empowered to declare the minimum sugarcane prices, because sugar and sugarcane are controlled by GOI, not State Governments. In Maharashtra, the Government advises different cane prices for different sugar factories. After the close of the crushing season, the final price proposed to be paid by each factory is placed before a Ministerial Committee headed by the Chief Minister, which lays down a broad guidelines on cane prices. Recently, the Government of Maharashtra has declared Rs. 460 per tonne of sugarcane as advance sugarcane price for the season 1996-97. The Committee[1] headed by Chief Minister of the State determines the policy for a particular year for cane price and for finalising the cane price of the last season.

In the States like U.P., Haryana, Punjab, Bihar and Madhya Pradesh, a uniform SAP is fixed for payment in one instalment after delivery of cane. It is not linked to recovery percentage of cane. Premium is allowed for early high sucrose varieties. SAP in U.P. is amounted only for public and co-operative sector sugar factories. Private factories fixes their own prices. In Gujarat also cane prices are fixed by the sugar factories even when all sugar factories belong to co-operative sector. The formula so developed in Gujarat is for, (a) Ex-field price = Minimum price declared by GOI + Add. cane price = Transport and harvesting charges, (b) Ex-factory price = Minimum price declared by GOI + Add. cane price. In Karnataka State SAP is linked to 8.5 per cent sugar recovery. SAP is compulsory to all factories in Karnataka. However, the sugar factories can pay higher prices after realisation due to increase in the prices of sugar and other by-products, or if their conversion cost is low. In Tamilnadu cane prices are fixed in consultation with the growers' associations belonging to each sugar factories. Whereas in Andhra Pradesh, SAP is fixed on the basis of cost of cultivation and other related aspects. For payment of additional cane prices Bhargav formula is worked out.

NOTES

1. The Members of the Committee are as follows :

1.	Chief Minister	—	Chairman
2.	Minister (Co-operation)	—	Member
3.	Minister (Irrigation)	—	Member
4.	Minister (Finance)	—	Member
5.	State Minister (Co-operation)	—	Member
6.	State Minister (Agriculture)	—	Member
7.	Chairman, Sakhar Sangh	—	Member
8.	Chairman, State Co-op. Bank	—	Invitee
9.	Secretary (Co-operation)	—	Invitee
10.	Secretary (Finance)	—	Invitee
11.	Secretary (Agriculture)	—	Invitee
12.	Secretary (Irrigation)	—	Invitee
13.	Commissioner of Sugar, Maharashtra, Pune	—	Invitee

TABLE 8 (A)

Statement Showing Cane Crushed, Sugar Production, Recovery per cent Cane and Some Technical Characteristics for the Season (1993-94) of Sugar Factories in Maharashtra

Sl. No.	Zone District Factory's Name	Inst. Cap. (TCD)	Cane Crushed (M.T.)	Sugar Production Net (Qtls.)	Sugar Production Gross (Qtls.)	Recovery Per cent Cane	Avalb. Days	Crush Rate Per Day 22 Hrs. (M.T.)	Filter Cake % Cane	Molasses Prod. Qty. (qtls.)	Molasses Prod. Per cent	Bagasse Prod. Qty. (m.t.)	Bagasse Prod. Per cent
1	2	3	4	5	6	7	8	9	10	11	12	13	14
	ZONE : SOUTH												
	DISTRICT : KOLHAPUR												
1.	B'VATI PARITE	4000	467210	573408	573605	12.27	148	3156	3.21	145770	3.12	136378	29.19
2.	CHH. RAJARAM	2200	248612	286244	286200	11.51	118	2102	3.91	91160	3.67	64315	25.87
3.	CHH. SHAHU	2500	265349	321957	321835	12.13	131	2026	5.35	96790	3.65	75014	28.27
4.	DATTA ASURLE	1250	160100	184665	194995	11.53	126	1272	4.69	60140	3.76	55570	34.71
5.	DATTA SHIROL	5000	562320	677462	677170	12.05	133	4219	4.02	213870	3.80	160542	28.55
6.	DAULAT	2000	297058	369161	378142	12.43	135	2194	3.57	106030	3.57	96187	32.38
7.	DUDH. VED.	3500	437809	530867	530587	12.12	126	3461	4.43	165260	3.77	121535	27.76
8.	GADHINGLAJ	2000	288122	337925	337778	11.73	148	1953	4.09	106300	3.69	88222	30.62
9.	JAWAHAR ($)	2500	228991	268944	270162	11.74	133	1725	3.76	84490	3.69	64644	28.23
10.	K. KASARI	3000	471985	595019	595180	12.61	136	3470	4.45	168380	3.57	134798	28.56

11.	P'GANGA	5000	698295	820863	822075	11.76	155	4516	3.83	268500	3.84	209977	30.07
12.	WARANA	4000	642020	821160	820050	12.79	161	3976	3.37	208860	3.25	164100	25.56
	DISTRICT TOTAL	36950	4767871	5787675	5797772	12.14	138	2839	4.06	1715550	3.06	1371282	28.76
	DISTRICT : SANGLI												
13.	H.K. AHIR	1250	290001	368210	367523	12.83	162	1786	3.50	101000	3.48	80707	27.83
14.	N'GANGA	1250	88500	88747	88670	10.03	113	780	3.34	35700	4.03	29629	33.48
15.	M'KALI	1250	148674	177906	177851	11.97	136	1089	4.28	58550	3.94	46787	31.47
16.	RAJARAMBAPU	4000	664098	809274	809260	12.19	167	3984	4.27	239540	3.61	187142	28.00
17.	TASGAON	2750	144370	159390	159615	11.04	103	1400	3.31	58620	4.06	43513	30.14
18.	V'DADA S'KARI	5000	745329	864293	889430	11.60	148	5020	3.83	248780	3.34	225313	30.23
19.	VISHWAS	1250	162439	197003	197040	12.13	126	1289	4.46	59290	3.65	46769	28.78
20.	V'WANT K'NAPUR	1250	155728	176355	176351	11.32	152	1027	2.90	62420	4.01	48228	30.97
	DISTRICT TOTAL	18000	2399139	2841178	2865704	11.84	138	2047	3.74	863900	3.60	708068	29.51
	DISTRICT : SATARA ($)												
21.	B. DESAI	1250	153841	182291	182313	11.85	126	1222	4.03	55150	3.58	45860	29.81
22.	KRISHNA	5000	840757	1043928	1046250	12.42	162	5191	3.78	303740	3.61	235664	28.03
23.	SAHYADRI	5000	546092	647607	650300	11.86	144	3783	3.22	210780	3.86	169616	31.06
	DISTRICT TOTAL	11250	1540690	1873826	1878863	12.16	144	3398	3.68	569670	3.70	451140	29.28
	ZONE TOTAL	66200	8707700	10502679	10542339	12.06	139	2637	3.90	3149120	3.62	2530490	29.06

(Contd.)

TABLE 8 (A) (*Contd.*)

1	2	3	4	5	6	7	8	9	10	11	12	13	14
	ZONE : CENTRAL												
	DISTRICT : SATARA (N)												
24.	AJINKYATARA	2500	350783	415094	415280	11.83	131	2683	3.32	121610	3.47	98710	28.14
25.	NEW P'TAN PVT.	1300	160337	176269	176794	10.99	134	1199	3.71	61710	3.85	48710	30.38
26.	SATARA	3000	351129	400173	399810	11.40	146	2399	3.63	137420	3.91	103934	29.60
27.	SHRIRAM P'TAN	2000	208706	229820	229770	11.01	118	1768	4.12	75550	3.62	68664	32.90
	DISTRICT TOTAL	8800	1070955	1221356	1221654	11.40	132	2012	3.70	396290	3.70	320018	29.88
	DISTRICT : PUNE												
28.	BHIMA PATAS	2500	459713	511280	511075	11.12	206	2227	3.57	161340	3.51	147246	32.03
29.	CHH. B'NAGAR	2500	302295	332828	332800	11.01	150	2014	4.11	124250	4.11	91081	30.13
30.	INDAPUR	1750	280934	308074	307826	10.97	206	1363	4.16	112030	3.99	83943	29.88
31.	MALEGAON	2500	404955	449158	449120	11.09	178	2272	4.00	150040	3.70	122012	30.13
32.	RAJGAD	1016	62664	65363	65440	10.43	95	658	3.01	25890	4.13	19764	31.54
33.	SOMESHWAR	2500	240911	270594	271105	11.23	152	1585	4.24	92470	3.84	72803	30.22
34.	VIGHNAGAR	1250	296213	343676	343525	11.60	161	1837	4.29	107800	3.64	86405	29.17
35.	Y'WANT THEUR	2500	416997	463085	462905	11.20	176	2365	4.89	149710	3.59	121054	29.03
	DISTRICT TOTAL	16516	2464682	2744058	2743816	11.13	166	1790	4.03	923530	3.75	744308	30.20
	DISTRICT : SHOLAPUR												
36.	ADINATH ($)	2500	130329	119600	120960	9.28	155	842	3.68	58640	4.50	39359	30.20
37.	B'VATI VAIRAG	1250	000	000	000	0.00	0	0	0.00	000	0.00	000	0.00
38.	BHIMA TAKLI	1250	286535	311750	311905	10.88	183	1564	3.86	112540	3.93	84785	29.59

39.	PANDURANG	1300	224660	234829	234650	10.45	178	1265	3.70	92510	4.10	69307	30.85
40.	S'SHWAR KUMATHE	2000	266386	267713	268385	10.05	157	1696	3.37	113710	4.27	81221	30.49
41.	S'WAD MALI PVT.	1750	179499	184891	184025	10.30	133	1350	3.81	80860	4.50	49685	27.68
42.	SANT DAMAJI ($)	2500	89954	87024	86765	9.67	106	848	3.75	36070	4.01	27085	30.11
43.	SHANKAR S'NAGAR	2500	277585	299604	299807	10.79	127	2188	3.89	98940	3.56	85690	30.87
44.	SMSM PATIL	4500	626846	661430	660700	10.55	160	3919	3.95	228870	3.65	201656	32.17
45.	VITHAL	3500	594558	631195	631195	10.62	174	3417	4.45	241350	4.06	197868	33.28
	DISTRICT TOTAL	23050	2676352	2799396	2797032	10.52	152	2031	3.85	1063130	3.95	836656	31.32
	DISTRICT : AHMEDNAGAR												
46.	AGASTI ($)	2500	117057	118395	118640	10.22	94	1248	3.28	44980	3.84	35550	30.37
47.	ASHOK	2600	183360	185532	185475	10.12	153	1196	3.90	74990	4.09	56291	30.70
48.	BELAPUR PVT.	1500	000	000	000	0.00	0	0	0.00	000	0.00	000	0.00
49.	DNYANESHWAR	3000	347512	367460	367258	10.57	148	2340	4.09	125670	3.62	113462	32.65
50.	DR. VIKHE PATIL	4000	495167	502439	528950	10.21	156	3180	4.74	180780	3.65	158304	31.97
51.	GANESH	1750	113231	111770	112940	9.87	105	1078	4.20	47450	4.19	35713	31.54
52.	JAGDAMBA	800	56696	61367	61263	10.82	122	462	5.35	21920	3.87	15954	28.14
53.	KOPARGAON	3000	332331	347856	347311	10.47	159	2094	4.81	146140	4.40	103687	31.20
54.	MULA	2000	300847	333206	333755	11.08	135	2221	4.45	116950	3.89	93262	31.00
55.	PARNER	1250	31622	29409	29320	9.30	55	578	4.12	12080	3.82	10084	31.89

(*Contd.*)

TABLE 8 (A) (*Contd.*)

1	2	3	4	5	6	7	8	9	10	11	12	13	14
56.	RAHURI	4250	448760	494641	495525	11.13	138	3239	4.04	190160	4.24	146340	32.61
57.	SANGAMNER	3500	348152	386718	386400	11.11	146	2375	4.59	130120	3.74	103644	29.77
58.	SANJIVANI	2100	391805	406261	406150	11.02	168	2355	4.22	158760	4.05	138659	35.39
59.	SHRIGONDA	2000	358860	395521	395615	11.01	168	2131	4.26	131660	3.67	114189	31.82
60.	VRIDHESHWAR	800	19198	16619	19508	8.66	76	252	3.94	9090	4.73	6145	32.01
	DISTRICT TOTAL	35050	3544598	3757194	3787660	10.60	131	1768	4.29	1390750	3.92	1131284	31.92
	DISTRICT : NASHIK												
61.	GIRNA	1500	000	000	000	0.00	0	0	0.00	000	0.00	000	0.00
62.	K.K.WAGH	1250	113894	106825	106807	9.38	137	831	3.22	50200	4.41	32437	28.48
63.	KADWA	1250	136195	152795	152675	11.22	125	1088	4.50	54990	4.04	40776	29.94
64.	NASHIK PALSE	1250	51562	53995	45088	10.47	89	580	3.71	20620	4.00	16515	32.03
65.	NIPHAD	3500	451818	513619	513260	11.37	131	3454	4.27	161800	3.58	123391	27.31
66.	RAVALGAON PVT.	1220	102120	108393	107900	10.61	104	986	3.07	42260	4.14	30666	30.03
67.	V'RAD DADA	2500	187990	198573	198445	10.56	120	1570	3.72	82240	4.37	58464	31.10
	DISTRICT TOTAL	12470	1043579	1134163	1124175	10.87	118	1419	3.75	412110	3.95	302249	28.96
	ZONE TOTAL	95886	10800166	11656167	11674337	10.81	140	1797	4.01	4185810	3.87	3334515	30.88

	ZONE : NORTH EAST												
	DISTRICT : DHULE												
68.	PANZARKAN	1250	88954	81987	81755	9.22	120	739	3.38	33290	3.74	27024	30.38
69.	SANJAY	1250	000	000	000	0.00	0	0	0.00	000	0.00	000	0.00
70.	SATPUDA TAPI	5000	657084	697846	697925	10.62	163	4031	3.87	232450	3.54	223342	33.99
71.	SHIRPUR	2500	166075	16615	166185	10.00	116	1430	3.67	68830	4.14	53891	32.45
	DISTRICT TOTAL	10000	912113	945948	945865	10.37	133	2067	3.64	334570	3.67	304257	33.36
	DISTRICT : JALGAON												
72.	BELGANGA	2500	232994	241910	243125	10.38	128	1825	3.69	99010	4.25	66286	28.45
73.	CHOPDA ($)	2500	4592	3099	1857	6.75	23	201	4.04	113820	3.87	100639	34.23
74.	MADHUKAR	2500	294011	285949	286018	9.82	140	2102	4.43	113820	3.87	100639	34.23
75.	VASANT KASONDA	1250	000	000	000	0.00	0	0	0.00	000	0.00	000	0.00
	DISTRICT TOTAL	8750	531597	530958	531000	10.02	134	1964	4.06	215130	4.04	168403	31.67
	DISTRICT : AURANGABAD												
76.	DEOGIRI ($)	2500	205196	198201	198340	9.66	140	1465	3.39	86070	4.19	63754	31.07
77.	GANGAPUR	2000	152733	158735	160505	10.39	108	1407	5.23	62460	4.09	47561	31.14
78.	KANNAD	1250	292360	305391	305275	10.44	181	1618	3.55	122190	4.18	83147	28.44
79.	S'SHWAR SILLOD	2000	265336	267109	267021	10.07	156	1696	3.71	106620	4.02	86924	32.76
80.	SANT EKANATH	1250	000	000	000	0.00	0	0	0.0	000	0.00	000	0.00
81.	VINAYAK	1250	000	000	000	0.00	0	0	0.0	000	0.00	000	0.00
	DISTRICT TOTAL	10250	915625	929436	931141	10.15	148	1547	3.98	377340	4.12	281386	30.73

(*Contd.*)

TABLE 8 (A) (*Contd.*)

1	2	3	4	5	6	7	8	9	10	11	12	13	14
	DISTRICT : JALNA												
82.	JALNA	1250	236073	237866	237775	10.08	163	1448	2.94	104890	4.44	70916	30.04
83.	SAMARTH	1250	93004	93748	93690	10.08	102	912	3.92	39890	4.29	27101	29.14
	DISTRICT TOTAL	2500	329077	331614	331465	10.08	132	1180	3.43	144780	4.40	98017	29.78
	DISTRICT : BEED												
84.	AMBEJOGAI	1250	92387	87340	88470	9.45	100	926	3.09	37890	4.10	30266	32.76
85.	GAJANAN	1250	000	000	000	0.00	0	0	0.0	000	0.00	000	0.00
86.	JAI BHAVANI	2500	000	000	000	0.00	0	0	0.0	000	0.00	000	0.00
87.	KADA	1250	000	000	000	0.00	0	0	0.0	000	0.00	000	0.00
88.	MAJALGAON ($)	2500	138628	138279	138150	9.97	116	1192	3.84	60720	4.38	42129	30.39
	DISTRICT TOTAL	8750	231015	225619	226620	9.77	108	1060	3.45	98610	4.27	72395	31.34
	DISTRICT : NANDED												
89.	GODAVARI (D)	1250	115521	122098	122518	10.57	115	1005	4.03	51430	4.45	38422	33.26
90.	MARATHWADA	1250	8490	6554	5130	7.72	34	249	3.90	3870	4.56	2941	34.65
91.	PURNA	2500	314700	330567	336640	10.61	162	1942	3.72	132490	4.21	109578	34.82
	DISTRICT TOTAL	5000	438711	459219	467288	10.47	104	1066	3.88	187790	4.20	150941	34.40

DISTRICT : NANDED												
92. GODAVARI (N)	2500	203827	211980	216175	10.40	131	1550	3.50	87710	4.30	67711	33.22
93. KALAMBAR	1250	83055	75580	76705	9.10	129	646	2.89	37670	4.54	28238	34.00
94. SHANKAR W'WADA	1250	146811	148228	148221	10.10	132	1113	3.85	54260	3.70	46509	31.68
DISTRICT TOTAL	5000	433693	435788	441101	10.05	131	1103	3.41	179640	4.14	142458	32.85
DISTRICT : OSMANABAD												
95. TERNA	3500	147287	135931	137300	9.23	106	1387	3.84	55080	3.74	59621	40.48
96. TULJA BHAVANI	1250	62194	61075	60777	9.82	101	614	3.87	20590	3.31	17905	28.79
DISTRICT TOTAL	4750	209481	197006	198077	9.40	104	1000	3.86	75670	3.61	77526	37.01
DISTRICT : LATUR												
97. J.JAWAN J. KISAN	1250	112521	115294	115282	10.25	114	985	3.00	39960	3.55	33970	30.19
98. MANJARA	1250	301753	356032	355900	11.80	158	1906	4.27	103060	3.42	91189	30.22
99. S'KARI KILLARI	1250	200526	204490	209755	10.20	160	1254	3.16	76240	3.80	59596	29.72
DISTRICT TOTAL	3750	614800	675816	680937	10.99	144	1381	3.48	219260	3.57	184755	30.05
DISTRICT : BULDHANA												
100. JIJAMATA	1250	000	000	000	0.00	0	0	0.0	000	0.00	000	0.00
DISTRICT TOTAL	1250	000	000	000	0.00	0	0	0.0	000	0.00	000	0.00

(Contd.)

TABLE 8 (A) (*Contd.*)

1	2	3	4	5	6	7	8	9	10	11	12	13	14
	DISTRICT : YAVATMAL												
101.	JAI KISAN	2500	45765	40329	39665	8.81	104	442	3.85	20860	4.56	14141	30.90
102.	SHANKAR S'KARI ($)	2500	14445	10663	9922	7.38	41	352	3.72	6730	4.66	5321	36.84
103.	VASNAT PUSAD	2500	262266	284809	289525	10.86	155	1687	3.97	101780	3.88	85052	32.43
	DISTRICT TOTAL	7500	322476	335801	339112	10.56	130	1065	3.92	129370	3.98	104514	32.20
	DISTRICT : AKOLA												
104.	BALAJI	1250	37305	34659	34660	9.29	75	498	3.62	16210	4.34	12094	32.42
	DISTRICT : AMARAVATI												
105.	S'KARI D'NGAON	1250	000	000	000	0.00	0	0	0.0	000	0.00	000	0.00
	DISTRICT : WARDHA												
106.	MAHATMA	1250	84339	89479	90050	10.61	115	733	4.09	34770	4.12	26119	30.79
	DISTRICT : NAGPUR												
107.	SHRIRAM N'PUR	1250	42125	41575	41100	9.87	129	327	3.37	21040	4.99	12877	30.51
	DISTRICT : BHANDARA												
108.	WAINGANGA	1250	55963	58641	58535	10.48	114	491	4.49	22150	3.96	17029	30.43
	ZONE TOTAL	73750	5158320	5291559	5316951	10.27	126	1254	3.74	2056330	3.98	1652771	32.03
	STATE TOTAL	235836	24666186	27450405	27533627	11.14	135	1830	3.90	9391260	3.80	7517776	30.48
	CO-OP TOTAL	230066	24224230	26980852	27064908	11.15	135	1851	3.91	9206430	3.80	7388715	30.50

(*Contd.*)

TABLE 8 (B)

Statement Showing Technical Characteristics for the Season (1993-94) of Sugar Factories in Maharashtra

Sl. No.	Zone District Factory's Name	POL.% Cane	Fibre % Cane	Recov. % Cane	Cap. Utlzn. %	Technical Performance				Sugar Lost%	Lost Hrs % to Available Hrs.			
						RHE	RME	RBHR	ROE		Cane Short	Mech +ELC	Other	Total
1	2	3	4	5	6	7	8	9	10	11	12	13	14	15
	DISTRICT : KOLHAPUR													
1.	B'VATI PARITE	14.12	13.54	12.27	78.90	94.77	94.83	91.49	86.70	1.86	2.86	1.53	6.05	10.44
2.	CHH. RAJARAM	13.24	12.18	11.51	95.55	95.19	95.18	91.06	86.68	1.75	10.98	3.35	1.29	15.62
3.	CHH. SHAHU	13.94	13.27	12.13	81.02	95.20	95.24	92.15	87.73	1.83	2.51	0.20	5.09	7.81
4.	DATTA ASURLE	13.45	15.38	11.53	101.80	95.23	95.39	90.96	86.62	1.94	16.83	2.85	2.18	21.86
5.	DATTA SHIROL	13.69	13.84	12.05	84.39	96.17	96.23	91.97	88.45	1.66	1.82	1.01	4.94	7.78
6.	DAULAT	14.22	15.40	12.43	109.69	95.89	96.05	91.53	87.77	1.81	0.70	1.12	5.34	7.17
7.	DUDH. VED.	14.08	13.12	12.12	98.88	96.08	96.10	88.73	85.25	1.98	3.18	1.35	3.44	7.97
8.	GADHINGLAJ	13.74	14.25	11.73	97.64	95.40	95.51	90.37	86.22	2.03	7.68	2.27	3.45	13.40
9.	JAWAHAR ($)	13.53	13.69	11.74	69.00	96.04	96.10	91.01	87.41	1.80	1.56	10.14	4.75	16.45
10.	K. KASARI	14.36	13.47	12.61	115.68	96.38	96.42	90.05	86.79	1.78	0.99	0.64	2.51	4.14
11.	P'GANGA	13.52	14.58	11.76	90.33	95.94	96.04	91.00	87.31	1.79	1.10	3.89	2.33	7.32
12.	WARANA	14.58	12.56	12.79	99.41	96.66	96.64	89.50	86.51	1.82	0.11	0.41	3.56	4.08
	DISTRICT TOTAL	13.96	13.77	12.14	93.81	95.75	95.81	90.82	86.95	1.84	3.98	2.36	3.77	10.12

(Contd.)

TABLE 8 (B) (*Contd.*)

1	2	3	4	5	6	7	8	9	10	11	12	13	14	15
	DISTRICT : SANGLI													
13.	H.K. AHIR	14.64	13.35	12.83	142.89	95.71	95.70	90.57	86.68	1.84	1.24	1.18	2.76	5.17
14.	M'GANGA	12.17	15.69	10.03	62.40	94.57	94.76	90.87	85.93	2.16	38.40	1.47	2.38	42.26
15.	M'KALI	13.97	14.81	11.97	87.13	95.29	95.38	91.43	87.12	2.02	16.84	1.44	4.21	22.49
16.	RAJARAMBAPU	14.04	13.39	12.19	99.59	96.28	96.33	90.22	86.86	1.87	0.89	0.11	2.15	3.15
17.	TASGAON	13.28	14.06	11.04	50.90	94.89	94.98	88.75	84.22	2.26	10.64	4.88	9.90	25.47
18.	V'DADA S'KARI	13.53	13.99	11.60	100.41	95.11	95.19	90.89	86.45	1.95	7.57	0.94	3.34	11.85
19.	VISHWAS	14.22	13.44	12.13	103.14	94.62	94.68	89.95	85.11	2.12	6.88	2.86	6.65	16.40
20.	Y'WANT K'NAPUR	13.57	14.43	11.32	82.17	94.32	94.47	90.10	84.98	2.27	16.96	1.23	2.54	20.73
	DISTRICT TOTAL	13.90	14.15	11.84	96.22	95.09	95.19	90.35	85.91	2.06	11.43	1.59	3.96	16.98
	DISTRICT : SATARA ($)													
21.	B. DESAI	13.84	14.00	11.85	97.75	94.97	95.06	92.12	87.48	2.01	5.58	2.58	3.45	11.62
22.	KRISHNA	14.18	13.44	12.42	103.82	96.52	96.53	90.26	87.12	1.78	1.54	0.99	3.80	6.33
23.	SAHYADRI	14.00	14.26	11.86	75.66	95.14	95.24	90.28	85.89	2.16	1.35	2.12	5.95	9.42
	DISTRICT TOTAL	14.12	13.90	12.16	95.05	95.54	95.61	90.89	86.83	1.98	2.65	1.83	4.42	8.90
	ZONE TOTAL	13.97	13.91	12.06	94.80	95.49	95.57	90.66	86.58	1.93	6.39	2.02	3.92	12.34
	ZONE : CENTRAL DISTRICT : SATARA (N)													
24.	AJINKYATARA	13.49	1.357	11.83	107.33	96.00	96.04	92.28	88.59	1.68	0.24	0.42	3.13	3.79

26. SATARA	13.26	14.19	11.40	79.97	96.01	96.05	90.07	86.48	1.88	1.02	3.88	5.06	9.97
27. SHRIRAM P'TAN	13.01	15.54	11.01	88.40	94.83	0.00	90.68	85.99	2.02	5.92	1.32	6.31	13.55
DISTRICT TOTAL	13.28	14.47	11.40	92.05	95.72	96.07	90.52	86.64	1.90	2.35	2.23	4.75	9.33
DISTRICT : PUNE													
28. BHIMA PATAS	13.11	15.03	11.12	89.07	95.11	95.25	90.46	86.04	2.01	0.98	4.25	4.08	9.31
29. CHH. B'NAGAR	12.76	14.28	11.01	80.54	95.95	96.01	91.22	87.53	1.77	1.66	2.22	4.97	8.85
30. INDAPUR	12.91	14.46	10.97	77.91	95.92	96.00	91.69	87.94	1.97	1.79	6.83	2.68	11.30
31. MALEGAON	12.97	14.14	11.09	90.86	95.64	95.69	90.70	86.74	1.90	1.43	1.86	4.98	8.27
32. RAJGAD	12.50	14.69	10.43	64.78	94.76	94.87	90.60	85.85	2.09	35.18	1.88	6.79	43.84
33. SOMESHWAR	13.26	14.02	11.23	63.39	94.96	95.04	90.06	85.52	2.05	20.54	0.94	7.26	28.73
34. VIGHNAHAR	13.34	14.16	11.60	146.94	96.10	96.17	91.58	88.00	1.76	0.00	0.14	3.92	4.06
35. Y'WANT THEUR	12.84	13.70	11.10	94.60	95.74	95.80	91.19	87.30	1.76	0.90	4.80	3.12	8.82
DISTRICT TOTAL	13.02	14.31	11.13	90.05	95.52	95.60	90.94	86.86	1.91	5.81	3.12	4.50	13.43
DISTRICT : SHOLAPUR													
36. ADINATH ($)	11.73	13.73	9.28	33.67	92.00	92.07	89.81	82.63	2.47	25.32	8.55	11.76	45.64
37. B'VATI VAIRAG	0.00	0.00	0.00	0.00	0.00	0.00	0.00	0.00	0.00	0.00	0.00	0.00	0.00
38. BHIMA TAKLI	13.15	13.81	10.88	125.09	94.15	94.25	89.42	84.19	2.29	0.31	2.05	5.99	8.35
39. PANDURANG	12.88	14.42	10.45	97.31	94.01	94.14	88.93	83.60	2.45	1.71	3.03	4.84	9.58
40. S'SHWAR KUMATHE	12.19	14.42	10.05	84.81	95.09	95.18	90.27	85.84	2.16	13.52	1.04	6.03	20.59
41. S'WAD MALI PVT.	12.31	13.68	10.30	77.12	96.13	96.19	89.62	86.15	2.03	2.72	3.99	5.92	12.62
42. SANT DAMAJI ($)	11.98	13.68	9.67	33.91	92.83	92.95	90.65	84.15	2.33	20.74	16.52	5.93	43.19

(Contd.)

TABLE 8 (B) (*Contd.*)

1	2	3	4	5	6	7	8	9	10	11	12	13	14	15
43.	SHANKAR S'NAGAR	12.61	15.05	10.79	87.54	95.64	95.77	91.82	87.82	1.84	3.71	1.81	6.98	12.49
44.	SMSM PATIL	12.63	15.25	10.55	87.09	95.20	95.35	90.63	86.28	2.10	0.40	3.35	7.02	10.77
45.	VITHAL	12.78	15.69	10.62	97.63	95.57	95.72	89.90	85.92	2.18	1.20	0.57	6.26	8.03
	DISTRICT TOTAL	12.67	14.50	10.52	86.66	94.83	94.94	90.15	85.49	2.17	4.75	3.47	6.09	14.32
	DISTRICT : AHMEDNAGAR													
46.	AGASTI ($)	12.12	14.11	10.22	49.91	94.15	94.23	90.50	85.21	2.03	19.79	2.36	4.39	26.54
47.	ASHOK	12.25	14.63	10.12	46.00	95.47	95.57	89.39	85.34	2.16	20.78	0.34	2.02	23.14
48.	BELAPUR PVT.	0.00	0.00	0.00	0.00	0.00	0.00	0.00	0.00	0.00	0.00	0.00	0.00	0.00
49.	DNYANESHWAR	12.22	15.48	10.57	78.00	96.30	94.43	92.01	88.60	1.67	9.12	0.34	3.95	13.41
50.	DR. VIKHE PATIL	12.01	15.19	10.21	79.49	95.07	95.23	91.64	87.12	1.88	6.54	0.80	2.92	10.25
51.	GANESH	11.81	15.03	9.87	61.60	95.35	95.49	90.94	86.71	1.96	23.11	0.76	5.68	29.54
52.	JAGADAMBA	12.74	13.11	10.82	57.81	94.31	94.35	91.85	86.62	1.94	47.21	1.68	6.76	55.65
53.	KOPARGAON	12.30	14.72	10.47	69.79	95.58	95.70	91.60	87.55	1.85	5.14	0.02	2.08	7.24
54.	MULA	12.90	14.89	11.08	111.05	96.16	96.26	90.22	86.76	1.85	1.17	1.54	4.45	7.15
55.	PARNER	11.21	15.16	9.30	46.26	94.56	94.72	91.57	86.58	1.93	44.93	0.62	7.15	52.70
56.	RAHURI	13.29	15.60	11.13	76.21	96.50	96.63	86.10	83.09	2.29	2.63	2.50	5.44	10.56
57.	SANGAMNER	12.67	14.24	11.11	67.86	96.47	96.52	92.10	88.84	1.58	0.66	0.13	2.64	3.43
58.	SANJIVANI	12.31	16.80	10.37	112.15	95.10	95.37	92.49	87.96	1.96	3.54	3.15	3.67	10.36

59. SHRIGONDA	12.96	14.48	11.02	106.54	96.27	95.34	90.57	86.29	1.96	1.22	1.41	5.13	7.77
60. VRIDHESHWAR	11.36	14.57	8.66	31.52	90.94	91.16	89.12	81.04	2.72	57.76	0.76	10.07	68.60
DISTRICT TOTAL	12.56	14.86	10.60	81.10	95.09	95.22	90.72	86.27	1.98	13.55	1.18	4.33	19.06
DISTRICT : NASHIK													
61. GIRNA	0.00	0.00	0.00	0.00	0.00	0.00	0.00	0.00	0.00	0.00	0.00	0.00	0.00
62. K.K. WAGH	11.41	13.40	9.38	66.46	93.70	93.79	90.80	85.08	2.05	27.56	1.01	2.88	31.40
63. KADWA	13.23	14.00	11.22	87.01	94.87	94.95	91.18	86.50	2.03	2.91	2.66	2.46	8.03
64. NASIK PALSE	12.67	14.79	10.47	46.38	93.60	93.79	91.47	85.61	2.22	39.77	5.70	2.14	47.61
65. NIPHAD	13.20	13.23	11.37	98.69	96.49	96.54	89.31	86.18	1.85	0.40	2.20	4.38	6.98
66. RAVALGAON PVT.	12.39	14.15	10.61	80.84	96.15	96.245	91.33	87.81	1.80	13.66	0.46	14.26	28.39
67. V'RAD DADA	12.67	14.52	10.56	62.82	94.84	94.95	91.29	86.58	2.12	2.84	3.09	3.67	9.61
DISTRICT TOTAL	12.86	14.01	10.87	80.93	94.94	95.62	90.90	86.30	2.01	13.45	2.39	4.80	20.00
ZONE TOTAL	12.80	14.51	10.81	85.48	95.16	95.27	90.66	86.27	2.01	8.74	2.39	4.85	15.98
ZONE : NORTH EAST													
DISTRICT : DHULE													
68. PANZARKAN	11.46	14.30	9.22	59.12	93.74	93.87	88.32	82.80	2.27	35.69	0.13	3.81	39.63
69. SANJAY	0.00	0.00	0.00	0.00	0.00	0.00	0.00	0.00	0.00	0.00	0.00	0.00	0.00
70. SATPUDA TAPI	12.56	15.67	10.62	80.62	95.30	95.47	90.83	86.56	1.96	1.85	2.84	4.80	9.50
71. SHIRPUR	11.94	15.18	10.00	57.19	94.69	94.88	91.89	87.01	1.96	11.33	1.52	7.63	20.48
DISTRICT TOTAL	12.42	15.05	10.37	78.28	94.57	94.75	90.35	85.44	2.07	14.80	1.64	5.33	21.77

(Contd.)

TABLE 8 (B) (*Contd.*)

1	2	3	4	5	6	7	8	9	10	11	12	13	14	15
	DISTRICT : JALGAON													
72.	BELGANGA	12.44	13.58	10.38	73.02	95.19	95.20	89.75	85.43	2.08	0.64	4.07	6.27	10.99
73.	CHOPDA	10.96	12.70	6.75	8.03	81.14	81.18	79.68	64.65	4.23	61.94	13.95	2.25	78.15
74.	MADHUKAR	11.89	15.99	9.72	84.08	94.48	94.70	90.00	85.03	2.17	1.49	2.90	6.23	10.63
75.	VASANT KASODA	0.00	0.00	0.00	0.00	0.00	0.00	0.00	0.00	0.00	0.00	0.00	0.00	0.00
	DISTRICT TOTAL	12.33	14.79	10.22	78.80	94.83	94.95	89.88	85.23	2.13	1.09	3.46	6.25	10.80
	DISTRICT : AURANGABAD													
76.	DEORIRI ($)	11.67	13.61	9.66	58.62	93.55	93.61	90.95	85.08	2.03	11.03	7.05	6.56	24.64
77.	GANGAPUR	12.46	14.76	10.39	70.35	95.31	95.46	90.08	85.86	2.08	6.87	0.95	4.81	12.63
78.	KANNAD	12.51	13.19	10.44	129.41	94.38	94.42	90.95	85.84	2.08	0.50	1.21	4.37	6.09
79.	S'SHWAR SILLOD	12.34	15.32	10.07	84.82	93.88	94.08	91.02	85.45	2.29	3.71	2.27	8.73	14.71
80.	SANT EKANATH	0.00	0.00	0.00	0.00	0.00	0.00	0.00	0.00	0.00	0.00	0.00	0.00	0.00
81.	VINAYAK	0.00	0.00	0.00	0.00	0.00	0.00	0.00	0.00	0.00	0.00	0.00	0.00	0.00
	DISTRICT TOTAL	12.25	14.22	10.15	80.68	94.28	94.40	90.75	85.56	2.12	5.06	2.84	6.14	14.04
	DISTRICT : JALNA													
82.	JALNA	12.03	14.13	10.08	115.86	95.00	95.09	91.52	86.94	1.97	0.58	0.89	2.68	4.16
83.	SAMARTH	12.17	14.23	10.08	72.99	95.16	95.26	90.44	86.07	2.11	36.72	3.18	6.19	46.09
	DISTRICT TOTAL	12.10	14.18	10.08	99.37	95.08	95.18	90.98	86.50	2.04	14.49	1.77	4.03	20.29

DISTRICT : BEED													
84. AMBEJOGAI	12.05	15.13	9.45	74.05	92.87	93.08	88.17	81.88	2.62	36.57	6.12	6.12	48.82
85. GAJANAN	0.00	0.00	0.00	0.00	0.00	0.00	0.00	0.00	0.00	0.00	0.00	0.00	0.00
86. JAI BHAVANI	0.00	0.00	0.00	0.00	0.00	0.00	0.00	0.00	0.00	0.00	0.00	0.00	0.00
87. KADA	0.00	0.00	0.00	0.00	0.00	0.00	0.00	0.00	0.00	0.00	0.00	0.00	0.00
88. MAJALGAON ($)	12.04	14.19	9.97	47.68	94.73	94.83	90.40	85.64	2.09	20.58	8.15	5.41	34.14
DISTRICT TOTAL	12.10	14.65	9.97	57.01	93.80	93.95	89.28	83.74	2.35	27.97	7.21	5.74	40.92
DISTRICT : PARBHANI													
89. GODAVARI (D)	12.90	15.54	10.57	80.43	94.26	94.49	89.65	84.51	2.35	18.97	3.70	6.42	29.10
90. MARATHWADA	10.82	16.02	7.72	19.90	92.21	92.49	79.78	73.57	3.23	57.93	2.90	15.53	76.36
91. PURNA	13.08	15.97	10.61	77.70	94.20	94.44	87.83	82.73	2.60	8.38	6.31	6.26	20.95
DISTRICT TOTAL	13.18	15.84	10.47	84.63	93.56	93.81	85.75	80.27	2.73	17.73	4.97	7.34	30.04
DISTRICT : NANDED													
92. GODAVARI (M)	12.44	16.07	10.40	62.00	95.68	90.88	90.52	86.61	2.06	6.17	3.86	4.52	14.59
93. KALAMBAR	11.81	16.18	9.10	51.65	93.39	93.67	86.04	80.36	2.73	20.22	7.46	5.55	33.22
94. SHANKAR W'WADA	12.05	15.26	10.10	89.07	95.17	95.33	90.85	86.46	1.97	16.77	0.53	4.70	22.00
DISTRICT TOTAL	12.28	15.84	10.05	66.38	94.75	94.96	89.14	84.48	2.25	14.34	3.92	4.92	23.18
DISTRICT : OSMANABAD													
95. TERNA	11.58	18.90	9.23	39.63	95.14	95.48	89.48	85.14	2.37	26.48	5.47	8.98	40.92
96. TULJA BHAVANI	11.63	14.10	9.82	49.09	95.20	95.28	91.05	86.68	1.83	28.02	0.13	5.38	33.54
DISTRICT TOTAL	11.48	16.50	9.40	42.50	95.17	95.38	90.26	85.91	2.10	27.23	2.86	7.22	37.32

(Contd.)

TABLE 8 (B) (*Contd.*)

1	2	3	4	5	6	7	8	9	10	11	12	13	14	15
	DISTRICT TOTAL	11.48	16.50	9.40	42.50	95.17	95.38	90.26	85.91	2.10	27.23	2.86	7.22	37.32
	DISTRICT : LATUR													
97.	J. JAWAN J. KISAN	12.15	14.16	10.25	78.78	94.04	94.13	93.09	87.54	1.93	23.37	1.03	3.73	28.12
98.	MANGARA	13.64	14.66	11.80	152.48	95.31	95.48	91.86	87.55	1.86	0.11	3.41	4.53	8.05
99.	S'KARI KILLARI	12.22	13.74	10.20	100.29	93.45	93.51	92.32	86.27	2.04	8.64	1.70	2.47	12.82
	DISTRICT TOTAL	12.91	14.19	10.99	113.71	94.27	94.37	92.42	87.12	1.94	9.41	2.15	3.56	15.12
	DISTRICT : BULDHANA													
100.	JIJAMATA	0.00	0.00	0.00	0.00	0.00	0.00	0.00	0.00	0.00	0.00	0.00	0.00	0.00
	DISTRICT TOTAL	0.00	0.00	0.00	0.00	0.00	0.00	0.00	0.00	0.00	0.00	0.00	0.00	0.00
	DISTRICT : YAVATMAL													
101.	JAI KISAN	11.19	13.80	8.81	17.66	92.47	92.58	91.34	84.46	2.38	41.12	6.00	4.96	52.08
102.	SHANKAR S'KARI	10.40	16.10	7.38	14.08	90.00	90.38	87.28	78.55	3.04	52.90	5.94	2.18	61.02
103.	VASANT PUSAD	13.16	15.09	10.86	67.48	94.25	92.42	89.74	84.58	2.32	4.01	8.08	7.41	19.50
	DISTRICT TOTAL	12.89	14.45	10.56	47.56	93.36	93.50	90.54	84.52	2.35	18.35	7.25	6.43	32.53
	DISTRICT : AKOLA													
104.	BALAJI	11.46	15.52	9.29	39.83	94.87	95.04	92.33	87.59	2.19	63.09	0.47	0.00	63.56

DISTRICT : WARDHA													
106. MANATMA	12.75	14.04	10.61	58.64	94.53	93.65	90.48	84.63	2.16	28.38	0.57	5.92	34.87
DISTRICT : NAGPUR													
107. SHRIRAM N'PUR	12.05	13.85	9.87	26.13	93.74	93.84	90.09	84.46	2.20	67.14	0.50	4.16	71.80
DISTRICT : BHANDARA													
108. WAINGANGA	12.64	14.12	10.48	39.29	93.35	93.45	91.32	85.24	2.18	50.46	1.88	2.47	54.81
ZONE TOTAL	12.45	14.88	10.27	72.73	94.28	94.43	90.07	84.92	2.20	17.82	3.22	5.34	26.39
STATE TOTAL	13.17	14.48	11.14	85.79	94.96	95.07	90.47	85.91	2.05\	10.87	2.55	4.76	18.18
CO-OP. TOTAL	13.18	14.49	11.15	85.73	94.92	95.03	90.48	85.89	2.05	11.02	2.54	4.67	18.24

7

FIXATION OF SUGARCANE PRICES IN MAHARASHTRA

Western Maharashtra was very famous in the production of jaggery (raw sugar) during early 20th century, particularly the taste of Kolhapuri jaggery is well-known even today to the Indian consumers. Besides it is being exported to other countries like U.K., U.S.A., Pakistan and Gulf countries. The favourable climate in Western Maharashtra helped to undertake the sugarcane crop at the beginning of the 20th century on a large scale basis. The beginning of sugarcane cultivation was made by the 'malis' of Sasvad in Maharashtra during 19th century. At that time sugarcane was used to produce jaggery. At the advent of the 20th century, the efforts were made to produce white sugar by using the modern technology. There were 3 such sugar factories in 1920s producing white sugar. Out of them two were closed down soon due to lack of sugarcane and growing prices of gur (See Table 10).

It was only after 1930s, the sugar industry had conceived good response in the state. However, it's growth upto 1950 was dwindling. The private sector was dominating in monopolising the industry in Bombay presidency. The number of private factories went upto 7 in 1936-37, and 13 upto 1940. There was a critical situation leading to the virtual stagnation during 1937-42, because of abundance in sugarcane harvesting, low sugar prices and rapid increase in excise duties etc. So, over-production lapsed into a state of stagnation. This affected the four factories of Bombay province, including other 19 big and small units of the country, not to join the Indian Sugar Syndicate. But the syndicate improved its performance by raising the selling prices of sugar. The Second World War enabled the industry push up its production, but even post-war experiences were adverse. The production of sugar declined due to shortage of sugarcane. The industry has to face severe competition with gur and khandsari units.

Dr. W.C. Shrishrimal (1967) has indicated that, the sugarcane prices in Maharashtra are not determined on the market forces of demand and supply. In fact the prices are fixed on the other considerations of the industrial management. By virtue of the provision in the by-laws of co-operative sugar factories in Maharashtra, the State Government fixes the sugarcane prices payable by all co-operative sugar factories except those who have repaid the State Government's contribution in share capital and paid fully the term loan and such other loans for which the State Government is the guarantor. Actually without the help of the government share capital and/or without State Government guarantor, a factory could not be ran. But an interesting point is that, there is no SAP for sugarcane in Maharashtra since the co-operative sugar is dominated in the State. The State Government by virtue of the provision in the by-laws is involved in controlling the industry. In co-operative sugar factories sugarcane price is nothing but distribution of income earned by sale of sugar in proportion to sugarcane supplied by the farmers. The State Govt. has powers to fix the sugarcane price payable by all such co-operative sugar factories every year, till these sugar factories have redeemed the Govt. share capital and repaid fully the term loan and such other loans for which the Govt. is guarantor.

Till 1979-80, different prices of sugarcane were being fixed by different co-operative sugar units for different group of members *e.g.*, members and non-members, etc. After 1989, equal prices are being paid to the members and non-members of the sugar co-operatives in Maharashtra. The Supreme Court verdict in 1989 clarified that the issue of different sugarcane prices paid to the non-members and members of sugar factories has to be stopped. The State Govt. had considered this aspect long back in 1980-81 that, the payment of sugarcane should not differ. This was introduced to attract the non-members to join the membership of the sugar co-operatives. Some other incentives were also provided in the form of fertilizer, insecticides, better seeds etc.

The sugarcane prices are paid in two-three instalments. The advance payments first and second are made by the sugar co-operatives as per the guidance and norms of the State Government's Ministerial Committee. Generally the advance of sugarcane price permitted to the sugar factories is the same, because of the steady growth and to avoid unhealthy competition between co-operative sugar factories. The advance prices are generally announced before the beginning of the crushing season. Experience shows that, the advance sugarcane price of the season is normally finalised by October/November. And the final sugarcane prices are being declared in December/January after finalising and tabulating the information by the Directorate of Sugar to State Govt. The first advance is decided considering the SMP, availability of cane, market prices of sugar and molasses and likely final cane prices of various factories during the last season. The Ministerial Committee headed by the Chief Minister lays down broad guidelines even for the final payment of the sugarcane prices. The Directorate of Sugar and State Federation of Sugar Co-operatives in consultation with the individual sugar factories place a proposal to set the final bill to the cane growers. This process generally starts after the close of the crushing season. Eventhough the payment of advance and final sugarcane prices differ from factory to factory. This is because of the norms fixed by the Ministerial Committee. The factories submit their necessary information to the Directorate of Sugar. The Directorate prepares necessary proposals to be submitted to the Ministerial Committee. On this basis, the Committee declares the advance price and final prices of individual factories. The decision of the Committee is communicated to each sugar factory (See Appendix-II) through Directorate of Sugar.

Generally the Ministerial Committee fixes two types of sugarcane prices *viz.*, Ex-field and Ex-gate. Ex-field price is the sugarcane crop price in the field. In this type, the responsibility of cane harvesting and transportation from cane field to factory rest on the sugar factories. The co-co-operatives have accepted this price. But now-a-days, because of the changing industrial relations of harvest and transport workers and the sugar industry, this responsibility now rest on to the farmers or the labour societies or trusts or some other types of institutions.

Ex-gate (factory) price of sugarcane is the price of sugarcane at the factory gate. The responsibility of cane harvesting and transportation rest on to the farmers or other bodies formed for the purpose. Some co-operative sugar factories have amended their bye-laws so as to get escaped from the provisions laid in BIR, 1946, that is, cane cutters and transport workers are the employees of the sugar industry.

The following points are generally taken into account while finalising the sugarcane price by the Ministerial Committee, Government of Maharashtra :

(i) Sugarcane crushed by the factory,

(ii) Total sugar production,

(iii) Recovery of sugar,

(iv) Sale of sugar,

(v) Stock of sugar,

(vi) Levy prices of sugar,

(vii) Open Market (stock) sugar prices,

(viii) Concessions under Samphat Committee,

(ix) Cost against ratoon crop,

(x) Bonus,

(xi) Education fund,

(xii) Audit fee,

(xiii) Subscriptions of State Federations,

(xiv) Deferred salary payments,

(xv) Deferred cost of harvest and transport of sugarcane,

(xvi) Depreciation,

(xvii) Loss if any.

Other than these norms, following principles are also considered :

(i) The minimum sugarcane price for the State is fixed for the season. No factory is allowed to pay less than the minimum price fixed by the State.

(ii) The sugar factory newly established, or old well established.

(iii) Prices of other co-operative sugar factories, which are located in the vicinity.

Any other sugar factory, if qualifies to pay substantially higher price than the neighbouring factories, it is not allowed to pay additional price in cash as a sugarcane price. The additional prices are authorized to be kept in fixed deposits with the sugar factories, so as to build up the reserves of the factories. Any sugar factories, if desired to pay the 'khodaki' (ratoon crop), it has to seek permission from the Ministerial Committee. This price is not paid to the non-members of the sugar factories. The final prices are arrived on the basis of working results of the sugar factories. Wide variations in recovery and working results compel them to have variations in prices.

Table 9 illustrates the consolidated information of the sugarcane prices paid by the co-operative sugar factories of Maharashtra from 1987-88 to 1993-94, which were declared by the Ministerial Committee from time to time and communicated the same to each sugar co-operative factories during the period. More detailed information of the corresponding prices are explained in Table 6 for the seasons 1993-94 to 1995-96.

During the 1993-94 season, nine sugar co-operatives have declared more than Rs. 900 sugarcane price per tonne. The final highest price for sugarcane in 1993-94 has been paid by Vignahar Co-operative Sugar Factory (Junner Taluka) at the rate of Rs. 1,011 per tonne. Rajarambapu (Sangli District) and Jawahar (Kolhapur District) Co-operative Sugar Factories were the other two sugar factories to pay the second highest prices in Maharashtra during the same period.

Considering the significance of the sugarcane pricing procedures, so far followed by the State Governments and the Central Government, the State Level Conference of the Co-operative Ministry and the Sugar Ministry in February 1994 resolved to request the Central Government to appoint a High Level Committee to recommend in respect of the sugarcane pricing procedures followed mainly by the State Governments. Accordingly a Ministerial Committee was appointed by the Central Government to recommend in respect of the uniform sugarcane pricing policy in India.

The Urban Development Minister of U.P. Government, Ramshankar Koushik was appointed as a Chairman of the High Level Committee. Other members were M. Chinnaswamy (Tamilnadu), Sajjankumar Jakhar (Punjab), Dr. Heggapa Lamani (Karnataka), Dr. Madhav Kinhalkar (Maharashtra) were other members of the High-Level Committee. The Committee submitted its report to Ajit Singh; then Minister of Food, Government of India.

The Committee with number of other recommendations suggested to establish the National Price Board for sugarcane. The Committee has firmly recommended to review the sugarcane price so far determined by the Central and State Governments simultaneously.

Maharashtra State Federation of Co-operative Sugar Factories is rather very much interested in having a different and fresh outlook of sugarcane prices, because sugarcane is the main raw-material of the sugar factories, whose yield, in Maharashtra is declining, and on the contrary, the number of sugar factories is increasing.

As stated earlier, the farmers have invested large amount of their capital in sugar industry in Maharashtra. Latter of, the farmers are shifting their cultivation habits of sugarcane to some other crops, mainly the oil seeds and horticultural products, which is yielding remunerative income to the farmers. This has created a problem to sugar factories. But the trend has yet to be set.

Following are the principles led, to be observed while fixing the sugarcane prices in Maharashtra :

(i) The minimum sugarcane prices are fixed for each sugar factory on the basis of the minimum statutory sugarcane price for 8.5 sugar recovery plus premium to be paid on 0.1% increase in sugar recovery as fixed by the Central Govt. For example the SMP for 8.5 recovery in 1995-96 season was Rs. 40 and premium for 0.1% of recovery was Rs. 0.54. If the average recovery of a sugar factory is around 12%, it means, the SMP for that sugar factory will be Rs. 40 + 3.5 excess sugar recovery × 0.54 premium = Rs. 58.90 per quintal of sugarcane for the said season as SMP.

(ii) The advance sugarcane prices are fixed at the beginning of every sugar season. No factory can pay high price than this. This has been introduced from 1980-81. The additional higher portion of sugarcane price over and above the limit is compelled to keep as fixed deposits with the sugar factories, so as to build the reserves. But actually some factories pay higher than the limit as it is set up after assessing their financial positions during previous seasons.

(iii) The price parity is generally maintained between the prices of the co-operative sugar factories among the factories located in the vicinity. Even if the working results of the factory does not permit payment of the price, the higher price (as compared to others) is allowed, even at the cost of making loss, so as to ensure sugarcane availability to the concerned sugar factories in the ensuing season and to maintain the incentive of the farmers (Kharche, 1986).

(iv) Sugarcane price is not decided on the basis of cost of production of sugarcane.

(v) The losses due to the payment of higher price of sugarcane are financed by postponing the depreciation and purchase tax payments and further by borrowing

TABLE 9

Final Cane Price Paid : Factorywise and Yearwise

(Pl. See Table 6 for corresponding data)

(Amount in Rs.)

Sl. No.	Name of the Factory & Address	CAP (TCD)	1987-88	1988-89	1989-90	1990-91	1991-92	1992-93
1	2	3	4	5	6	7	8	9
	KOLHAPUR REGION							
	KOLHAPUR DISTRICT							
1.	BHOGAWATI SSK LTD.	4000	400.00	402.00	490.00	434.00	439.00	667.00
2.	CHHATRAPATI RAJARAM SSK LTD.	2200	360.00	401.00	405.00	405.00	437.00	600.00
3.	CHHATRAPATI SHAHU SSK LTD.	1250	390.00	404.00	458.00	466.00	490.00	676.00
4.	DATTA SSK LTD.	1250	365.00	364.00	370.0	417.50	426.00	669.00
5.	DATTA SHETKARI SSK LTD.	5000	405.00	405.00	410.00	410.00	435.00	686.00
6.	DAULAT SHETKARI SSK LTD.	3500	368.00	406.00	461.00	461.00	501.00	705.00
7.	DUDHAGANGA VEDGANGA SSK LTD.	3500	345.00	350.00	401.00	357.00	392.00	646.00
8.	GADHINGLAJ SSK LTD.	2000	353.00	395.00	490.00	465.00	510.00	702.50
(A)								
9	JAWAHAR SSK LTD.	2500	0.00	0.00	0.00	0.00 — Under Erection —	0.00	0.00
10.	KUMBHI KASARI SSK LTD.	3000	382.00	401.00	465.00	450.00	435.00	670.00
11.	SHRI PANCHAGANGA SSK. LTD.	5000	405.00	405.00	490.00	460.00	486.00	676.00
12.	WARANA SSK LTD.	4000	419.00	442.00	475.00	435.00	450.00	700.00

(*Contd.*)

TABLE 9 (*Contd.*)

1	2	3	4	5	6	7	8	9
	KOLHAPUR REGION							
	SANGLI DISTRICT							
13.	HUTATMA KISAN AHIR SSK LTD.	1250	425.00	475.00	620.00	530.00	475.00	703.00
14.	MAHANKALI SSK LTD.	1250	340.00	396.00	495.00	495.00	450.00	675.00
15.	MANGANGA SSK LTD.	1250	290.00	325.00	370.00	405.00	410.00	500.00
16.	RAJARAM BAPU PATIL SSK LTD.	4000	427.00	466.00	525.00	460.00	400.00	0.00
(A)								
17.	TASGAON SSK LTD.	2750	0.00	0.00	0.00	0.00	444.00	0.00
				— Under Erection —				
18.	VASANTDADA SHETKARI SSK LTD.	5000	365.00	391.00	475.00	449.00	446.00	0.00
19.	VISHWAS SSK LTD.	1250	346.00	348.00	450.00	427.50	416.00	679.00
20.	YASHWANT SSK LTD.	1250	336.00	395.00	494.00	492.00	427.00	540.00
	PUNE REGION							
	SATARA DISTRICT							
21.	BALASAHEB DESAI SSK LTD.	1250	377.00	386.00	465.00	408.00	413.00	626.00
22.	KRISHNA SSK LTD.	5000	371.00	381.00	511.50	440.00	400.00	0.00
23.	SAHYADRI SSK LTD.	5000	399.00	405.00	465.00	470.00	450.00	625.00
24.	AJINKYATARA SSK LTD.	2500	415.00	425.00	525.00	436.50	426.80	620.00
25	SATARA SSK LTD.	2000	240.00	240.00	250.00	400.00	421.00	575.00
26.	SHRIRAM SSK LTD.	2000	240.00	240.00	250.00	260.00	296.80	540.00

TABLE 9 (*Contd.*)

1	2	3	4	5	6	7	8	9
	PUNE DISTRICT							
27.	BHIMA SSK LTD.	2500	344.00	328.00	343.00	300.00	337.00	511.00
28.	INDAPUR SSK LTD.(A)	1750	0.00	0.00	0.00	307.00	361.80	525.00
					— Under Erection —			
29.	RAJGAD SSK LTD. (A)	2500	0.00	0.00	0.00	0.00	306.80	440.00
					— Under Erection —			
30.	SHRI CHHATRAPATI SSK LTD.	1800	353.00	361.00	385.50	461.50	460.80	613.00
31.	SHRI SOMESHWAR SSK LTD.	2500	324.00	320.00	371.50	351.00	296.80	450.00
32.	SHRI VIGHNAHAR SSK LTD.	1250	0.00	310.00	350.00	427.00	485.00	575.00
33.	THE MALEGAON SSK LTD.	2500	390.00	320.00	451.00	461.50	441.00	621.00
34.	YASHWANT SSK LTD.	2500	336.00	395.00	494.00	492.00	427.00	556.00
	PUNE REGION							
	SHOLAPUR DISTRICT							
35.	BHIMA SSK LTD.	1250	344.00	328.00	343.00	300.00	337.00	544.00
36.	BHOGAVATI SSK LTD.	1250	0.00	252.00	276.00	312.50	306.80	0.00
37.	SHRI PANDURANG SSK LTD.	1300	0.00	0.00	0.00	0.00	351.80	460.00
					— Under Erection —			
38.	SHRI SANT DAMAJI SSK LTD.(A)	2500	0.00	0.00	0.00	0.00	0.00	0.00
					— Under Erection —			
39.	SHRI SHANKAR SSK LTD.	1250	318.00	345.00	421.00	380.00	379.00	496.00
40.	SHRI SIDDHESHWAR SSK LTD.	2000	355.00	414.00	414.00	380.00	361.00	425.00

(*Contd.*)

TABLE 9 (*Contd.*)

1	2	3	4	5	6	7	8	9
41.	SHRI VITTHAL SSK LTD.	3500	335.00	365.00	425.00	427.00	400.00	577.00
42.	S.M.S. MOHITE PATIL SSK LTD.	4500	319.00	346.00	469.00	377.00	370.00	499.00
(A)	**AHMEDNAGAR REGION**							
	AHMEDNAGAR DISTRICT							
43.	AGASTI SSK LTD.	2500	0.00	0.00	0.00	0.00	0.00	0.00
				— Under	Erection —			
44.	ASHOK SSK. LTD.	2600	260.00	142.00	375.00	410.00	369.00	0.00
45.	DR. V. VIKHE PATIL SSK LTD.	4000	295.00	285.00	310.00	360.00	375.00	0.00
46.	GANESH SSK LTD.	1750	240.00	0.00	315.00	325.00	340.00	0.00
47.	KOPARGAON SSK LTD.	2200	345.00	335.00	380.00	400.00	0.00	0.00
48.	MULA SSK LTD.	2000	290.00	283.00	361.00	363.00	401.00	0.00
49.	PARTNER TALUKA SSK LTD.	1250	0.00	268.00	306.50	325.00	330.00	429.00
50.	SANGAMNER BHAG SSK LTD.	3500	360.00	375.00	425.00	400.00	420.00	0.00
51.	SHRI DNYANESHWAR SSK LTD.	3000	325.00	325.00	381.00	381.00	425.00	645.00
52.	SHRI JAGDAMBA SSK LTD.	800	240.00	273.00	330.00	307.50	326.80	425.00
53.	SHRI VRIDHESHWAR SSK LTD.	800	0.00	257.00	290.00	305.00	355.00	0.00
54.	THE RAHURI SSK LTD.	4250	278.50	267.00	306.75	305.00	350.00	0.00
55.	THE SANGIVANI SSK LTD.	2100	350.00	340.00	390.00	410.00	390.00	0.00
56.	SHRI SHRIGONDA SSK LTD.	2000	306.00	306.00	353.00	395.00	390.00	525.00
	AHMEDNAGAR REGION							
	NASHIK DISTRICT							
57.	K.K. WAGH SSK LTD.	1250	300.00	335.00	376.50	375.00	351.80	474.00

TABLE 9 (*Contd.*)

1	2	3	4	5	6	7	8	9
58.	NASIK SSK LTD.	1250	240.00	242.00	300.00	299.00	316.80	00.00
59.	THE GIRNA SSK LTD.	1500	261.00	300.00	301.00	275.00	296.80	00.00
60.	THE KADWA SSK LTD.	1250	280.00	312.00	372.00	372.00	389.00	586.00
61.	THE NIPHAD SSK LTD.	3500	349.00	200.00	201.00	275.00	296.80	637.00
62.	VASANTRAO DADA PATIL SSK LTD.	1250	302.00	325.00	376.50	382.50	330.00	450.00
	AURANGABAD REGION							
	DHULE DISTRICT							
63.	SHIRPUR SSK LTD.	2500	301.00	321.00	321.00	357.00	351.00	401.00
64.	SHRI PANZARAKAN SSK LTD.	1250	244.00	242.00	300.00	275.00	326.80	396.00
65.	SHRI SATPUDA TAP P. SSK LTD.	5000	363.00	300.00	425.00	430.50	430.80	516.00
66.	THE SANJAY SSK LTD. (B)	1250	240.00	242.00	275.00	290.00	0.00	0.00
	AURANGABAD REGION							
	JALGAON DISTRICT							
67.	BELGANGA SSK LTD.	2500	272.00	300.00	325.00	332.50	336.80	418.00
68.	MADHUKAR SSK LTD.	2500	279.00	253.00	308.00	356.00	471.00	471.00
69.	VASANT SSK LTD.	1250	260.00	280.00	291.00	275.00	306.80	380.00
	AURANGABAD DISTRICT							
70.	DEOGIRI SSK LTD.	2500	0.00	0.00	0.00	0.00	0.00	0.00
				— Under Errection —				
71.	GANGAPUR SSK LTD.	2000	271.00	265.00	325.00	350.00	361.80	500.00
72.	KANNAD SSK LTD.	1250	266.00	300.00	343.00	307.50	320.00	410.00
73.	SHRI SANT EKNATH SSK LTD.	1250	240.00	242.00	306.00	307.50	325.80	368.00

(*Contd.*)

TABLE 9 (*Contd.*)

1	2	3	4	5	6	7	8	9
74.	THE SIDDHESHWAR SSK LTD.	2000	314.00	321.00	375.00	419.00	375.00	500.00
75.	VINAYAK SSK LTD.	1250	0.00	242.00	325.00	318.50	337.80	318.00
	JALANA DISTRICT							
76.	JALANA SSK LTD.	1250	273.00	325.00	362.00	430.00	430.00	491.00
77.	SAMARTH SSK LTD.	1250	284.00	268.00	326.00	350.00	375.00	400.00
	AURANGABAD REGION							
	BEED DISTRICT							
78.	AMBEJOGAI SSK LTD. (A)	1250	271.00	275.00	300.00	292.50	306.80	0.00
79.	JAI BHAVANI SSK LTD.	1250	261.00	332.00	355.00	309.50	339.80	0.00
80.	KADA SSK LTD.	1250	240.00	242.00	300.00	307.50	306.80	0.00
81.	MAJALGAON SSK LTD.(A)	2500	240.00	0.00	0.00	0.00	0.00	0.00
				— Under	Erection —			
82.	SHRI GAJANANAK SSK LTD. (B)	1250	255.00	262.00	271.00	321.00	306.00	0.00
	NANDED REGION							
	PARBHANI DISTRICT							
83.	GODAVARI DUDHANA SSK LTD.	1250	240.00	242.00	300.00	350.00	368.00	460.00
84.	MARATHWADA SSK LTD.	1250	240.00	242.00	265.00	275.00	306.80	310.00
85.	PURNA SSK LTD.	2500	286.00	313.00	329.00	307.50	375.00	475.00
	NANDED DISTRICT							
86. (B)	GODAVARI MANAR SSK LTD.	1250	240.00	242.00	310.00	350.00	356.80	400.00
87.	KALAMBAR VIBHAG SSK LTD.	1250	0.00	0.00	0.00	0.00	0.00	0.00

TABLE 9 (*Contd.*)

1	2	3	4	5	6	7	8	9
88.	SHANKAR SSK LTD.	1250	0.00	272.00	305.00	359.00	365.00	447.00
	NANDED REGION							
	OSMANABAD DISTRICT							
89.	SHRI TULJABHAVANI SSK LTD.	1250	260.00	320.00	365.00	514.00	428.00	423.00
90.	TERNA SHETKARI SSK LTD.	3500	240.00	297.00	303.00	325.00	321.80	400.00
	LATUR DISTRICT							
91.	JAI JAWAN JAI KISAN SSK LTD	1250	240.00	265.00	312.00	339.00	376.00	426.00
92.	MANJARA SSK LTD.	1250	269.00	315.00	410.00	522.00	525.00	590.00
93.	SHETKARI SSK LTD.	1250	266.00	283.00	325.00	340.00	347.00	0.00
	AMARAVATI REGION							
	BULDHANA DISTRICT							
(B)								
94.	JIJAMATA SSK LTD.	1250	240.00	240.00	250.00	260.00	296.80	0.00
	YAVATMAL DISTRICT							
(A)								
95.	JAI KISAN SSK LTD.	2500	0.00	0.00	0.00	0.00	0.00	0.00
					— Under Erection —			
96.	VASANT SSK LTD.	1250	266.00	284.00	296.50	275.00	346.00	383.00
	AKOLA DISTRICT							
97.	BALAJI SSK LTD.	1250	240.00	242.00	281.50	307.00	313.00	375.00
	AMARAVATI DISTRICT							
98.	SHETKARI SSK LTD. (B)	1250	266.00	283.00	325.00	340.00	347.00	0.00

(*Contd.*)

TABLE 9 (*Contd.*)

1	2	3	4	5	6	7	8	9
	NAGPUR REGION							
	WARDHA DISTRICT							
99.	MAHATMA SSK LTD.	1250	240.00	242.00	250.00	275.00	296.80	318.00
100.	SHRIRAM SSK LTD.	1250	282.00	207.00	400.00	350.00	350.00	0.00
	BHANDARA DISTRICT							
101.	WAINGANGA SSK LTD.	1250	240.00	240.00	250.00	260.00	296.80	0.00

Note : (A) = Under Erection (From 1987-88 to 1990-91/1991-92/1992-93)

(B) = Not in Operation (During Season 1992-93)

Cane prices in respect of rest of the factories are yet to be fixed.

TABLE 10

Harvest Prices of Jaggery (Raw-Sugar) in the Bombay Presidency

(Price per Maund 82 2/7 16)

Years	Prices	
	Rs.	Annas
1916-17*	9	4
1917-18*	8	10
1918-19	11	7
1919-20	15	12
1920-21	14	1
1921-22	14	14
1922-23	12	7
1923-24	10	0
1924-25	12	3
1925-26	11	0
1926-27	9	1
1927-28	8	6
1928-29	9	15
1929-30	9	5

* Average annual market prices.

Source : Agricultural Statistics of India, Vol. I, 1917-18 to 1929-30.

by borrowing funds from outside sources. In October 1996, as a policy of State Govt., the losses of sugar factories have been converted into Government's shares. Around 86 sugar factories in the State have benefited by this policy.

Thus, the task lies with the Government, to decide the issue. Due to the collective influence of the co-operative sugar factories in most of the states, the issue may get compliance in due course. In fact the issue deserves, a review and an alternative policy issues to dole out.

Thus the foregoing analysis, obviously, illustrates, how complications have been simplified. Thus the policy has a great bearing on the operations of the sugar factories in Maharashtra. Moreover, it is an issue of a great interest, on the part of the cane growers of Maharashtra, because the cost of cultivation of sugarcane is inherently increasing. The prices of agricultural inputs are rather growing higher than the agricultural output prices.

8

TRENDS IN SUGARCANE PRICES FROM 1950 ONWARDS

On the basis of the norms so far discussed earlier, the Central Government and the CACP announces the sugarcane prices at the different levels. Table 11 illustrates the national trend in detail. The SMP is measured in terms of Rs. per quintal. From 1950-51 to 1961-62 the sugarcane prices were fixed by Central Government on the basis of weight of sugarcane. The trend during the period was decreasing. In 1950-51 the SMP was Rs. 4.60 per quintal, which was declined to Rs. 3.85 and Rs. 4.34 during the period referred above.

From 1962-63 onwards the SMP is linked to the basic recovery of 9.8 with a premium of Re. 0.04 per 0.1 per cent increase in sugar recovery. The premium of additional recovery of sugar in sugarcane price is allowed only from 1970-71 onwards.

After the establishment of APC, the range of SMP has been drawn as shown in column 5 and the range of actual price paid by sugar factories from 1968-69 onwards is as shown in column 6 of Table 11.

In August, 1967, when a partial decontrol was introduced, the minimum price was raised significantly to Rs. 7.37 per quintal and from 1967-68 season, a premium of 5.36 paise per quintal has been allowed for every 0.1 per cent increase in sugar recovery. During the season, 1967-68 and 1968-69, sugar factories have paid much higher sugarcane prices as compared to SMP.

During the period from 1967-68 to 1971-72, the minimum

price of sugarcane was fixed at Rs. 7.31 per quintal linked to a basic recovery of 9.4 per cent. The practice in northern states was different. The Govt. Notification of September, 1967 provided that, the sugarcane delivered at any purchasing centre connected by rail and transported by rail, payment shall be made at 32 paise per quintal less than the notified minimum price. Further a rebate not exceeding 2.5 paise per quintal per K.M. subject to a maximum of 32 paise per quintal would be allowed, to be deducted out of the minimum price of sugarcane transported by such producers by road on his own transport from the purchasing centre to the factory gate.

The Price Commission recommended that, Govt. may announce the basic level of recovery with reference to which the price is fixed would progressively lowered by 0.2 per cent every year until it reached 8.4 per cent by 1972-73. This recommendation stemmed from the belief that progressive lowering of basic recovery linked to the minimum price would result in improvement of quality of cane. But the quality of cane could not improve with this recommendations. It involves propagation of varieties suitable for different areas, their protection from pests and diseases, improved agricultural practices, irrigation and the inputs. The above recommendations would have adverse effect on the price received by the cane growers in comparatively low recovery zones / states. Therefore, Govt. did not consider it advisable to make an announcement.

Sugar mills generally pay the minimum price fixed by the Govt. In 1972-73, the sugarcane price had been raised to Rs. 8.0, but the recommended recovery had been reduced from 9.4 per cent to 8.5 per cent, which is kept constant since then. The SMP for the seasons 1993-94 and 1994-95 have been fixed in advance by the CACP. The SMP for the season 1997-98 was fixed at Rs. 48.45 (see Table 11). This rate has been hiked to Rs. 50.70 with a premium of Re. 0.62 for every 0.1 per cent increase in recovery. Generally the Govt. announces the price as recommended by CACP. In the last 12 years (1985-86 to 1996-97) Government have deviated from the recommendations of CACP only in four occasions. In 1990-91 and 1993-94, Government announced SMP lower, by

Re. 1 and Rs. 2 respectively, in 1992-93 and 1994-95 it announced SMP higher, by Rs. 4 and paise 60 respectively (Mahajan Committee, Report 1998, p. 177).

Thus the price is generally fixed taking into account the cost of production of sugarcane, the returns to the growers from alternative crops and the general trend of prices of other agricultural commodities and the fair price of sugar paid by the customers. Over the period 1952-53 to 1964-65, the acreage under sugarcane in the country increased at the compound rate of 4.03 per cent per annum, while the corresponding increase of acreage under foodgrains was only 0.98 per cent. In Maharashtra the respective rates were 6.02 per cent and 0.32 per cent. The acreage under cane constituted less than 2 per cent of the total cropped areas in the country, in money terms cane production contributed almost 7 per cent of aggregate agricultural income (APC, 1967).

TABLE 11

SMP and Actual Prices Paid for Sugarcane

(1950-51 to 1998-99)

Seasons	SMP@ in Rs. (per Qtl.)	Basic Recovery	Premium (t)	Range of SMP (Rs./QHS)	Range of Actual Price paid by Factories
1	2	3	4	5	6
1950-51	4.69	—	—	—	—
1951-52	4.69	—	—	—	—
1953-54	3.52	—	—	—	—
1954-55 to					
1958-59	3.85	—	—	—	—
1959-60 to					
1961-62	4.34	—	—	—	—
1962-63	4.34	9.8	0.04	—	—
1963-64	4.69	9.0	0.04	—	—
1964-65	5.36	10.4	0.04	—	—
1965-66	5.36	10.4	0.04	5.36-6.48	—
1966-67	5.68	9.4	0.04	5.68-6.84	—

(*Contd.*)

TABLE 11 (*Cont.*)

1	2	3	4	5	6
1967-68	7.37	9.4	0.0536	7.37-9.35	—
1968-69	7.37	9.4	0.0536	7.37-9.35	7.37-15.0
1969-70	7.37	9.4	0.0536	7.37-9.09	7.37-10.0
1970-71	7.37	9.4	0.066	7.37-9.22	7.37-11.55
1971-72	7.37	9.4	0.066	7.37-9.48	7.37-18.50*
1972-73	8.00	8.5	0.094	8.00-11.57	8.0-15.50*
1973-74	8.00	8.5	0.094	8.0-11.29	8.00-18.0*
1974-75	8.50	8.5	0.10	8.50-12.40	8.50-18.65
1975-76	8.50	8.5	0.10	8.50-12.40	8.50-17.50*
1976-77	8.50	8.5	0.10	8.50-12.70	8.50-16.60*
1977-78	8.50	8.5	0.10	8.50-12.40	8.50-16.50*
1978-79	10.0	8.5	0.117647	10.0-14.59	10.0-14.71*
1979-80	12.50	8.5	0.147059	12.50-18.68	12.50-22.00*
1980-81	13.0	8.5	0.152941	13.0-18.35	13.0-28.0
1981-82	13.0	8.5	0.152941	13.0-18.81	13.0-26.0
1982-83	13.0	8.5	0.152941	13.0-19.12	13.0-23.0
1983-84	13.50	8.5	0.158824	13.50-19.69	13.50-26.20
1984-85	14.0	8.5	0.164706	14.0-20.42	15.0-35.0
1985-86	16.50	8.5	0.194118	16.50-24.07	16.50-32.19
1986-87	17.0	8.5	0.20	17.0-25.0	17.60-28.10
1987-88	18.50	8.5	0.21765	18.50-26.77	18.50-38.60
1988-89	19.50	8.5	0.2294	19.50-27.99	19.50-49.50
1989-90	22.0	8.5	0.2588	22.0-32.09	22.0-56.10
1990-91	23.0	8.5	0.270588	23.0-34.36	30.0-60.10
1991-92	26.0	8.5	0.305882	26.0-38.54	26.0-60.0
1992-93	31.0	8.5	0.3647706	31.0-47.41	71.90
1993-94	34.50	8.5	0.405882	34.50-53.17	65-0
1994-95	39.10	8.5	0.46 upto 10% 0.60 above 10%	39.10-66.40	71.0

(*Contd.*)

TABLE 11 (*Cont.*)

1	2	3	4	5	6
1995-96	42.50	8.5	0.54	42.50-68.96	N.A.
1996-97	45.90	8.5	0.57	45.90-72.69	N.A.
1997-98	48.45	8.5	0.60	-	N.A.
1998-99	50.70	8.5	0.62	-	N.A.

Notes : @ = SMP - Rs./Quintals
t = Premium payable of every 0.1 per cent increase in recovery
* = Advance prices paid by factories

Source : Various Issues of Co-operative Sugar.

The price policy during 1967-68 was aimed to stabilise the sugarcane acreage. This role of price fixation during the period thus emphasised on, (a) to leave undistributed, the present relative gains to the growers from sowing cane and from cultivating other crops, and (b) to encourage the production of cane of superior varieties (APC, 1967).

The Govt. of Maharashtra, in the beginning of the 1994-95 season had declared to pay, the sugarcane prices on the basis of the quality of sugarcane. But it is difficult to test the recovery of sugar in the sugarcane at farm level. At present the pol percentage (*i.e.*, maturity of sugarcane) in sugarcane can be tested by an instrument called refractometer.

Now-a-days the SMP for sugarcane is fixed with the object of ensuring payment of guaranteed price for cane by the factory to the cane growers. The main elements of the SMP as practiced today can be summarised as :

(a) a minimum cane price fixed on the norms as stated earlier,

(b) a basic level of sugar recovery,

(c) a premium of every 0.1 per cent increase in sugar recovery over the basic level, and

(d) the average sugar recovery of the factory during a fixed period (optimum period).

The Central Government considers the first three constituents of the above formulae which is changing from time to time.

The millwise SMPs are fixed by the GOI. The average percentage of recovery is taken into consideration while fixing the SMP of each factory. The SMP is fixed on the basic recovery rate of 8.5 per cent. The recovery more than this rate is taken up and multiplied with the premium rates for estimating SMP of each sugar factory.

9

SUGARCANE PRICING IN INDIAN STATES AND FOREIGN COUNTRIES

The determination of sugarcane prices is a matter of critical importance both for the sugar industry and the cane growers. The industry-agriculture linkages become more emperic and theoretic at the point of controversy in fixing the prices of agricultural produce. When the sugarcane prices are too low, the cane growers suffer a lot due to fall in their expected income and unrecoverable costs incurred with an intention to earn expected level of income. Particularly, the farmers get discouraged and frustrated, when the prices of alternative crops are remunerative. This is like an opportunity loss compelled to be borne on farm accounts due to lack of market forecasting abilities of the farmers. Consequently the farmers will switch over to another crops in the next season. This attitude throws the sugar industry in trouble leading to fall in production and adverse effects of the financial conditions of the sugar mills. On the contrary, if the sugarcane prices are higher, (or artificially kept higher) the cost of production and consequently the price of sugar will rise, and the general consumers will suffer. On the Govt. part, this situation keeps them in trouble. Partial control or full control becomes inevitable as has been happening frequently in the past. The outcome, then, will be ill-health of the industry, cane appears mount and sugar factories are left with no funds to invest in expansion or modernisation of the industry and cane development. Industrial sickness alarms.

The existing system of SMP in India is under the provision of Sugarcane (Control) Order, 1966. The CACP determines the SMP based on various norms and principles. The levy prices of sugar are fixed by the Govt. computed on the basis of BICP norms and principles. The actual cane price paid by the farmers has been announced by the State Govts. except in case of Co-operative Sugar Factories in the States of Maharashtra, Gujarat, where they are fixed by the factories themselves with the approval of the respective State Govts.

The GOI fixes SMP which can be computed factorywise based on the premium for each 0.1% of sugar recovery. Therefore, the actual SMP varies from factory to factory depending on the recovery percentage during peak season in the particular season.

In a judgment (Petition No. 36889-1996) given by the Allahabad High Court, it has been held that, the State Govts. do not have any power whatsoever to declare the price of sugarcane, as under law this power rests on the Central Govt. The Central Govt. exercising under Essential Commodities Act promulgated the Sugarcane (Control) Order, 1966, Clause 3 (1) States that,

> "The Central Government any after consultation with such authorities, bodies or associations as it may fit, by notification in the official Gazette, from time to time fix the minimum price of sugarcane to be paid by producers of sugar or their agents for the sugarcane purchased by them...."

In practice, State Govts. have been announcing SAPs compelling the sugar factories to pay accordingly. Every State Govts. in India follows different method of fixing SAPs.

SUGARCANE PRICING IN INDIAN STATES

In Northern States like U.P., Haryana, Punjab, Bihar and Madhya Pradesh, a uniform SAPs were fixed for payment in one instalment after delivery of cane. The SAPs were not linked to recovery per cent. Premium was allowed for early high sucrose varieties. From 1996-97 season the Government of U.P. is announcing SAP of sugarcane for only Public Sector and Co-operative Sector factories. Private Sector Factories are now fixing their own prices based on SMP announced by GOI.

The genesis of SAPs are found in Sugarcane Act, 1934 Section 3(2) of the said Act entitled the State Govts. to fix by notification the minimum price for purchasing in any controlled area sugarcane intended for use in any factory. But this Act was by implication repealed by the Essential Commodities Act, 1955, which is a Parliamentary Law under which the 1966 sugarcane order was made. The implications of provisions in 1934 Act Section 3(2) came to end.

The U.P. Sugarcane (Regulation of Supply and Purchase) Act, 1953 Section 16 permits the State Government to regulate the purchase and supply of cane in reserved areas, it does not provide for fixation of a SAPs.

In Maharashtra State SAP is fixed by the Ministerial Committee headed by the Chief Minister. Other members of the Committee consists of Ministers of Co-operation, Irrigation and Finance, State Ministers of Co-operation and Agriculture, Chairman of Sakhar Sangh as its Members and State Co-op. Bank (invitee) and Secretaries of Co-operation, Finance, Agriculture, Irrigation and Commissioner of sugar as its invitee members.

In Maharashtra, more than 95% of sugar factories belong to co-operative sector. They are governed by Co-operative Societies Act and the bye-laws framed thereunder. Bye-laws 63, 64, 64A, 65A and 65B deal with fixation of price of cane. Bye-law 64, empowers the State Govt., to fix the price of cane so long the amount invested by it in setting up of sugar factory is not repaid. There is only one sugar factory, (Hutatma Kisan Ahir, Walva) who has paid all invested amount of Govt. of Maharashtra. However, there are other obligations of the State Govts. on the sugar co-operatives in terms guarantee to the different types of loans borrowed by the sugar factories.

The Ministerial Committee takes into account the ex-gate minimum price declared by the Central Government, the estimated sugar production and availability for production by the factories, the estimated average recovery of sugar factories, the estimated conversion charges and the present day levy and free sale sugar price while fixing the sugarcane price for a season. The price is not the final sugarcane price, it is termed as first advance price determined on the basis of SMP, market price of sugar, molasses and likely final sugarcane price. The SAP is ex-field, it does not include transport and harvesting charges. These charges are borne by the sugar factories. The SAP is always higher than SMP and do not vary from factory to factory unlike SMPs. The Committee takes decision about some norms for final price of the proceeding season.

In Gujarat State all sugar factories belong to co-operative sector. The cane prices are decided by the sugar factories themselves. Bhargava formula is not applied in the State. Ex-field price and ex-factory prices are fixed under ex-field price formula; SMP + additional cane price – transport and harvesting charges are taken into account. While ex-factory price is fixed as SMP + additional cane price. Sugarcane price is paid in three and two instalments in South Gujarat and Sourashtra region respectively. The final price is fixed by Board of Directors. Very small amount of price is paid in second and third instalments.

In Karnataka State, SAP of sugarcane is fixed like that of SMP, linked to 8.5% sugar recovery. All sugar factories in the State have to pay the SAP. However, if a sugar factory willing to pay higher sugarcane price than SAP, no restrictions are imposed on it. There is a possibility of higher sugarcane price to be paid by a factory due to higher realisation of sugar prices and other by-product or if its conversion cost is comparatively low.

For fixing the SAP, the Karnataka State Govt. has constituted a High Power Committee under the Chairmanship of the Chief Minister to advise the Govt. The HPC advise the Govt. about the fixation of a suitable sugarcane price to be paid to the growers. The HPC meeting is convened every year, which is attended by the managements of sugar factories, representatives of the cane growers, M.Ps. MLAs and MLCs of sugarcane growing area and the concerned officers of the State Govt. The HPC bears the views and suggestions of the participants which can be considered while fixing the SAP alongwith following norms :

(A) Realisation Aspects

(i) Realisation from the sale of free and levy sugar,

(ii) Realisation from sale of molasses and other by-products,

(iii) Purchase tax rebates to the farmers (Rs. 12 per tonne).

(B) Expenditure Aspects

(i) Conversion cost of sugar (weighted average),

(ii) Purchase tax and turn over tax,

(iii) Cane cost.

The ex-factory prices are paid by some factories in Southern and Central Karnataka, whereas in Northern Karnataka the ex-field prices are fixed (factories meet harvesting and transport expenses).

Payment of remunerative SAP of sugarcane without affecting the sugar mills is in practice in Tamilnadu, which is decided after taking note of the views and suggestions of Grower's Representative Associations and the management of sugar factories. The SAP, normally remains more than SMP and simultaneously higher than Additional Cane Price (ACP) (final price) fixed under Bhargava formula. Since a reasonable level of SAP is fixed by the State Govt., no factory is defaulting in payment of cane dues.

The peak averages of sugar recovery of the previous crushing season are taken into account by the State's Commissioner of Sugar while fixing the factorywise sugarcane prices.

In Andhra Pradesh SAP is fixed, based on the cost of cultivation of sugarcane and other related aspects. The SAP is higher than SMP. Bhargava formula is worked out to compute ACP.

Payment of sugarcane price arrears is a headache to the factories. Cane arrears were higher in 1991-92 and 1995-96. As the sugar co-operatives are owned by the cane growers, the surplus after deducting conversion cost goes directly to the cane growers, which is paid in the form of advances (first instalment). Second and third instalments are paid after realisation of sugar prices.

Fixation of SAP by the Govts. in different states of India basically depends on the pressure of a lobby in the State. The lobbies may be of co-operatives, private mill owners, joint-stock companies, or farmers (cane growers). In most cases the confusion eventuate, when the issue of realisation of sugar prices and prices of by-products are taken into account while fixing the sugarcane prices. Particularly, this becomes, an important issue to private and joint-stock company undertakings. Co-operatives are directly disbursing the surpluses after deducting the conversion cost. Sometimes, Govt.'s political economy either obstruct or enhance the issue in a different fashion. Cane politics in States of Maharashtra, Karnataka and Gujarat is very crucial.

Allahabad High Court held an important verdict in 1998 that, the fixation of SAP by State Govts. is illegal. All powers relating to it are restored with Central Govt. The court further stated that, "When there is conflict between the law and equity, it is law which is to prevail in accordance with the Latin Maxim, "Dura Lex Sed Led", which means "the law is hard but it is the law". ....The Court mentioned to modify the outdated laws relating to sugar industry and sugarcane, and suggested to appoint a High Power Committee to review the laws and regulations relating to the industry in foreign countries. GOI appointed the Mahajan Committee to review the whole things.

Mahajan Committee suggested to appoint a Sugarcane Pricing Board headed by an Economist. The Committee also suggested to make suitable amendment in Clause 3 of Sugarcane Control Order, 1966. To give justice to the efficient cane growers, the Committee suggested to fix the sugarcane prices based on sugarcane varieties. This is actually brought in practice in co-operative sugar factories in Karnataka and Maharashtra.

SUGARCANE PRICING IN FOREIGN COUNTRIES

Sugarcane pricing in foreign countries was the major issue to the High Power Mahajan Committee as directed by Allahabad

High Court. Allahabad High Court, obviously held that, the laws and regulations relating to sugar industry should be reviewed and reframed, they are now become outdated. To investigate this in foreign countries, H.P.C. has made visit to 12 major countries including Australia, Indonesia, Mauritius, Philippines, Taiwan, Thailand, Mexico, South Africa and USA etc. and tried to investigate the licensing procedure, cane area reservation, price control, sugarcane pricing, import-export, Govt. help, R & D etc.

In Australia, sugarcane prices are determined through agreement on the basis grower's share of revenues, while fixing the growers share, the averaged cane quality and efficiency of a sugar mill is taken into account, which is around 60 to 65 per cent. Sugar mills are obliged to pay for the cane transport out of their proceeds.

Cane payment formula is made helpful and beneficial to both Farming and Milling Committees with an incentives to protect and retain their efficiencies in their respective areas. The H.P.C. (1998) noted that, "the cane price formula is only one part of a whole series of contracts and arrangements to determine the real share of proceeds between farmers and millers". In such arrangements advance system, transport allowance, crushing allowance, sharing of irrigation and drainage cost, R & D etc. are taken into account.

From May 1998, the Brazilian Govt. is fixing the sugarcane price through an agreement between cane growers and mill owners. However, this price control is proposed to be liberalised later on. While fixing the sugarcane prices, sugar recovery exceeding 12.25% is taken into account as minimum official premium sale. The sugar prices are not linked to the sugarcane prices. Payment of sugarcane bills are made in four instalments. The first 70% instalment is paid within a month of cane harvest, and the rest in three parts within 30, 60 and 90 days thereafter. The North-East region of Brazil is receiving 25% more cane prices as compared to the South Central region.

In European Union the beet and sugarcane growers make contract annually with the mill owners for supply of cane/

beet. But as the cane/beet prices are regularised, no independent negotiations are made between growers and processors. Cane/ beet prices are linked to the quota sugar. The cane/beet processed to produce quota sugar receive the basic price, which is derived from white sugar intervention price (normally stands 58%) after deducting the processing margin, beet transport allowance and a credit for molasses sales. Minimum price is fixed for standard quality of 16% sugar content.

In Indonesia the farmers get a kind of yield share which is determined on basis of the sucrose content. There is no institutional mechanism to fix the cane prices. The grower's share in yield with below 8.5% sucrose is 68% and for the redemption above 8.5% is 70%.

Similar type of pricing is followed in Mauritius. The Arbitration and Control Board carries out all the analysis and computation of sugar accruing to growers and mill owners. The growers receive 76% and remaining 24% by the sugar producers. Nearly 64% of cane supply to the sugar factories comes from the land owned by mill owners. The price of sugar to be paid to them is based on the price obtained by the Mauritius Sugar Syndicate (MSS) for all sales. Advance payments against the delivery of sugarcane is made one week before the actual supply of cane. The corresponding payment are also regularly made. The final payment is made in June of the ensuing season.

In Mexico the sugar factories have a standard contract for buying and selling cane. The cane price paid to its producer constitute 54% of the value a kilogram of sugar multiplied by the factory production. Sugar producers provide various forms of credit for a minimum period of one year or one ratoon.

In South Africa, there is a facility of testing sucrose content in canes by an independent Cane Testing Service run by the South Africa Sugar Association (an equal membership organisation of mill owners and cane growers). The cane prices are based on the proceeds sharing partnership agreement. The grass proceeds consists of domestic/export sales of sugar/molasses. All relevant industrial costs are deducted from this gross proceeds.

The net proceeds are distributed according to a formula (64:36) agreed by both mill owners and cane growers. The cane payments to growers are made on monthly basis depending on the ratio of 64:36. This ratio changes from time to time. A few years back, the ratio was 62:38. About 97.5% of payment for cane are made initially and rest after the test of sucrose content. Every sugar mill has a sucrose testing station run by SASA.

Sugar companies in Sri Lanka, determine the sugarcane prices without any agreement between cane growers and mill owners. There is a discretionary practices in sugar companies to fix the sugarcane prices either on the average sucrose content or at a flat-rated. Cane payments are made within the period of 14 days after supply of sugarcane to the sugar companies.

Farmer's sugarcane is not purchased by the Sugar Mills in China (Taiwan) directly. Taiwan Sugar Corporation (TSC) initiates in determining the sugar sharing system for contract farmers. Cane growers grow sugarcane for TSC. In exchange of sugarcane, the farmers receive the processed sugar. The sharing ratio fixed by TSC is 55:45 in favour of the cane farmers. The portion of farmer's sugar is purchased by TSC at a guarantee price. Lump-sum cane payments are made within a fixed period. The TSC has set a Sugar Stabilisation Fund out of the portion of the export sales. When the export price fall below the guaranteed price offered by TSC, the difference is compensated from the SSF.

The Thai Sugar Industry is highly regulated by the office of Thai Cane and Sugar Board. The cane growers, sugar producers and Govt. are the representatives to this Board. This board undertaken three types of policy measures *viz.* (a) processing capacities, (2) domestic and export marketing and (c) distribution of revenues between growers and mill owners. The system of quality based cane payment is the recent induction of the sugar policy in 1992-93. Majority of sugar is marketed privately by mill owners. There is no single marketing body as it is in Australia and South Africa. Cane growers receive 70% of industry's net sugar revenues. Cane quality is taken into account while paying the cane prices. Cane payment formula has been developed. In addition to cane price per tonne, the cane growers get additional price out of the sale of by-products (10 bant .per tonne of sugarcane).

In United States also beet growers and mill owners share revenues earned out of sale of sugar, molasses independently. There are similarities between many such contracts. The beet growers receive around 50-55% of net selling sugar price of sugar (*i.e.*, sugar price – marketing costs). This share in cane sector is around 60-65%. Sugar producers are free to market their sugar to whom they wish and at whatever price they wish.

In conclusions, it can be stated that, in most of sugar producing major countries of the world, sucrose content is taken into account while fixing the sugarcane prices. The percentage share of growers in the net proceeds varies in various countries. However, the grower's share is greater than 55%. Sugarcane price in most countries is fixed on the contract basis.

There is no restrictions in any country on the agencies through which sugar factories have to obtain cane from the growers. Similarly no cane is supplied at a subsidised rate.

Co-operative type of organisation of sugar factories is the most suitable set up to give justice to the cane growers, because cane growers themselves are the owners of the sugar co-operatives.

10

DEDUCTIONS FROM SUGARCANE PRICES

Some deductions from the sugarcane prices are statutory and obligatory on the sugar factories. As a result the cane growers have to suffer. The input cost of the sugarcane has gone high as compared to the sugarcane prices, the farmers are receiving from the sugar factories. The terms of trade between sugar factory and sugarcane farming are not favourable today. Simultaneously the sugarcane yield is also deteriorating. Therefore, the cane growers are trapped in a triangular obstructions of Govt. deduction, growing input costs and declining yield of sugarcane.

Initially the deductions from sugarcane prices have been introduced to generate funds from the internal sources so as to strengthen the economic condition of the sugar factories. Some sugar factories in the State have raised the share capital of their members, automatically deducted from the sugarcane prices of the same members. Deductions are made to create various reserves. Such deductions are either backed by the provision in the bye-laws or by the decisions of the Ministerial Committee on sugarcane pricing.

Similarly as told earlier, the additional sugarcane prices beyond mark-up sugarcane prices fixed by the State Govt. goes to create deposits with the respective sugar factories, or State Govt. may ask to keep in its account in a State Co-operative Bank, so as to avoid competition in sugarcane prices. The refundable and nonrefundable deposits are also collected from the sugarcane prices. Such deposits are used to redeem the long-term-loans taken from the industrial credit institutions.

Appendix-I and II exhibits number of deductions from the final sugarcane prices to be paid by the sugar factories for a specific sugar season. All types of deductions have to be approved by the Ministerial Committee.

The Ministerial Committee examines, the income and expenditure of the sugar factories exhibited in a proforma (see Appendix-I). Such reports are generally sent to the Directorate of Sugar immediately after the crushing season. The Directorate scrutinises the details given in the proforma and same is sent to the Ministerial Committee for the final approval. The Ministerial Committee, look into the details of the sugar sales, balance sugar quantity, the cost of balanced (stock) sugar, concession given as per the Sampat Committee recommendations, losses, loans, deposits, transport cost of sugarcane, etc. Simultaneously arrangements have also been made, as per the clause of the cooperative laws, or the decision of the Ministerial Committees, to decide upon the expenses for Khodaki (ratoon crop) and Vechani for members and non-members. Other deductions in the statement consists of bonus payment (%), educational fund, audit fees, contribution to the State Sugar Factories' Federation, salaries, expenses incurred on sugarcane harvesting and transport, depreciation charges, VSI subscription, interest etc. All above deductions are made from the income earned by selling the sugar to Govt. and by tendering the auction sale. These are indirect deductions from sugarcane prices, because after deducting all types of costs and expenses, whatever surplus remains, that is distributed among the cane growers, who have supplied the sugarcane during the season.

Direct deductions made from the sugarcane bill includes, (a) deductions as per the bye-laws, (b) non-refundable deposits, (c) refundable deposits, (d) sugarcane development funds, (e) Chief Minister's fund, (f) small savings, (g) area development, (h) funds for educational institutions and trusts, (i) payment of interest on loans and loan instalments, (j) rehabilitation, (k) sugarcane purchase tax etc.

(a) Deductions as per the Resolutions/Bye-laws

The General Body of a Co-operative Society is a supreme

body to resolve the important resolutions for the benefit of the general members of the factory. The deductions from the sugarcane can be made in accordance with the General Body resolutions. Sometime, when Govt. feels essential, makes the sugar factories to resolve some important resolutions by the concerned co-operative sugar enterprises. Govt. may ask the co-operatives to pass the resolutions as required by Govt. to deduct some amount for the welfare of the general masses. For example Chief Minister's fund, VSI subscription etc. Table 6 illustrates the financial position of the sugar co-operatives in Maharashtra. Simultaneously Appendix-I also discloses the details of deductions from the sugarcane prices. Helping funds for educational institutions, trusts and other social institutions are also made by deducting some portion of sugarcane prices.

(b) Non-refundable Deposits

A co-operative sugar factory deducts at the rate of Rs. 5 to Rs. 15 stipulated by the term lending institutions, while sanctioning the block capital loan at the time of its erection. Such deductions are termed as N.R.Ds. As per the provision in the bye-laws of the co-operative sugar factories, these deposits are converted into shares of the concerned members. An interest at the rate of 12% per annum is being given to the members. But no sugar factory in Maharashtra have converted these deposits into the share capital (Kharche, 1986). Even no interest is also paid on such deposits. This may burden the sugar factories as an increasing cost of production. The members do not demand the conversion of these deposits into the share capital, because share will not yield return, whereas the deposits render returns in the form of interest at 12%.

(c) Refundable Deposits

Refundable deposits are taken from the non-members by deducting at the rate of Rs. 5 to Rs. 10 from the sugarcane prices normally for the period of 5 years. The rate of interest paid on such deposits is 10%. This was imposed to avoid the members' attitude to send their sugarcane in the name of a non-member to get escape from N.R.Ds.

(d) Chief Minister's Fund

The co-operative sugar enterprises have received a favourable response from the Govt. authorities since its beginning. Ultimately it is the responsibility of the sugar industry to help the Govt. in carrying out some social work through it. In view of this the deductions like contribution to the C.M. fund at the rate of Re. 0.50 to Rs. 2.00 per tonne is made every season. Similarly hutment fund, area development fund, are made available to the beneficiaries located in the operational areas of the sugar co-operatives.

(e) Hutment Fund/Earthquake Fund

Under the 20-Point Programmes, construction of houses for the landless poors was financed under the Govt. scheme. The sugar cooperatives have also deducted some portion from the sugarcane price to contribute towards the hutment fund. As a social organisation, the sugar factories have contributed to the rehabilitation fund for the earthquake affected people in Maharashtra.

(f) Area Development Fund

A.D.F. is created with a view to finance for undertaking various timely development activities in the operational area of a sugar co-operative. The development activities includes, construction of roads, social costs, irrigation schemes, medical and health facilities, etc. The detailed rules to use A.D.F. has been framed by the National Federation of Sugar Co-operatives in 1980. In certain cases, the expenses made under area development by sugar factories have been reimbursed by the Govt. *e.g.*, road construction. Now this scheme has been stopped.

(g) Sugarcane Development Fund

Sugarcane is the main raw-material of the sugar factories. Obviously, it is the duty of the sugar factories to enhance the sugarcane cultivation so as to produce quality raw-material to the sugar factories. S.D.F. is created to make R&D in connection with sugarcane crop. This includes demonstration plot, production of quality seeds, pilot schemes of sugarcane cultivation, invention of new varieties, crop protection measures, irrigation, farm management etc. But in most of the sugar factories this section is dormant dealing nothing about improving the quality of sugarcane though it is essential.

(h) Small-Scale Saving

To enhance the saving habits among the farmers, the sugar factories deduct very little amount of money from the sugarcane prices and is invested in Government's SSS on account of the individual farmers.

(i) V.S.I. Contribution

Vasantdada Sugar Institute (former Deccan Sugar Institute) has been established to promote research and development concerned to sugar industry in Maharashtra. It undertakes research, education, extension activities under various disciplines of sugar industry for promoting and guiding to the sugar factories to improve the managerial efficiency of the sugar factories. The institute collects and assess the working results of the sugar factories and guide the sugar factories in case of any technical / managerial obstructions. The institute also finances for the development of quality of sugarcane to the sugar factories. The VSI subscription has been deducted from the sugarcane prices at the rate of Re. 0.50 to 1.00 per tonne of sugarcane supplied by the cane growers.

Besides number of other small and major deductions are made at the level of individual sugar factory to meet the social costs arising in the regions or for protecting the interests of the farmer members of the co-operative sugar factories. Occasional deductions are also decided in the General Body Meeting (See Table 6).

11

TERMS OF TRADE : PARITY PRICES AND COST OF SUGARCANE CULTIVATION

The concept of terms of trade, normally, is used in the context of international trade. The changing ratios of export prices and import prices are being described in the context of international terms of trade. This analysis reflects the gains/ losses arising out of differential rates of changes in the ratios of exports and imports.

The idea of terms of trade can also be used in two sector analysis *e.g.*, agricultural and non-agricultural. In this context the concept of terms of trade would imply to a comparison between the prices received by agricultural sector and the prices paid by it for purchasing its inputs from non-agricultural sector. Though the application of concept of terms of trade to two-sectoral analysis is limited, it has been used in U.S.A. in the form of parity prices (see Kahlon and Tyagi, 1983).

In India, the question of parity principle (policy) for agricultural prices was in discussion since long. The Janata Party in 1977 manifested to consider the parity prices between the prices paid and prices received by agricultural sector. Accordingly in 1980, the CACP has been required to revise agricultural prices on the basis of changes in terms of trade. Even before their incident, number of studies had been worked out to explore the fact based on the different varieties of crops. Similarly the price movement between industry and agriculture sector was worked out. Besides the two-crop terms of trade was also analysed by using different methods of computing it.

It has been always proclaimed by the sugarcane growers that, the cost of sugarcane cultivation has gone up phenomenally, while the sugarcane prices have not. On the contrary the sugarcane prices have gone down in 1995-96 as compared to the sugar season of 1994-95. Consequently the farmer's reluctancy to undertake the plantation of sugarcane has persisted during the following sugar season. As a result the sugar industry had faced the problem of supply of raw-material (*i.e.,* sugarcane) during the sugar season.

Terms of trade can be estimated with references to the (a) prices of other competing crops like jowar, wheat and rice, (b) prices of competing commodities like gur and sugar, (c) input prices like fertilizers and the prices of sugarcane.

Table 12 exhibits the terms of trade between sugarcane and competing cereals crop jowar in Maharashtra. Jowar was the competing crop to sugarcane during 1960s and 1970s. The terms of trade for sugarcane were not favourable during the period from 1962-63 to 1965-66 as compared to the prices of competing cereals jowar in Maharashtra. Same is the case even with the rest of the sugarcane producing states like U.P., Bihar, Punjab, Andhra Pradesh, Madras and Mysore with their competing cereal crops (*i.e.*, Wheat in U.P., Bihar and Punjab; rice for Andhra Pradesh, Madras and Mysore).

Even after 1965-66, the minimum prices of sugarcane were high as compared to the competing crops like maize and wheat in Maharashtra. The percentage change over, in minimum sugarcane price (related to the levels of average recovery realised in the preceding years) in 1969-70 over 1965-66 was (+) 49.7. The percentage change in procurement price of wheat during the same period was (+) 16.9 and the percentage change in minimum price of maize for same period was (+) 15.4 and that of procurement price of maize was (+) 24.4.

Table 14 indicates the movement in wholesale price indices of sugar *vis-a-vis* other commodities like food and agricultural commodities. It is seen that over the 15 years period, an increase

TABLE 12

Terms of Trade Between Sugarcane and Jowar in Maharashtra

Years	Minimum prices of sugarcane* (1962-63 = 100)	Wholesale prices index of jowar	Terms of Trade (Sugarcane as denominator)	
1962-63	100.0	100.0	100.0	* Minimum price of sugarcane related to levels of recovery realised in the preceding year.
1963-64	111.9	135.1	120.7	
1964-65	110.9	192.7	173.8	
1965-66	107.9	195.0	180.7	

Source : APC, 1966-67.

TABLE 13

Sugarcane, Wheat, Maize and Paddy : Minimum Prices in Maharashtra

		Range of Min. Price	% change
Sugarcane	Sept. 1966	5.36	
		6.48	(+) 50.6
	Dec. 1968	8.07	
		9.35	(+) 44.3
Wheat	Sept. 1966	49.50	
	Dec. 1968	59.0	(+) 19.2
Maize	Sept. 1966	36.0	
	Dec. 1968	44.0	(+) 22.2
Paddy	Sept. 1966	39.0	
	Dec. 1968	44.0	(+) 12.8
Paddy Procurement prices :	Sept. 1966	45.0	
	Dec. 1968	56.0	(+) 24.4

Source : APC, 1969.

in wholesale price of sugar has been substantially lower at 125% than that for agricultural commodities (230%), food article (236%) and for all commodities (196%). Increase in gur price (169%) has been — somewhat higher than sugar while Khandasari prices have increased by almost the same extent (123%).

TABLE 14

Movement in Wholesale Price Indices — Sugar vis-a-vis other Commodities

Years	Wholesale price indices (Base Year 1981-82 = 100)					
	Sugar	Agri. Comm.	Food article	All Comm.	Gur	Khandasari
1981-82	100	100	100	100	100	100
1985-86	114.8	129.1	134.1	125.4	119.7	99.7
1990-91	141.9	198.3	200.6	182.7	166.3	141.2
1991-92	156.7	236.7	241.7	207.8	166.6	145.2
1992-93	177.5	255.6	271.0	228.7	187.0	152.6
1993-94	207.2	271.2	284.4	247.8	279.7	192.6
1994-95	230.5	307.7	312.7	274.7	297.1	228.6
1995-96	225.5	330.5	335.7	295.8	269.3	222.6

Source : Office of the Economic Adviser, Ministry of Industry, Quoted in Mahajan Committee Report, 1998, p. 90.

As it is seen in Table 13 the price indices of sugarcane prices as compared to other price indices except wheat is less. Even it is less than price indices of all commodities in India.

Similar data has been exhibited by Maharashtra State Co-op. Sugar Factories Association (see Table 16). While pleading before the Third Wage Board, the Sugar Federation proclaimed the fact that, as compared to price indices of related aspects of sugar factories, sugarcane prices were discouraging. An income of actual average cane price per quintal since 1973-74 is negative. From 1979-80 season to 1985-86 an increase in the actual average price has gone up to 140. In the next corresponding year, there is a sharp decline in actual average price of sugarcane (see Table 16).

TABLE 15

Price Trends
(Wholesale price indices)
(Base 1970-71)

Years	S.	Sc.	Gur.	Khand	Rice	Wh.	Van	Veg. & fruits	Pulses	All
1973-74	150	117	202	144	140	107	140	145	177	149
1974-75	167	123	205	236	183	183	185	160	216	175
1975-76	169	128	233	234	179	160	160	139	182	173
1976-77	173	129	223	227	157	152	143	143	145	177
1977-78	159	126	188	187	162	157	168	177	215	186
1978-79	147	150	148	135	161	151	163	161	247	185
1979-80	177	189	260	208	184	161	195	191	244	218
1980-81	250	194	437	385	206	176	211	213	323	257
1981-82	259	193	371	356	226	192	235	243	330	231
1982-83	229	191	275	251	257	214	258	250	202	239
1983-84	231	195	341	258	592	218	255	301	347	316
1984-85	244	212	321	286	273	640	275	304	431	338
1985-86	290	253	446	356	284	226	299	358	463	358
1986-87	304	262	456	345	303	239	369	430	408	358
1987-88	313	283	436	353	326	259	430	440	498	405
1988-89	339	291	479	300	364	294	444	435	658	435
1989-90	365	291	582	448	372	292	465	470	633	458

Source : Compiled and presented by S. Rajagopal - Sugar Industry Profile, IBA, 1992, p. 9.

All above exercises except APC, expresses the sugarcane prices are discouraging since 1970s.

This indicates the fact that, the percentage change in the minimum price of sugarcane was not suffered as compared to competing crops in Maharashtra. The relative minimum prices or procurement price or even open market prices of computing foodgrains in sugarcane was not relatively fared better. Thus the sugarcane prices were in more advantageous than competing foodgrains crops. It would be better if income data is available for analysing the comparative status of the crops, but it is very difficult to get such data base. Besides double or sometime tripple cropping pattern can be followed in case of foodgrain crops (cereals and pulses). In this regard it would be worthwhile to consider the comparative cost of cultivation of foodgrain crops and sugarcane crops also. To measure the comparative profitability of the crops is another topic of great interest to the researchers.

12

COST OF CULTIVATION : INPUT PRICES

As it is seen earlier, while deciding upon the minimum sugarcane price, the Commission takes into account the comparative prices of alternative competing crops to sugarcane. Similarly, the Commission has to take into account the recent increases in the prices of input used for sugarcane crop alongwith competing crops also. The references of such farm management studies are being referred by the Commissions to arrive at the particular level of minimum prices. The data of costs is based on the data collected under the comprehensive scheme for studying the cost of cultivation of principal crops. The field data are generally collected by Mahatma Phule Krishi Vidyapeeth, Rahuri for sugarcane in Maharashtra.

Total cost of cultivation includes expenses incurred in cash and kind on hired human labour, bullock and machine labour (both hired and owned), seeds (both farm produced and purchased), insecticides and pesticides, fertilizers and manures, irrigation charges, land revenues, taxes and cesses, depreciation on implements, farm buildings, rent paid for lease-in land and the imputed rental value of owned land, imputed interest on fixed capital and imputed value of family labour etc. The per quintal estimated total costs are obtained by dividing the corresponding estimates per hectare (net of the value of by-product) by the yield per hectare.

In 1969-70 the cost of sugarcane production was estimated at Rs. 3.79 per quintal, which has gone up to Rs. 4.56 in 1973-74. The systematic study of cost estimation has been made under the comprehensive scheme in 1974-75, and 1977-78 through Mahatma Phule Krishi Vidyapeeth, Rahuri in Maharashtra. Further details are illustrated in Table 17 (b).

TABLE 16

Comparative Trends of Wholesale Prices, Consumer Prices and Cane Prices

Sl. No.	Year	Wholesale Price Index of Sugar		Minimum Monthly Salary of an Unskilled Worker		Consumer Price Index in Industrial Worker		Actual Average Cane Price per Qtl.	
		Index No.	Increase over 1972-73	Rupees	Increase over 1972-73	Index No.	Increase over 1972-73	Rupees	Increase over 1972-73
1.	1972-73	144	--	177.35	—	210	—	11.02	—
2.	1973-74	150	4.17	226.34	27.62	264	25.71	12.77	15.80
3.	1974-75	167	15.97	323.00	82.12	326	55.24	10.97	- 0.45
4.	1975-76	169	17.36	346.00	95.09	298	41.90	10.32	- 6.35
5.	1976-77	173	20.14	314.00	77.05	307	46.19	11.33	2.81
6.	1977-78	159	10.42	341.00	92.27	325	54.76	10.91	- 1.00
7.	1978-79	177	2.08	404.00	127.80	332	58.09	10.57	- 4.08
8.	1979-80	177	22.92	439.95	148.07	371	76.67	14.57	32.21
9.	1980-81	250	73.61	491.82	177.32	411	95.71	21.11	91.56
10.	1981-82	259	79.36	596.97	236.50	455	116.67	20.75	88.29
11.	1982-83	229	59.03	639.53	260.61	495	153.71	19.48	77.77
12.	1983-84	231	60.42	745.82	320.53	563	169.09	19.83	79.94
13.	1984-85	244	69.44	848.57	373.47	588	180.00	25.57	132.02
14.	1985-86	300*	108.33	901.37	408.24	631	200.48	26.50£	140.47
15.	1986-87	—	—	995.42	461.27	678	222.86	27.50£	49.55

* = August, 1986

£ = Provisional January every year.

Index No.

	March, 1971	March, 1986	Increase
(i) Minimum Wages	161.586	8995.42	516%
(ii) CPI (Nos.)	184	678	269%

TABLE 17 (A)

Cost of Production of Sugarcane in Maharashtra (Rs.)

Sl. No.		1974-75	1977-78
1.	Total cost of cultivation per hectare (Rs.)	7057.34	A1-4963.50 A2-5047.86
2.	Rental value of owned land per hectare	1930.10	B-6651.84 C- 6920.78
3.	Interest on fixed capital per hectare	277.12	
4.	Cash & Kind exp. + Value of family labour per hect. [1-2(2+3)]	4850.12	
5.	Yield per hectare (Qtls.)	826.67	829.36
6.	Value of the main product per hectare	12377.12	9613.88
7.	Value of by-product per hect.	624.98	502.83
8.	Total cost (c) of prod. per qtl.	7.78	
	Avg. recovery of sugar (%)	11.17	A1-5.26 A2-5.36
9.	Total cost (c) of prod. per quintal in terms of recovery of 8.5%	5.92	B-7.29 C-7.62

*Cost A1 : Pertains to paid out costs or exp. incurred in cash and kind on material inputs, hired human capital, bullock and machine, labour (both hired and owned) etc. when rent paid for leased-in is added to cost A1 one gets A2 *i.e.*, paid out of a tenant cultivators. Cost B is obtained with the addition to cost A2 of imputed rental value of owner land and interest on owned fixed capital and cost C with the further addition of the impugned value of family labour.

TABLE 17 (B)

Estimates of Cost of Cultivation/Production and Related Data

STATE : MAHARASHTRA

CROP : SUGARCANE

ITEMS	1982-83	1983-84	1986-87	1987-88	1988-89	1989-90	1990-91
COST OF CULTIVATION PER HECT. (Rs.)							
A1	8965.56	9354.63	9319.18	10044.35	11300.42	13125.60	11272.87
A2	8965.56	9354.63	9319.18	10044.35	11300.42	13125.60	11272.87
B1	9502.82	9788.90	10081.98	10528.42	11818.83	13787.93	12297.08

ITEMS	1982-83	1983-84	1986-87	1987-88	1988-89	1989-90	1990-91
B2	11545.76	12583.05	13221.01	13860.92	15315.82	17840.10	16080.76
C1	10208.09	10541.23	10975.29	11293.20	12543.18	14648.41	13839.63
C2	12251.04	13335.39	14114.82	14625.70	16040.16	18700.56	17623.31
COST OF PRODUCTION PER QTL. (Rs.)							
A1	10.78	11.22	11.42	11.80	12.78	13.07	13.45
A2	10.78	11.22	11.42	11.80	12.78	13.07	13.45
B1	11.52	11.81	12.31	12.36	13.37	13.75	14.72
B2	13.81	15.05	16.00	16.07	17.34	17.71	19.17
C1	12.41	12.67	13.41	13.18	14.17	14.58	16.68
C2	14.71	15.91	17.10	16.89	18.14	18.54	21.12
VALUE OF MAIN PRODUCT/ HECT. (Rs.)	12366.80	16701.78	18075.86	19532.36	19741.86	23364.25	21963.66
VALUE OF BY-PRODUCT/ HECT. (Rs.)	779.77	960.53	1581.85	1350.85	2162.98	1852.82	1524.38
IMPUT QTY. PER HECT.							
SEED (Qtls.)	39.26	23.45	33.56	33.50	23.34	33.67	26.23
FERTILIZERS (KG. NUTRIENTS)	459.26	454.77	299.47	418.81	464.43	568.93	501.25
MANURE (Qtl.)	36.20	36.24	30.94	43.93	31.10	26.67	32.83
HUMAN LABOUR (Man Hrs.)	2998.80	2763.56	2317.14	2187.61	2361.69	2745.68	2009.94
ANIMAL LABOUR (Pair Hrs.)	109.04	97.25	146.75	128.62	129.15	106.19	139.26

ITEMS	1982-83	1983-84	1986-87	1987-88	1988-89	1989-90	1990-91
RATE PER UNIT (Rs.)							
SEED (Qtls.)	17.66	28.66	32.36	29.14	36.32	41.39	45.26
FERTILIZERS (Kg. Nutrients)	5.20	5.02	5.16	4.70	4.63	4.78	4.78
MANURE (Qtl.)	7.98	7.54	14.31	11.36	12.45	13.34	13.23
HUMAN LABOUR (Man Hrs.)	1.10	1.23	1.68	1.88	1.80	2.11	2.23
ANIMAL LABOUR (Pair Hrs.)	2.71	3.61	3.45	4.62	5.68	6.38	4.61
HOLDINGS IN SAMPLE (No.)	84	73	76	45	54	72	76
TEHSILS IN SAMPLE (No.)	22	16	22	15	17	23	26
YIELD PER HECTARE (Qtl.)	781.38	791.63	750.50	809.90	798.75	934.46	780.39

Break-up of Cost of Cultivation Per Hectare

STATE : MAHARASHTRA

CROP : SUGARCANE

ITEMS	1982-83	1983-84	1986-87	1987-88	1988-89	1989-90	1990-91
OPERATIONAL COST	9414.82	9846.69	9954.44	10552.15	11713.96	13689.35	12545.05
HUMAN LABOUR							
CASUAL	2411.05	2487.98	2771.67	3238.26	3251.45	4596.52	2805.68
ATTACHED	128.78	157.66	226.80	115.17	271.69	335.49	128.22
FAMILY	705.27	752.33	893.81	764.78	724.35	860.47	1542.54
TOTAL	3305.10	3397.97	3892.27	4118.21	4247.49	5792.48	4476.44
BULLOCK LABOUR							
HIRED	46.22	54.40	175.33	182.81	366.12	150.98	220.27
OWNED	249.04	296.77	331.42	410.79	367.84	526.23	421.33
TOTAL	295.26	351.17	506.75	593.60	783.96	677.21	641.60

ITEMS	1982-83	1983-84	1986-87	1987-88	1988-89	1989-90	1990-91
MACHINE LABOUR							
HIRED	96.58	180.20	63.42	112.16	459.33	112.95	186.51
OWNED	2.36	0.00	0.00	12.94	33.06	11.14	0.46
TOTAL	98.94	180.20	63.42	125.10	492.39	124.09	186.97
SEED	693.22	672.16	1085.97	976.43	847.70	1383.81	1187.19
FERTILIZER & MANURE							
FERTILIZER	2390.43	2281.85	1544.42	1970.43	2149.97	2721.69	2396.21
MANURE	288.97	273.41	442.80	499.23	387.29	355.44	434.43
TOTAL	2679.40	2555.26	1987.22	2469.66	2537.26	3077.13	2830.64
INSECTICIDES	0.21	44.75	0.00	15.34	0.00	1.03	0.00
IRRIGATION CHARGES	1820.04	2110.22	1885.32	1678.09	2208.72	1868.97	2575.01
INT. ON WORKING CAPITAL	512.33	534.96	532.98	575.73	646.45	754.64	647.21
MISC.	10.31	0.00	0.00	0.00	0.00	0.00	0.00
FIXED COSTS	2836.22	3488.70	4160.88	4073.55	4326.20	5011.22	5078.26
RENTAL VALUE OF OWNED LAND	2042.94	2794.26	3139.03	3332.50	3496.99	4052.16	3783.68
RENT PAID FOR LEASED IN LAND	0.00	0.00	0.00	0.00	0.00	0.00	0.00
LAND REVENUE, CESSES & TAXES	148.59	150.15	137.91	148.73	154.55	151.53	131.77
DEP. ON IMPLEMENTS & F. BLDG.	107.42	110.13	120.65	108.25	156.25	145.20	138.59
INT. ON FIXED CAPITAL	537.26	434.26	762.80	484.07	518.41	662.33	1024.21
TOTAL COST (C2)	12251.04	13335.39	14114.82	14625.70	16040.16	18700.57	17623.31
C2						18533.51	
C3						20386.86	
C3 (Rs./Quintal)						24.43	

Source : Cost of Cultivation of Principal Crops in India, 1996, Directorate of Economics and Statistics DAC, Ministry of Agriculture, GOI.

Suresh Gavali (11 March, 1997, Sakal) has estimated the cost of cultivation of various items for sugarcane which has gone up by 100 to 1000 percentage during the period, 1993-94 to 1995-96 (see Table 18).

TABLE 18

Cost of Cultivation of Sugarcane (Per acre Rs.)

Items	1993-94	1995-96	Increase
Ploughing	175	375	200
Plantation	200	1200	1000
Furrowing - I	400	800	400
Furrowing - II	500	1000	500
Widing (Labour charges)	400	500	100
Fertilizer (Urea)	120	165	45
Fertilizer (Suphala)	225	650	425
El. Charges	1000	1500	500

The study further highlights the per hectare cost of sugarcane cultivation. Accordingly, the sugarcane cultivation render loss to the cane growers (See Table 19). The farmers generally are undertaking the sugarcane cultivation because of the following reasons :

(a) There is no competing alternative crop to sugarcane.

(b) Crop loan of Rs. 5000 to 6000 per acre is available from PACS at low rate of interest (12%).

(c) Sugarcane crop is less labour intensive, so farmer's hardships are less.

(d) Its harvesting schedule is prepared by sugar factories.

(e) The farmer's worries are less.

(f) Sugarcane crop is market-linked or process-linked.

The other alternative crops, like oil seeds and horticultural crops are more remunerative, but requires more attention, to be given to protect the crop. Similarly, marketing or processing of horticultural crop is not assured. So, the trend has yet not set.

An average yield of sugarcane per hectare in Maharashtra has come down to 85 tonnes, whereas an average yield rate in Tamilnadu is 113 tonnes. This decline in yield, deserve careful farm management studies in Maharashtra. Normally farmers know the art of cultivating any new crop, but do not dare to cultivate it, because there is no assured capability of the farmers to market it or to process it. Once the facility of processing or marketing is made known, the farmers can undertake the crop cultivation on a larger scale. This is the case with strawberry and soyabean cultivation in Western Maharashtra.

TABLE 19

Per Hectare Cost of Cultivation of Sugarcane (Current Prices) 1996-97

Sl. No.	Items	Input Units per hectare	Input Cost per hect. (Rs.)	Total Cost per hect. (Rs.)
1	2	3	4	5
1.	Hired labour (Days)	82.86	29.61	2543.48
	Male Worker (")	67.90	23.00	1561.70
2.	Bullock labour (Pair Days)	15.73	76.51	1203.50
3.	Implements (Rs.)	—	—	501.11
4.	Seeds (Kg.)	7038.46	0.71	4997.31
5.	Manure (bullockcart)	18.26	82.59	1508.09
6.	Chemical fertilizers (Kg.)			
	N	115.90	7.21	4394.29
	P	115.90	17.82	2065.34
	K	69.33	9.33	3468.82
7.	Irrigation cost (Rs.)	—	—	—
8.	Pesticides (Rs.)	—	—	142.96
9.	Land revenue surcharge and taxes (Rs.)	—	—	660.00
10.	Depreciation on implements and godown (Rs.)	—	—	111.57
11.	Cost of acquiring inputs (Rs.)	—	—	3029.98
12.	Interest on working capital (Rs.)	—	—	24032.81
13.	Total Cost (A) (1-12)	—	—	11551.31
14.	Rent (Hire) (Rs.)	—	—	418.24
15.	Interest on fixed capital (Rs.)	—	—	—
16.	Cost-B 1-14	—	—	36002.36
17.	Domestic labour			
	Male	82.45	37.01	3051.47
	Female	14.92	27.44	409.40

(Contd.)

1	2	3	4	5
18.	Supervision	—	—	2403.28
19.	Cost-C 1-16	—	—	41866.51
20.	Cost of cultivation (per hectare)	—	—	41866.51
21.	Yield per hectare (Qtls.)	—	State average for 10.77% sugar recovery	762.67 (for 8.5 recovery)
22.	Cost per quintal of sugarcane	—	54.89	43.32
23.	(a) 20% profit on production cost	—	10.98	8.66
	(b) Transport Cost	—	6.75	6.75
24.	Sugarcane price entitled to be paid (22 + 23)	—	72.62	58.73
25.	Sugarcane prices (CACP) (1996-97)	—	47.19	45.90
26.	Loss per quintal (Rs.)	—	25.43	12.93

Source : Bhav Nasalyane Vos Kami, Karakhane Dhokyat (Marathi), Suresh Gavali, Sakal (daily) 11-3-1997.

13

ECONOMICS OF SUGAR RECOVERY

Overall efficiency of a sugar factory depends on the rate of sugar recovery. Sugar recovery means, the ratio of the sugar quantity produced in kilograms to the sugarcane quantity crushed per tonne for a specific period. It can be written as :

R = Sq. (kg.)/ Scq. (M.T.)

Where

R = Recovery

Sq. = Sugar quantity produced in Kilograms

Scq. = Sugarcane quantity in M.T.

As stated earlier, the mill efficiency depends on various factors like RME, RBHE, ROE, which can be maintained at various stages of the sugarcane processing activities. Although all such norms affect the sugar recovery, more appropriately sugar recovery depends on the harvesting and transportation schedule of the sugar factory. Sugarcane once harvested, should be crushed within 4.30 hours, so that sucrose content in the cane and the weight would not deteriorate. According to the thesis from Deccan Sugar Technologist Association, it is stated that, the weight of sugarcane and sugar contents in the cane get deteriorate as the time passes after cane harvest (see Table 20). This, in fact, is an essential norm to keep the unit to operate efficiently.

The final sugarcane prices are generally determined (or fixed) on the basis of the recovery rate during a specific season. This, no doubt rewards the cane growers. But unfortunately the advance sugarcane prices are being paid on the basis of the weight of the sugarcane rather than the quality of sugarcane and the recovery. However, of late, Government of Maharashtra has reiterated, to consider the advance sugarcane prices, to be paid on the basis of the cane maturity and the recovery rate; which is a strenuous job to the sugar factories.

TABLE 20

Sugar Recovery

Sl. No.	Time Required for Cane Crushing after its Harvesting	Loss of Weight (in Kg. per M.T. of Cane)	Loss of Sugar (in Kg. per M.T. of Cane)		
			R.S.Ratio	Pol. Loss Ratio	Average
1.	After 0 Hours	0.000	0.000	0.000	0.000
2.	8 Hours	14.000	1.045	—	1.045
3.	16 Hours	17.500	1.900	—	1.900
4.	24 Hours	29.500	3.990	2.640	3.315
5.	32 Hours	39.800	5.225	3.280	4.253
6.	40 Hours	57.500	7.125	4.880	6.003
7.	48 Hours	64.700	8.645	6.040	3.343
8.	56 Hours	73.800	10.450	7.280	8.865
9.	64 Hours	77.000	12.447	9.920	11.183
10.	72 Hours	83.000	13.870	15.160	14.515

Source : Deccan Sugar Technologist Association.

According to the geo-climatic conditions prevailing in Maharashtra State, there are 11 types of soils (See Map 1). Similarly, the state area can also be divided into nine geo-climatic divisions (See Map 2). The geo-climatic conditions prevailing in the area determines the cropping pattern of the region. This has a direct link to the sugarcane cultivation, and the establishment of sugar factory and *vice-versa*. The geo-climatic conditions, the soils and rainfall have a direct impact

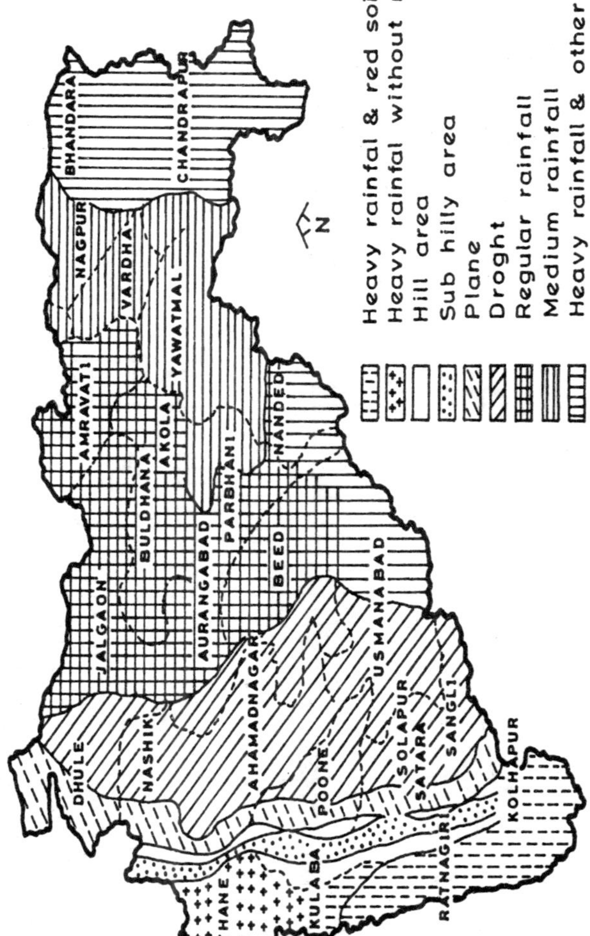

Map. 1 — CLAMATIC DIVISIONS OF MAHARASHTRA

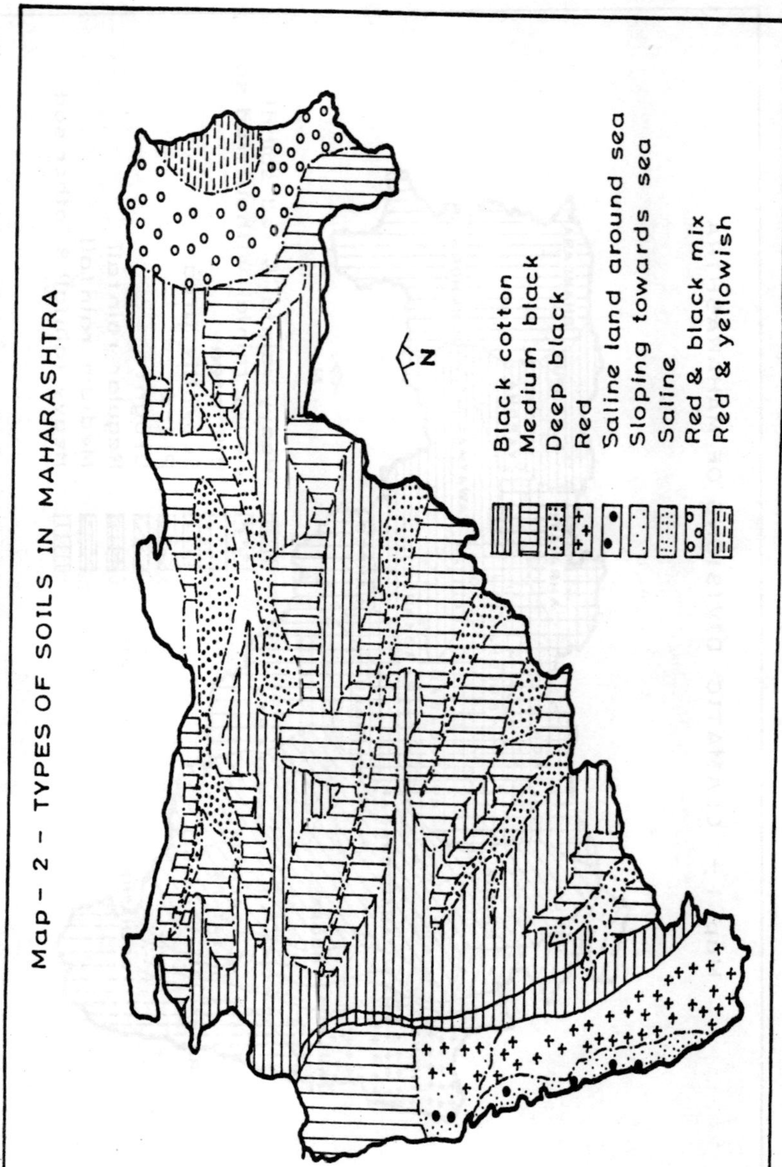

Map - 2 - TYPES OF SOILS IN MAHARASHTRA

on the sugarcane cultivation and the sugar recovery etc. The sugar recovery differs according to the conditions of geo-physical situations, soils and irrigation avenues.

Based on the conditions above, we have three zones classified, according the sugar recoveries in Maharashtra *viz.* High, Medium and Low recovery zones. High recovery zone is confined on the basis of average sugar recovery more than 11.00. Medium sugar recovery zone can be identified, where the average recovery rate ranges between 10.25 to 10.99; and the least recovery zone is demarcated, where the recovery rate is less than 10.25. Kolhapur, Sangli and Satara (South) districts come under the high sugar recovery zone, whereas Ahmednagar, Pune, North Satara, Nashik and Sholapur district area comes under the zone of medium sugar recovery. The districts of the Khanadesh, Marathwada, Vidarbha and Konkan regions have a least average sugar recovery. In fact an average cane yield is higher in medium recovery zone as compared to high recovery zone. *Cateris paribus* the sugarcane yield in least recovery zone remains less. Some times the rate of sugar recovery remains less, even when the sugarcane yield is phenomenal; which is because of early and immature cane harvesting during a particular season.

Table 8 highlights, the factorywise distribution of recovery percentages. Hutatma Kisan Ahir is well-known for its high sugar recovery, and had attained the highest sugar recovery in 1993-94. Even during the corresponding years, the position has been retained by the sugar factory. Chh. Shahu Sugar Co-operative of Kagal (Dist. Kolhapur) had attained the highest sugar recovery (12.82%) during the season; 1998-99.

An average recovery during the season; 1993-94, was 11.15 which is less as compared to the maximum recovery in high recovery zone (12.06). In 1988-89, an average recovery in high recovery zone was 13.50. The sugar recovery of some sugar factories during the high recovery period went around 14. Table 8(A) explains the recovery of sugar factories in Maharashtra for the season 1993-94.

TABLE 21

Sugar Recovery in 1995-96

	Crushing	Production	Recovery
1	2	3	4
KOHLAPUR			
Warana	8.38 (6.42)	10.74 (8.22)	12.82 (12.22)
Panchganga	9.89 (6.98)	11.92 (8.22)	11.92 (12.16)
Bhogawati	5.43 (4.67)	6.79 (5.73)	12.50 (11.61)
Doodhganga	6.23 (4.38)	7.67 (5.30)	12.31 (12.11)
Kumbhi-Kasari	5.68 (4.72)	7.11 (5.96)	12.49 (12.14)
Datta (Aasurlay-Porlay)	3.32 (1.60)	3.66 (1.85)	11.04 (11.23)
Datta (Shirol)	9.78 (5.62)	11.85 (6.80)	12.09 (11.91)
Daulat	4.03 (2.97)	4.90 (3.79)	12.10 (12.14)
Gadhinglaj	4.45 (2.88)	5.38 (3.38)	12.07 (12.52)
Shahu	4.38 (2.65)	5.40 (3.21)	12.32 (12.82)
Rajaram	5.00 (2.48)	5.62 (2.86)	11.23 (11.73)
Jawahar	5.60 (2.29)	6.89 (2.70)	12.32 (12.30)
	72.15 (47.66)	87.93 (58.02)	12.19 (12.07)
SANGLI			
Vasantdada (Sangli)	11.60 (7.45)	12.35 (8.11)	11.44 (12.19)
Vishwas (Chikhlee)	3.03 (1.62)	3.68 (1.97)	12.17 (12.57)
Rajarambapu (Sakharale)	9.18 (2.90)	11.32 (3.69)	12.40 (12.57)
Kisan Ahir (Walwa)	3.53 (6.64)	4.58 (8.09)	12.97 (12.47)
Mahakali (Kavathe Mahakal)	3.52 (1.49)	4.28 (1.78)	12.10 (N.A)
Manganga (Atapadi)	3.99 (0.88)	3.34 (0.89)	10.88 (N.A)
Yashwant (Nagewadi)	2.94 (1.59)	3.30 (1.76)	11.22 (N.A)
Tasgaon Taluka	3.79 (1.44)	4.19 (1.60)	11.04 (N.A)
	40.69 (23.98)	48.05 (28.69)	11.62

Note : 1. The data in parenthesis of Col. 2 and 3 indicates the position during season 1994-95.
2. The data in parenthesis of Col. 4 indicate position as on March 1999.

Table 21 discloses the overall good performance of sugar factories in Kolhapur and Sangli districts in sugar recovery even when the sugar season extended due to excess supply of sugarcane in 1995-96. Hutatma Kisan Ahir Sugar Factory has retained its highest sugar recovery (12.97%) among the sugar factories located in high sugar recovery zone of Maharashtra

State in 1995-96. Kolhapur district is dominating in keeping its highest position of recovery by almost all sugar factories except Panchganga and Chh. Rajaram. In Sangli district four sugar factories have the sugar recovery beyond 12% and rest four have less than 12% sugar recovery.

Since 1980s the sugar recovery in Maharashtra is increasing with minor up-downs during the period. Before that the recovery rate was found declining. The recovery rate also varies even during the particular season of a sugar factory (See Fig. 1). The recovery remains high during February and March, which is because of the climatic change during the months. With an increasing intensity of the cold, the sugar recovery increases. An early and later season of the sugar factories have a low recovery.

However, the geo-physical and climatic conditions in Maharashtra are more favourable for sugarcane cultivation. Even if, there is a proper crop planning with scientific use of water and fertilizers, and if the cane is harvested timely, then the per hectare yield of sugarcane may go upto 140 M.T. At least on an average the per hectare yield of sugarcane may reach upto 120 tonnes during a crop season. The minimum sugar recovery assumed at this situation is 12%.

If the problems associated to the sugarcane cultivation are properly tackled with timely considerations, then both sugarcane yield and sugar recovery may further improve and render good benefits to the factories and the farmers. Even to maintain the existing sugar recovery is also a problem to some factories. Day-by-day the intensity of the problem is increasing. The zonewise problems are discussed in the chart (on the next page) (Hapse in seminar papers : 1st Conference of Sugar Factories, Shirol).

As mentioned earlier, to increase the recovery rate, the harvested crop has to be crushed within 4.30 hours after it's cut. For this, transport efficiency should get improved. The location of a sugar factory in fact should depend on this norm. Cane harvesting and transport includes cane cutting, pruning and making a sizable bundles, loading of cane bundles

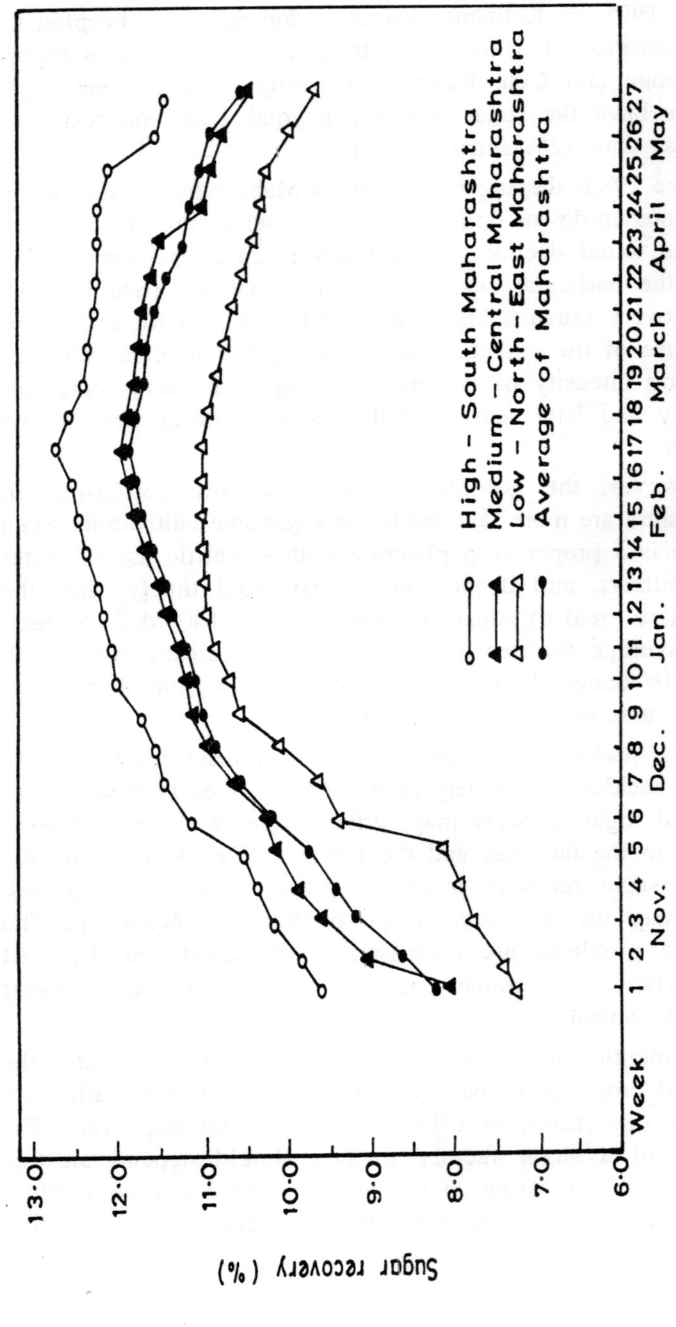

Fig. 1 — SUGAR RECOVERY IN A SEASON.

Problems in High Recovery Zone	Problems in Medium Recovery Zone	Problems in Low Recovery Zone
1. Scarcity of Water during summer	1. Scarcity of Water throughout the crop season	1. Scarcity of water throughout the crop season
2. Unbalance use of fertilizers	2. Irregular and· unbalanced use of fertilizer	2. Irregular and less use of fertilizer
3. Lack of micro-food contents in the soil	3. Lack of soil-fertility and manures	3. Traditional plantation method. No use of HYV
4. Pest problems	4. No crop protection measures	4. No crop protection measures
5. Crushing of immatured cane	5. Crushing of over matured cane	5. Late plantation
6. Inadequate time period for proper growth of cane	6. Adsali plantation takes time to crush	6. Immature cane for crushing
7. Irregular rotation of Suru and Ratoon crops	7. Ratoon crop is neglected	7. Ratoon crop is neglected, third year ratoon is kept
8. Soil salinity	8. Soil salinity	8. No proper land tilling
9. Rate of fertility is declining	9. Rate of fertility is declining, cost is increaşing, low profit	9. To protect the fertility is essential

in the cane fields and unloading the same at the "gavan centre" after weighing it in the factory site, which takes sufficient time and cannot be carried out within the post-harvest time limit of 4.30 hours. However, the loss can be kept at minimum.

The existing licensing policy do not consider this aspect of industrial profiteering. The existing policy of demarking the operational area within the radius of 15 K.M. for a factory is indeed required to be reviewed properly. Not only this but a factory should not be allowed to expand its crushing capacities more than 2,500 T.C.D.

It is also observed that, a sugar factory operating for

more than optimum crushing period of 160 days, also face the problem of deteriorating recovery. Only in February and March (winter period), the recovery remains high. So, every efforts be made to increase the crushing rate during these months. So a small size of sugar factory is justifiable as compared to a large size.

The sugar recovery of Kisan Ahir Co-operative Sugar Factory is high because of efforts carried out by the factory from crop harvesting to cane crushing. The factory ranked first in the country for six times since its installation in 1984-85. Of course this is possible because of the following reasons :

(i) The operational area is of only 15 villages with 8,529 (1985) shareholders.

(ii) The land area is of 24,168.09 acres.

(iii) River flows within the operational area with mandatory curves, so the area under irrigation is larger.

(iv) Night harvesting schedule is prepared carefully, so that, day-night crushing of fresh cane is made possible.

(v) The extra earnings due to high sugar recovery is equally distributed among the factory workers, farm workers, cane growers and Area Development Fund. This is an incentive to the concerned.

(vi) Night harvesting workers are paid higher wages based on the quantity of the sugarcane harvested and transported.

Low sugar recovery is one of the significant cause of the industrial sickness existing in this 'lead industry'. It is essential to study the cost of conversion per kilogram of sugar by different sugar factories. It is obvious that cost differs, therefore, the causal relations be identified properly. To get the recovery improved, is not possible within a short period. The managerial rigour at all stages of conversion be properly maintained and made attentive. An industrial professionalisation is must in this 'lead industry'.

14

CONSEQUENCES OF DELICENSING AND DECONTROL OF SUGAR INDUSTRY

The history of Industrial Policy in Maharashtra reveals the fact that, whenever the sugar industry was adhered to face some likely problems, the State Government initiated to solve them immediately because of the domination of the lobby in the Government and the significance of sugar industry as "lead industry" in the State. But today, in the framework of liberalisation, it is contemptible to expect some protection from the State Government or Central Government. The poor performance of the sugar co-operatives in Maharashtra has been abused and pondered upon by the political leaders and the academicians. Number of alternatives have come up either to ferule the industrial leadership or to improve the economic conditions of the industry.

It is because of the multi-dimensional problems, the industry is facing, the rural life has to stir up because of the industry's forward and backward linkages. Simultaneously, the problem of existence and survival of farms and farmers has been activating due to soil salinisation in sugarcane growing belt of Western Maharashtra; which is because of the interminable plantation of sugarcane and use of chemical fertilisers and mismanaged water supply by the cane growers in the region.

The crisis can be depressed by a perspective, foresighted and integrated outlook with turn around management tricks to be followed by the leaders of sugar co-operatives. The Western Maharashtra has a great heritage of such managerial tricks being exhibited in managing the sick spinning mills in other parts of Maharashtra. Today's crisis, in fact, is an occasion to get improved the overall health of the industry, because people, very soon will forget the tricks to be implemented, when remunerative sugarcane prices would have been paid by the sugar factories as a result of shortage of sugarcane and increasing sugar prices in coming future. For every three-four years the sugarcane price swings up, because of the distortions in the supply and demand of sugarcane. Sugarcane cannot be produced soon when its demand increases. The supply response to the sugarcane prices always distorts.

Number of alternative tricks and strategies have been brought up by the academicians, policy makers and well-wishers of the industry.

Delicensing and decontrol of the sugar industry is an unvil policy to be implemented with full text as a part of liberalisation policy in India. The procedure of simplifying the process of licensing has been noticed by the Government of India. The policy issues of decontrol has also been seriously thought of by the GOI. These two policy issues have crucial significance as on the part of fate of sugar industry in Maharashtra.

Since the passing up of the Sugar Industry (Protection) Act, 1932, the industry received a very attentive and perspective process of its development. Upto 1950, the private sector had took the benefits accruing due to the policy decisions related to sugar industry in Maharashtra. Since the installation of Pravara Co-operative Sugar Factory at Pravaranagar (Maharashtra) in 1949, the licensing policy was made patronaged to the Co-operative Sector. The co-operative set up has rewarded the cane growers and the ruralites in developing the rural infrastructure. So, the economic feasibility in expanding the co-operative enterprises was worth rewarding in almost all aspects of the industry.

Gundurao Committee, 1963 was the next effort made by the Government of India to rehabilitate and modernise the sugar industry during the corresponding year 1964. S.R. Sen Committee was appointed to study the economics of sugar industry in India. Bhargav Committee, Sampat Committee, Ram Kumar Committee, Mahajan Committee are some of the later additions to the perspective policy decisions by the Government.

To protect the interest of the Maharashtra State Government, in respect of zoning of the sugar factories, a Committee was appointed to suggest the consequences and implications of zoning in the State in 1983. Similarly, zoning for the levy prices was also dealt with to give justice to the sugar factories having better recovery. For example, Maharashtra State earlier was considered as only one zone. Now the State has been divided into high and middle sugar recovery zones. Whereas the Sugar Factories' Federation demand three zones of high, medium and low recovery areas in Maharashtra.

Maharashtra Government has also appointed various working groups and expert committees to deal with the problems faced by the sugar industry in the State. For example, Committee on Sick Sugar Co-operative (1986), Zoning Committee (1983), S.B. Patil Committee, Dadasaheb Rupwate Committee, Review Committee on Zoning (1997), Godbole Committee, Prem Kumar Committee etc. are some of the examples of State Level Committees in Maharashtra.

LICENSING POLICY

Up till 1950, the sugar industry was under the control of Provincial Governments. Later on the Ad-hoc Licensing Committee (1951) was appointed to deal with the norms and procedures of licensing to the sugar factories. The Committee sought its recommendations in 1954. The Committee had recommended the following norms while issuing the licenses to a particular sugar factory :

(i) Availability of sugarcane and sugarcane transporting;

(ii) Possibilities of increasing the sugarcane area;

(iii) Technical and economic viability of the project;

(iv) Leadership capabilities of the Chief Promoters to complete the project.

Initially, it was permitted to set up a sugar mill, wherever the possibilities of sugarcane cultivation were existing and an urge of the local leadership to install a sugar mill in the region was justified. The economies of scale were fallen into an account as per the perception of the local leadership and the Chief Promoters. However, there was a rigour in it. Shortage of sugarcane supply was the grave problem during 1950s. As a condition of licensing, to increase the area under sugarcane cultivation, most of the sugar factories in 1960s had begun to install co-operative lift irrigation schemes through financial assistance from the sugar co-operatives in their localities. Pilot schemes to increase the area under sugarcane cultivation were instituted. Simultaneously logistic links have been developed with the idea of demonstration plots, seedling plots, sugarcane development programmes, subsidy to cane growers etc. which were the incentives to assist for the expansion of sugarcane cultivation in the localities. This abstained to amplify the economy of the sugar industry and the locality. The yield rate of sugarcane went up to a maximum level. So the industry since then began to face the problem of surplus of sugarcane supply in selected localities of the co-operative sugar factories in Maharashtra. As a result, new sugar mills were demanded. Since then there is a phenomenal growth of this industry in Maharashtra. Today, there are 116 operating co-operative sugar factories, 4 private sugar mills and 54 co-operative sugar mills have received the letter of intent from the Central Government. But hardly 10 per cent have begun their erection, rest are quiet.

As a result of unplanned location of sugar factories, the issue of zoning and operational area has been augmented during the time of shortage of sugarcane. Shortage of sugarcane is because of two reasons *i.e.,* (i) Number of sugar mills has gone up; (ii) The unremunerative sugarcane prices paid to the cane growers. The idea of zoning normally has been raised by the mill owners during 1984 for their convenience and benefit to have an assured cane supply from their localities. The locational feasibilities were not taken into account, when they receive the accreditation from the Centre. Ultimately zoning became a debatable issue. The cane growers and the sugar mills have evoked series of offsprings of zoning in Maharashtra.

Number of cluster group villages come under the operational area of two-three sugar factories. The farmer's organisations are combating the zoning issue. It has been introduced for the convenience of the sugar factories. At the time of excess supply of sugarcane, the seed of zoning is being taken up by the farmers, whereas shortage of sugarcane is being taken up seriously by the sugar factories. Although, it goes very easy to set a plan schedule of sugarcane crushing by a sugar factory for a particular season.

The organisational pattern of sugar factories is normally advocated by the Government. However, it was stated in the Sixth Five Year Plan that, in case of inability of public or co-operative sector to install a sugar mill in a deserving locality, the private sector may be given a free hand to errect a sugar mill. This was in fact the beginning of liberalisation policy. Now it has been fully delicensed.

Determination of the productive capacity of a sugar unit is normally the subject to be contemplated on the ground of technology and economies of scale. The Sen Committee had recommended the minimum productive capacity of 2000 TCD, whereas Sixth Plan had arrived at the maximum limit at 3,500 TCD. Taking into account the operational area of the factory and the economics of sugar recovery, the desideratum and conceivability of the mini-sugar plants has been signified by the industrial group.

Initially when the issue of zoning was raised, the operational area of a factory had been fixed to 40 K.M. The limit has been brought down to 25 K.M. in general cases and 15 K.M. in the specific cases. Now the operational area has been further brought down to 15 K.M. as its radius of operational area. In practice, there are no hard and fast rules and regulation in this respect, because the initial locations were not as per the existing zoning policy. Some sort of overlapping in the operational area of the sugar factories has created a chronic problem in Western Maharashtra. As a result, zoning was the problem in 1983 and even the issue is controversial as an outcome of political strategy rather than actual need from both sides *i.e.*, sugar factories and cane growing farmers. Majority of cane growers have a membership of more than one sugar factory. Ultimately this deviate the interest and the sense of belongingness of the members. The non-members who have cultivated the sugarcane they have been locked up in a peculiar situation. Neither they were sending their sugarcane to the sugar factory of their jurisdiction since they are not members nor they send it to other sugar factories because of the condition of zoning.

EFFECTS OF DELICENSING

In the process of earlier system of licensing, the Chief Promoter of a sugar factory had to forward a proposal to the State Government first with all details of the project. The concerned State Government use to examine the technical and economic feasibilities of the project. The feasibility norms; such as supply of cane, irrigation potentials, transport conveyance, economics of the proposed factory and direct implications if any on other existing sugar factories in the localities were checked up. Once the State Government feels satisfactory, the same proposal is forwarded to the Central Ministry of Food. The concept of 'satisfactory' depends on political and economic considerations. The Food Ministry was appointing a Screening Committee to examine the technical and economic feasibilities. The Committee use to review, the area of operation, technical aspects and viability of the project. The factory in its operational area was entitled to crush the sugarcane available for a season. The Food Ministry, after receiving the feasibility report from the Screening Committee, was sending the proposal to the Ministry of Industry. The letter of intent was being issued by the Industry Ministry to the Chief Promoter. The concerned State Governments normally contribute 32.5% of share capital to the proposed and approved co-operative sugar factories. Same procedure was normally followed in case of expansion of productive capacity of a sugar industry. To get all these procedures completed, it normally required six months to six years depending on the influence of a leader (Chief Promoter). The licensing policy was more dominated by political considerations. As a result, zoning, scale of economies, location have become a debatable issues.

Now, all procedures and political considerations come to an end. No doubt, the professional and economic considerations shall have to be taken into account while installing a new sugar factory in a particular area. The private sector is well-known for its professional and economic considerations. The managerial skills of the private sector, no doubt try to harness the benefits as compared to co-operative sector, Co-operative sector lacks in professional and economical management of the industry. Its social considerations are overriding the professional considerations. Moreover, they are sincerely involved only in processing the sugarcane and manufacturing the sugar not else. After deducting the conversion cost of sugar, the surplus income earned by a sugar co-operative by selling the sugar is equally distributed among the cane suppliers as per their quantity of sugarcane in tonnes. The provision of Statutory Minimum Prices (SMP) and State Advised Prices (SAP) are nothing applicable in this regard. Some sick co-operative sugar factories in Maharashtra are even enable to pay the minimum sugarcane prices fixed by the CACP. The excess of SAP limit normally expected to go to the fund specially created by the State Government for the benefit of the Sugar Factories in the State. But most of the sugar co-operatives instead of contributing to the fund try to display the benefits to their members by number of other ways.

It has been noticed that, the entrepreneurs, who wish to avail of the delicensing of sugar industry should file an Industrial Entrepreneurs Memorandum (IEM) with the Secretariat of Industrial Assistance in the Industry Ministry as laid down for all delicensed industries. Those who have been given letter of intent, they have been exempted from IEM. However, they have to file Part-B of the IEM at the time of commencement of commercial production against LOI issued to them. In fact the issue of decontrol and delicensing has been guided by World Bank (Draft Report on India's Sugar Industry : Priorities for Reforms, April, 1997). More details of IEM operations have yet to come. After which one can diagnose the degree of freedom, the government has laid in it. Immediately after declaration of delicensing, around 368 proposals were registered in Maharashtra. Some have applied to make speculation with MNCs.

The co-operatives, in fact have a better jeopardy to take the blessing of delicensing, because the members of the co-operative sugar factories are the cane growers. To private sector, it goes very difficult to acquire the required raw material *i.e.*, sugarcane from the cane growers. This was the difficulty faced by private sugar mills during the period of 1950s. Still it goes very difficult to private sector to establish their rapport in sugar industry in Maharashtra State. The co-operative giants (*i.e.*, big sugar factories) and the co-operative culture spread throughout the rural Maharashtra will not concede the private sector to enter into the industrial enterprising even when the delicensing policy is introduced. Besides the private sector has to compete with well set sugar co-operatives with all types of infrastructure in the rural area. The private enterprises have to first introduce some incentives to the canegrowers, which is costly on the part of the private sector. Co-operatives are basically run on 'no loss no profit' principle, whereas the moto of the private sector is profit. If profit is not earned, the private sector will move away the activity and the frequency of take over will increase. Industrial relations will also get spoiled and industrial unrest will be an outcome. The workers and the farmers today in Maharashtra are united and unionised by number of ways. Lot of awareness has been grown up even among the canegrowers. So, the process of unionisation against the private sector will soon be shaped upto serve the purpose. Co-operative sugar undertakings were opposed by the trade union leaders in 1950s, because they were suspected that, co-operative efforts would abort the strength of trade unions and a kind of colonial monopoly would be set up in rural areas. And this has happened. Now the workers are also the members of the sugar co-operatives and also activate as a member of canegrower's family, of which his family head is normally a member canegrower of a sugar factory in Maharashtra. Ultimately a sense of belongingness is being created among the workers; as an employee and as a member of a sugar factory. The relation may not allow the workers to agitate against the factory management irrespective of political and individualistic considerations. Simultaneously, due to the day-to-day touch with local leaders (Directors of Board of Executive Council), the sugar workers are generally reluctant to strike against a particular sugar factory. The sugar workers in normal cases participate in State and National level agitations.

Sugar Co-operatives in rural Maharashtra are well-known in creating and developing socio-economic infrastructure in their operational areas. The private sector will not enter in generating infrastructural facilities in rural area. It will try to activate government in infrastructural sector. In fact, they mostly depend on the Government efforts to facilitate the rural infrastructure. Social justice and social welfare activities will erode the profits of private sector, whereas in co-operatives, that is the fundamental principle of the co-operative movement. The sugar co-operatives in Maharashtra have developed their forefronts in all social endeavours even by paying remunerative sugarcane prices to the canegrowers since 1950s. Like all other commercial crops, sugarcane is also a supply response crop to its prices. For every 7 to 8 years the problem of excess supply of sugarcane prominently rose up. As a result, unfavourability on the part of canegrowers begin due to unremunerative sugarcane prices. The glut was occurred in 1991-92 and it repeated in 1995-96.

Mr. Sharad Pawar, two years back had consulted the World Famous Brooke and Layele (Brooke and Tate) Consultancy Service to make a survey of experience of the countries who have accorded the policy of delicensing and to assess the performance of the sugar industry after delicensing. Brazil, Australia and Thailand are the only three countries, who have delicensed and decontrolled the sugar industry. However, in Australia sugarcane area (zoning) is strictly followed. The experiences were reported worst and unsatisfactory. This was referred and quoted in the Parliament.

The small privately owned sugar units will have to compete with big giants, which will strategically compel them to quit the industrial activity. Simultaneously, the existing sugar mills will try to expand their productive capacities as a result of delicensing. This no doubt will save money, but may spoil the performance of better sugar recovery. The experience in most cases reveals this fact.

Competition, no doubt enhance the efficiency in private sector. But it goes very difficult to increase the managerial efficiency in co-operatives due to number of constraints involved in managing a sugar factory. The Sugar Factories Federation, as a representing organisation of the co-operatives has to come forward to shoulder extra responsibilities in managing the day-to-day functioning of the sugar factories. As a result of delicensing, every co-operative sugar factory will have to stick to the policies of the Federation.

An important consequence of delicensing of sugar industry is the problem of capital formation to run the industry. The State Government will not contribute towards the share capital of a sugar factory. At present 32.5% of share capital is being contributed by the State Government and 60% by the financial institutions in the form of loans and remaining amount of capital from the members in a co-operative set up. The cost of errection of a sugar factory at current prices has gone up to 50 crores. The problem of capital accumulation will be a task before the co-operatives and to private sector also. Particularly, it goes very difficult to the co-operatives to collect the required amount of capital.

In August, 1991, Dr. Ram Kumar Committee was appointed to study how the cost of erection can be curtailed. The Committee after a detailed review of the cases proclaimed that, around 3 crores of cost of erection can be saved, particularly from the expenses on account of building and machineries. Thus borrowing will be the only alternative to erect a co-operative sugar factory as an outcome of delicensing. As a result, the interest cost will hike. According to the IFCI's estimation, the interest cost for each bag of sugar will go up by Rs. 140 which is Rs. 106 per bag in 1994-95. Some co-operative sugar factories in Western Maharashtra are paying the interest cost to the tune of Rs. 350 to 400 crores for every season and some other are paying between the range of Rs. 50 to Rs. 120 crores.

SUGAR RECOVERY AND LICENSING

Sugar recovery is the main aspect of the economies of scale and location of the sugar factories, which unfortunately is not taken into account, while approving the proposals of sugar factories either at the State level or at the Central level.

To attain high level of sugar recovery, a factory has to improve the transport efficiency. According to the Deccan Technologists Association, the harvested cane should have to be crushed within 4 to 5 hours. Irrespective of which the weight and recovery declines. The sugar recovery, in high recovery zone of Maharashtra comprises of 12 to 13 per cent.

Normally, the sugar recovery depends on climate, soil, irrigation, season and variety of cane etc. The topography of the region is also an important aspect of its determinant. No licensing policy today, has taken note of the economics of sugar recovery. While considering the case of sugar recovery, the economies of scale should be taken into account. The sugar recovery remains high during the crushing period from November to February. Ultimately, it is obvious that, maximum use of capacity should be made during the period.

While pleading before the Talwar Committee (Attwood, 1992) the issue of sugar recovery was raised and pleaded by the Indian Sugar Mills Association that, the sugar recovery can be improved only in the Mill Section, it has nothing to do with the quality of sugarcane. Whereas the Indian Co-operative Sugar Factories Federation pleaded that, the sugar recovery is being created and built up in the sugarcane farms and not in the Mill Section. This issue was raised on the background of payment of additional sugarcane prices against the realisation of higher sugar prices during the corresponding period, after sugarcane crushing season.

The Mill Section efficiency, as it is seen earlier, depends on (i) Reduced Mill Extraction Efficiency (RME), (ii) Reduced Boiling House Efficiency (RBHE), (iii) Overall Mill Efficiency (OME), (iv) No. of crushing days, (v) Percentage of waste hours, (vi) Use of cent per cent productive capacity, (vii) Percentage of waste of sugar etc. The technical efficiency of sugar co-operatives in Maharashtra is much higher than required standard norms. It is obvious however that, the Mill Section as it is essential, also contributes to increase sugar recovery. But cannot determine the percentage share of it in attaining the higher sugar recovery.

The sugar recovery also depends on the sugarcane cultivation techniques, farm management, variety of cane, irrigation, use of organic and inorganic fertilizers, crop protection measures, climatic conditions, growth of sugarcane, harvesting techniques transport efficiency etc. Mill Section efficiency changes with the change in the quality of sugarcane. Simultaneously, a good quality sugarcane may not yield good recovery, if there is loss and waste of sugar in the Mill Section. Mill Section efficiency can only be improved by developing a technical skill. But it goes very difficult to increase the quality of sugarcane, because the sugarcane quality is individualistic and scattered throughout the farm varieties with varying farm management techniques so far followed by different group of the canegrowers.

At the time of shortage of sugarcane, the sugar factories tend to administer number of incentives to the cane growers, so as to fulfil their want of supply of raw-material. Every sugar co-operatives in Maharashtra have established Cane Development Sections, but actually they carryout, the activities other than the cane development. The declining yield of sugarcane and deteriorating quality of sugarcane are the severe problems set before the industrial group and the Government.

The Mill Section is expected to perform its efficiency upto its maximum level, since all sections in the Mill belongs to the technical expertise. And it is obviously performing better no doubt. However, the farmers should improve the quality of sugarcane; and the transport efficiency of the factories in bringing the canes from farm to factory for immediate crushing should also get improved. Lot of negligency towards these aspect tends to deteriorate sugar recovery.

One more important aspect of the sugar recovery is that, while determining the final sugarcane prices, an average sugar recovery is being taken into account since 1950s. However, there was a uncertainty in fixing the minimum level of sugar recovery for fixing statutory minimum prices. The issue was controversial during the period from 1962-63 to 1968-69. At the very first instance, the minimum recovery for determining SMP was fixed at 9.8, which was raised to 10.4 in 1965-66 and then brought down to 9.4 in 1968-69. It has been kept constant at 8.5 per cent since last 30 years.

With this, it can be stated that, the private sugar factories may raise, the issue of paying additional cane price to the canegrowers. In co-operatives, cane is being crushed, even when the factory could not pay minimum price to its canegrowers. The private sector will never do like this. They will close down the factory. This will be a loss to the canegrowers in the area. Actually, there is no problem of paying the minimum sugar prices in sugar co-operatives, since they are operating on 'No Profit, No Loss' basis. The sugarcane prices in co-operatives are paid after deducting the conversion cost of sugar production from the surpluses earned out of selling the sugar. Co-operative marketing efforts are not reaching at the grass-root level consumers in a big way. The value-added in the process of marketing is being harnessed by the middlemen and the vendors. The private sector is very keen in earning the value-added through trading. The Private Sector's intention will be, on to keep the farmers only in the production front. The agro-produce will be processed, or a new commodity would be manufactured by the private sector and, would be sold in the market with huge amount of value-addition. This is a sort of colonial economics rather than development economics. This is the case with almost all marketable surplus in agricultural sector. Therefore, the co-operative efforts, in processing and marketing of agro-produce should be rectified with vertical and horizontal links. Liberalisation, in fact is a boon to the co-operative sector and also a challenge to it.

DECONTROL

Decontrol means withdrawal of the Government control or regulations imposed on the various activities of sugar industry.

The industry is under the control of GOI since 1932. Various industrial activities have been directed and regulated by both Central Government and State Government. For example, levy on sugar, levy sugar prices, sale of sugar, sugarcane prices (SMP, ACP, SAP) zoning, dual prices of sugar, government's contribution to share capital, export-import of sugar, supply of sugar through PDS, control on molasses, Government guarantee, commodity credit policy, buffer stock etc. Partial or full decontrol means partly or fully government will not interfere in the oversaid activities of the sugar industry.

Decontrol is different from delicensing. In the process of delicensing, as stated earlier all procedures of getting a factory sanctioned to crush the sugarcane for production of sugar comes to an end. Simplified procedures of IEM has been introduced in place of restrictive licensing policies. There will now be free entry and free exit of the sugar enterprises as a result of delicensing. Decontrol rules out all types of controls and therefore, it has been criticised by both private as well as co-operative lobbies at the national level. Decontrol of the industry will harshly shoot up the performance of small and new units either in co-operative sector or in private sector or in joint stock company sector.

Following are some of the implications of the decontrol :

(1) Sugarcane prices (SMP, ACP, SAP) will be determined as per the will and vims of the industrialists. The private sugar mill owners will begin to exploit the canegrowers by paying low prices. Profit will be the principle of their business. Such exploitations are not existing in sugar co-operatives. Today, the economics of sugarcane cultivation and terms of trade between input prices and sugarcane prices have totally disturbed. The input prices are greater than the sugarcane prices. Similarly, the prices of sugar have also gone up as compared to the prices of sugarcane. This tends to shift in the cropping pattern from sugarcane to more remunerative crops. This tendency will harm the economy of sugar industry. Huge amount of capital investment will go waste if people find an alternative crop to sugarcane.

In this respect partial decontrol is more preferable rather than total decontrol.

(2) Decontrol leads to sell all sugar produced by the factories in the open market. This leads to competition among the mill owners to sell their produce, particularly on the occasion of rising prices. As a result, the sugar prices will crash down. This creates uncertainty and instability in sugar prices. Supply of sugar through PDS, now has come to an end. This was in fact demanded by the industrial sector since long, because levy prices were not remunerative to the industry.

Government will have to purchase sugar from open market at the prevailing market rates to distribute the same through PDS, if it desires, and for the consumption of the military force. This leads to a loss of Rs. 1,400 crores and generate burden on the central treasury, which could not be recovered even by imposing excise duties on sugar. The overall excise duty will go around 53 crores. Government requires 3.69 lakh tonnes of sugar for PDS and 2 lakh tonnes for military purpose every month. Today, atleast 45 per cent of sugar produced by the factories is being purchased by the Government at the levy prices. Recently, levy prices have been revised after 7-8 years. There was a great demand from the industrial group to increase the levy sugar prices. Levy sugar prices have been fixed by the BICP on nine-point norms for computing the conversion cost of sugar. The cost incurred on sugarcane harvesting and transport of sugarcane is not included in the nine-point norms of costing by BICP. The Co-operative Sugar Factories' Federation is demanding to compute this cost while fixing the levy sugar prices. Further, there is a demand from the industrial group that the levy prices should be linked to the actual conversion cost of sugar with a periodical review.

(3) The industrial relations have been changed since the award of various court decisions on BIR Act, 1949 that, 'the harvest and transport workers are the employees of the industry'. The industry is not in a position to accept these workers as their employees, they term them as the 'Mazdoors' not the 'Kamgars' (for details see Jugale, 1997). As a result of decontrol, the industrial relations will once again get disturbed with new

trends in it. Wage agreements of sugar workers has been expired in December, 1997. Now they want to sign next tripartite agreements.

(4) No new sugar factory will amicably get rewarded by decontrol. The problem of capital accumulation to erect a sugar factory will be a grave problem. Most of the new entrants will prefer to install mini sugar plants rather than big giants. New entrants will not receive any concessions in their operation.

(5) Decontrol may lead to determine the sugarcane prices on demand and supply forces which is impracticable. Similarly, there will not be an imposition of zoning. Recently the Supreme Court has held to free the sugarcane zoning. The effects of this will have to be tested during corresponding seasons. Moreover, the equity share members (canegrowers) may not have a liability towards their own sugar co-operatives. Sugar co-operatives simultaneously may jerk towards privatisation. Maharashtra Government is prepared to privatise the sick co-operative units. Privatisation of sugar factories may not reward the canegrowers. The situation will be worst. It would be far better to introduce a scheme of rehabilitation of sick co-operatives on the line of BIFR. The growing sickness is a headache in the co-operative sugar scenario in Maharashtra, whatever we have achieved since 1950s by way of this 'lead industry' will be demolished soon after total decontrol. Decontrol measures should carefully be introduced. Phase-wise experiments can be tested. In fact, Indian Government is very careful and tactful in introducing the reforms in various sectors.

(6) Now-a-days, Government interference in co-operative administration is growing and has created number of debatable issues both on the lines of theory of co-operation and the practice of co-operation. Reforms in giving free hand to the co-operative enterprises will definitely help to conserve and protect the co-operation. The reforms should not be political oriented and revengeful to kill the political rivalry at the grass-root level. It is true that, there are some mistakes made by the management of some sugar factories, but that can be corrected through co-operative principles and philosophy. In

Maharashtra Co-operatives have been accorded as an instrument to play with the politics and to develop the political career at the grass-root level. The co-operative sector should be depoliticised. In fact such type of reforms and restructurisations are essential in future.

CONCLUDING REMARKS

Agro-industrial sector is rather more convenient to the co-operative sector. The sector should have to be administered and managed on the basis of business tricks with the moto of welfare of the common people. The marketing and processing activity should be restructured properly on the background of the globalisation.

Each sugar factory should have a transferent operations in its financial accounts and all other economic and social activities. The co-operative units should be administered on the will of their members. Government interference should totally be minimised. To encourage the co-operative activities means to protect the co-operation. Co-operation is a rural hope, that should not be killed. Although radical reforms in the co-operative movement are necessary, whose vision should be to uplift the rural masses.

India is a poor country. To rule the poor country means to eradicate the poverty. Poverty can never be eradicated without planning. Delicensing and decontrol are part of the planning. Of course, planning should not be exaggerated. We have a long tradition of democratic control. Policy, planning and control in co-operatives are essentially be based on the democratic principles. Democratic decision helps to arrive at the level of sustained development with ecological and environmental values. Development should not take us to decay. Development should reorient and regenerate the human capital rather than physical capital. Co-operatives and NGOs (Collective action sector) will perform well to-do-away the odds created by the mixed economy. Market economy can only be driven away by markets.

15

CONCLUDING REMARKS

The foregoing analysis extensively discloses the gamut of overall processes and links of sugarcane prices in India in general and Maharashtra in particular. Simultaneously other links of studies to sugarcane prices like the parity prices of sugarcane as compared to the prices of competing crops has been taken into account. Now-a-days the issue of terms of trade is in grace, particularly farmer's reluctancy to undertake sugarcane plantation due to the falling prices of sugarcane and rising prices of inputs have been accounted for by the farmers. The sugar industry always express its fear of cultivating alternative crops to sugarcane crop by the farmers. Shortage of sugarcane is a grave problem to sugar factories, because it is the only raw-material required to manufacture sugar. Since their installation, the co-operative sugar factories in Maharashtra have not concentrated on the improvement of quality of sugarcane and cane development activities except few. However, at the time of shortage of sugarcane, the incumbents including Govt. agencies try to propagate for undertaking the cultivation of sugarcane. This normally happens at the time of shortage of sugarcane. Warana pattern is becoming popular in this respect.

The prices of sugarcane cannot be determined by supply and demand forces as it happens in manufacturing commodities. The crushing capacities of the sugar co-operatives have been already fixed. It means demand for sugarcane is fixed. In normal cases the sugar co-operatives expect to crush extra 25% more sugarcane, than the established capacity. The sugar industry generally operates for 160-180 days, commencing from October to May of the year, which is termed as sugar season.

The sugar factories during the off season initiates to survey the cane availability for the coming season. If they diagnose the shortages of cane, they may begin to crush sugarcane late, and try to close it shortly. The crushing operation is being managed during the period of high sugar recovery, that is from December to February, the sugar recovery remains highest (see Fig. 1). In case of excess supply of sugarcane, sugar factories begin their crushing early in the month of October and ends the season by the May end. The sugar recovery during the first week of October remains at 7% or below to that, and in the month of May it remains between 8 to 9%. During the peak the sugar recovery (some times) may go up to more than 14%. However in normal cases it remains between 12 to 13%.

The organizational features of co-operative set up compel the sugar factories to crush the sugarcane cultivated by its members who have enrolled the area of sugarcane cultivation in their respective offices. The advance prices of sugarcane are being paid to the farmers after 15 days of its harvesting. Whatever sugar is produced, is normally sold to Govt. and in the open market as per the quota determined by the Central Govt. After deducting the conversion cost of sugar production, whatever surplus remains is being distributed among the cane growers (who have supplied the sugarcane during the sugar season) as per their quantity of sugarcane supply. Therefore, the sugarcane prices cannot be determined according to the demand and supply forces.

However, the supply response to the sugarcane prices always remains non-beneficial to the cane growers. When the sugarcane prices goes up for a season, during the corresponding cultivation season, the plantation of sugarcane goes up. Consequently sugar is being produced in a great quantity. Sugar being a agro-produce manufactured commodity, its prices may come down due to excess supply of sugar. As a result the cane suppliers may get less prices. This may again creates the reluctancy to undertake sugarcane plantation for the next season.

The conversion cost of sugar production varies due to number of reasons. However, extravagant expenses can be curbed by economising the process of conversion. For example store expenses can be minimised. Collective or Group store units may be created at the central places of the factories' location. Similarly extra efforts be made to crush the sugarcane within a short span of time after its harvesting. Night harvesting gangs may be created to harvest sugarcane even at night, so that there will be a regularity in the supply of fresh sugarcane.

Proper guidance to the farmers by the sugar factories is necessary so as to acquire fresh and quality sugarcane from the cane growers. The plantation and harvesting plans should be earmarked before the crushing season begins. A computer network of cane plantation and harvesting of sugarcane may be installed at the state level. This will facilitate the Govt. and the industry to plan for the economic use of raw-material and to produce the sugar at lowest costs. This sort of macro planning will help even to plan at micro levels. Professionalisation of sugarcane cultivation initiated by the sugar factories should spread among the farmers.

The consequences of structural reforms which are entering in this industry by way of delicensing and decontrol should better be understood by the group of co-operators, and try to modify their way of managing the co-operative sugar industry. The co-operatives should have to convert this challenge into an opportunity by reforming themselves with a new democratic outlook.

Each sugar factory should have a transferent business operations reflected in its financial accounts and with all other economic and social activities. The co-operatives should be administered on the will of the members. Govt. interference should be minimised. To encourage the co-operative activities means to protect the co-operation.

APPENDICES

APPENDIX - I

Statement Showing the Receipt and Expenditure for Crushing Season 1995-96

(To be submitted by each sugar factory)

1. Name of the Co-operative Sugar : Factory, Tal._____, Dist. _____

2. Crushing capacity (original) :

3. Year of Ist crushing season :

4. Expansion of the capacity Factory : Year
   capacity ________ ________

5. Capacity for the 1995-96 crushing season :

6. Total cane required for the full capacity (Lakh M. Tonne) (last 3 years) : 1993-94 ______ 1994-95 ______ 1995-96 ______

7. Total cane crushed during season: (Table 2)
   (a) Members : ______ ______ ______

   (b) Non-members : ______ ______ ______

(c) From out of area : ______ ______ ______

TOTAL : ______ ______ ______

(d) Recovery : (1) Upto 31-3-96 ______

(2) Full season ______

(a) Cane crushed from		From Area		Out of Area	Total
		Members	N. Members		
1. 1-4-95 to end of season	:				
2. 1-10-95 to 31-3-96 (Table 2)	:	______			
3. Total for ______ 96 (Table 2)	:	______			
4. 1-4-1995 to end of season (95-96 crushing) season (Table 2)	:	______			

		From Area		Out of Area	Total
		Members	N. Members		
5. Total for 1995-96 crushing season (Table 2)	:				
6. Total cane for which price is to be fixed (Table 6)	:	______			
7. %age of utilisation of capacity for the 94-95 crushing season (Table)	:				

8. (a) Total bags produced during 94-95 year i.e. 1-4-95 to end of season ———— 95 : Levy ____ Free ____ Total ____

(b) (95-96)-1-10-95 to 31-3-96 : ____ ____ ____

(c) Total for 1-1-95 to -/-/96 end of season : ____ ____ ____

10. Opening sugar stock as on 1-4-1995 (Table 14) : Quantity (bag) | Rate (per bag) | Value (Rs. in Lakhs)

(a) Levy : ____ ____ ____

(b) Incentive : ____ ____ ____

(c) Free : ____ ____ ____

(d) Total : ____ ____ ____

12. Total of (10 + 11)

(a) Levy : ____ ____ ____

(b) Incentive : ____ ____ ____

(c) Free : ____ ____ ____

(d) Total : ____ ____ ____

13. Sales realisation from 1-4-95 to 31-3-96 (Table 13) : Quantity (bag) | Rate (per bag) | Value (Rs. in Lakhs)

(a) Levy : ____ ____ ____

(b) Incentive (difference) : ____ ____ ____

(c) Free : ____ ____ ____

(d) Total : ____ ____ ____

14. Closing stock as on 31-3-1995 (Table 11)

(a) Levy : ________ ________ ________

(b) Incentive (difference) : ________ ________ ________

(c) Free : ________ ________ ________

(d) Total : ________ ________ ________

(1) Valuation for free sale Rs. /- per Qtl. : ________ ________ ________

(2) Molasses (Table 11) : ________ ________ ________

15. Total value of sugar produced during (1995-96 year) (13 + 14–10)

(a) Levy : ________ ________ ________

(b) Incentive (difference) : ________ ________ ________

(c) Free : ________ ________ ________

(d) Total : ________ ________ ________

16. Other receipt (Vide Table No. 11 + 14 + 15) : ________ ________ ________

(1) Profit from B.P. —

(a) Dist. (Table) : ________

(b) Paper (Table) : ________

(c) (Table) : ________

(2) Others (Table) : ________

17. Total Receipt ( ) : ________ ________

18. (a) Deduct Loss if from other units (1)	:			
19. Total Receipt	:			
20. Expenditure for 12 months *i.e.,* during 1-4-95 to 31-3-96 (Table 17)	:	— (Rs. in Lakhs) —		
		Actual for 1995-96	Rate PMT (95-96)	Rate PMT (94-95)
(a) H.T. Commission	:			
(b) H.T. Charges	:			
(c) Purchase Tax	:			
(d) Cane feeding	:			
(e) Salary and wages	:			
(f) Store consumption	:			
(g) Other overheads	:			
(h) Interest (Table 20)	:			
Total amount	:			
(a) On term loan	:			
(b) Working capital	:			
(c) On deposits	:			
Total	:			
Total (a to h)	:			

Depreciation fund = Rs. in lakhs
as on 31-3-95 = Rs.

(i) Depreciation : ——— ——— ———

(j) Other expdr/provision :
provision vide (Table 2)

(a) Khodki at Rs. 25/- : ——— ——— ———

(b) Bonus @ Rs. : ——— ——— ———
(Table 21)

(c) Education fund as per : ——— ——— ———
Act (Table 21)

(d) Sakhar Karkhana Sangh : ——— ——— ———

(e) Audit fee : ——— ——— ———

(f) VSI contribution
(per bag 1/-) : ——— ——— ———

(g) Cane development : ——— ——— ———
expenditure

Total production cost : ——— ——— ———
(a to g)

21. Accumulated losses as on
(Rs. in Lakhs) 31-3-95
(Table 21) Rs. ——— :

(a) 1/8th losses to be written off: ——— ——— ———

22. Gate/contracted cane cost : ——— ——— ———
(for 95-96 season)

23. Cane cost paid for the crushed during 1-4-95 to end of season (1994-95-season)	:	———	———	———
24. Total expenditure	:	———	———	———
25. Surplus	:	Rs. ———	Lakhs Rs.	———PMT
26. Cane price on merit	:	———	———	———
27. Differed provision on account of loss/dep.	:	———	———	———
(a) Depreciation	:	———	———	———
(b) 1/8th losses	:	———	———	———
(c) .	:	———	———	———
Total expenditure	:	———	———	———
27. Surplus (25–26)	:	———	———	———
28. Provisions — REPAYMENT OF CURRENT INSTALMENT				
(i) Financial Institution	:	———	———	———
(ii) NCDC	:	———	———	———
(iii) SDF	:	———	———	———
(iv) Project loans etc. from DCCB/MSCB	:	———	———	———
(v) Govt. loan	:	———	———	———

(vi)	Govt. S/C	:	———	———	———
(vii)	Govt. guarantee fee	:	———	———	———
	Total provision for current repayment	:	———	———	———
29.	Provision for overdue	:	———	———	———
(i)	(a) Total F.I. overdue	:	———	———	———
	(b) Repayment of NCDC overdue	:	———	———	———
(ii)	(a) Total Govt. S/C overdue	:	———	———	———
	(b) Repayment of Govt. S/C overdue portion	:	———	———	———
(iii)	(a) Total Govt. loan overdue	:	———	———	———
	(b) Repayment of overdue portion	:	———	———	———
(iv)	(a) Total NCDC overdue	:	———	———	———
	(b) Repayment NCDC overdue	:	———	———	———
(v)	(a) Total SDF overdue	:	———	———	———
	(b) Repayment of SDF portion	:	———	———	———
(vi)	(a) Total overdue project loans etc. CCD/MSCB	:	———	———	———
	(b) Repayment of overdue portion	:	———	———	———

(vii) (a) Total overdue : ________ ________ ________

(b) Provision for overdue repayment : ________ ________ ________

30. Total provision for current overdue liabilities : ________ ________ ________

31. Surplus : Rs.______ Lakhs Rs.________

32. Cane price after all provision : ________ ________ ________

33. Deductions — : Rs. (PMT) Total (Rs. in Lakhs)

(a) Area Development Fund : ________ ________

(b) Cane Development Fund : ________ ________

(c) Chief Minister's Fund : ________ ________

(d) Any other deduction : ________ ________

(e) : ________ ________

Total : ________ ________

34. Deposits : (PMT) (Total Rs. in lakhs)

(a) N.R.D. (for repayment of F.I. dues overdues) : ________ ________

(b) NRD (without intt. for pre-seasonal loans) from members and non-members of area : ________ ________

(c) Sampat Committee (Benefits) interest on long term loan diff. to be taken as deposits : ________ ________

(d) Deposit for expansion/ modernisation as per bye-laws (A.G. Resolution) (refundable for 5 years with intt.) : ________ ________

Total : ________ ________

Total deductions : ________ ________

35. Net cane price : ________ ________

36. Cash payment : ________ ________

37. Net balance in Bank's pledge Accounts available for the cane price : Rs. per M.T. Total (Rs. in lakhs)

: ________ ________

38. Arrears of cane price : ________ ________

(a) Due to the Members/Non-Members : ________ ________

Year

(1) : ________ ________

(2) : ________ ________

(b) Due to other SSKs : ________ ________

Year

(1) : ________ ________

(2) : ________ ________

39. (a) Amount required for the cash payment by way of the final cane price difference : ________ ________

(b) Repayment of deposits with interest : ________ ________

Total : ________ ________

APPENDIX - II

Outward No./Sugarcane rate/
2093/139/Divi-7/Finance-2
Director of Sugar,
Maharashtra State, Pune-42.

Date :

To

The Managing Director

____

____

Sub.: *Final rate for sugarcane the crushing of (year)*

Sir,

In accordance with the by-laws of your factory and considering the recommendations of the Director of Sugar, Maharashtra State Co-operative Sugar Mills Association, and as per the resolutions passed in the meeting of Ministerial Committee Sugarcane rate fixed (ex-field) for your factory is Rs.______ in words __________________________________ per tonne for the crushing year _________.

2. The following aspects are taken into account in the meeting of the Ministerial Committee, while fixing this rate.

(i) Sales of sugar : In the year *i.e.*, from April 1 to March 31. ____________.

(ii) Balance Sugar Quantity : The cost of balance sugar quantity by the end of 31st March _______ in respect of levy sugar, available for open sale, excluding the Central Excise tax, is fixed as follows :

(a) The cost of the balance sugar quantity controlled (levy) sugar, is in accordance with the cost, fixed by the Central Government.

(b) The balance, out of the deceived extra quota, as per the 'Sampat Scheme' is calculated as cited above.

For the open quota, per bag of one quintal Rs. ________ is thought of.

(iii) Sampat Concessions : As per the recommendations of the Sampat Committee, the extra income earned from the concessions, granted to the sugar factories, is to be utilised only for the repayment of loans taken for the capital expenses. Accordingly, sugar factories are expected to reserve the same for the repayment of loans. As per the suggestions made by the Sugar Federation, Maharashtra State and as per the system approved by the Govt., the additional income earned from the Sampat concessions, is taken into account and the sugar factory is to deposit (unrefundable) that much amount. The additional income in (year) earned from the Sampat concessions is to be utilised as constructed below :

Details	Amount in Lakh Rs. Rate per M.T.
A. Total income from the concessions granted by the Sampat Committee	________
(i) Extra income actually received	________
(ii) Difference in (value) the balance quota	________
B. Utilization of the above cited amount	________
(i) To make up losses	________

(ii) To repay loans taken for capital expenses ____________

(iii) To receive the deposit (unrefundable) in lien of transport of sugarcane ____________

____

TOTAL : ============

There is no need to utilize the additional income, received from the concessions of the Sampat Committee to curtail further the unrefundable deposits, if the rate of interest of the financial institutions, is more than the rate of interest on the refundable deposits, deducted from the total bills. However, the factories have to take caution that the amount utilized to make up losses, is to be compensated from the unrefundable deposits.

3. Arrangements to be made as per the sub-clause, of the co-operative laws / rules / decisions of the Ministerial Committee.

Details of the Arrangement	Arrangements made in Lakhs
3.1 Expenses for Khodaki and vechani (Rs.________ per M.T.) for member/non-member	____________
3.2 Bonus ________________ %	____________
3.3 Educational funds as per the Act of co-operative, for the State Co-operative Education Fund	____________
3.4 Auditors fees	____________

3.5 Contribution to Maharashtra State Sugar Federation ______________

3.6 For salaries ______________

3.7 Funds for harvesting and transport of sugarcane ______________

3.8 Depreciation charges in year ______________

3.9 For other Expenses ______________

3.10 To make up previous losses ______________

3.11 V.S.I. subscription (Vasantdada Sugar Institute) ______________

____

TOTAL : ==============

Note : Permission/consent is granted to allow the factory for the expenses of Rs.______ lakhs as Khodaki expenses.

4. Arrangements thought of/considered taken into account

4.1 Provision of the interest or levy guarantee, being court matter, is excluded from the expenses.

4.2 As per the suggestion of the Ministerial Committee, that at least 1/8th loss be made up, to enable your factory to compensate the loss, an amount of Rs.______ lakhs, is made available for your factory.

4.3 Depreciation amount of Rs.______ lakhs, out of the total depreciation of Rs.______ lakhs, in (year), is not considered while fixing the final rate.

5. Deductions to be made from the sugarcane bills.

5.1 As per the arrangements in the by-laws of the factory and the condition of the financial institutions and by K.W. No : 2.3 of the Sampat Committee the unrefundable deposits are to be deducted.

5.2 As per the Ministerial Committee's recommendations for (year), crushing season, the maximum rate for cash payment is fixed at Rs.________ per M.T. The amount, more than Rs.__________ per M.T. is to be deposited refundable into the factory, for a period of 5 years after making all other deductions. The factory has to pay interest on their deposits, interest, as per the provisions made.

5.3 In case of non-members while giving the same rate to them, refundable deposits for the period of 10 years, are to be taken at the rate of interest for non-refundable deposits.

5.4 The factory has to deduct from the sugarcane bills considering the above suggestions.

Details of Deductions to be made from the sugarcane bills	Rate of Deductions from the bill Rate per M.T.
DEPOSITS :	
1. Bye-law deductions as per the condition of financial institutions	________________
(a) Unrefundable Deposits from the the members	________________
(b) Refundable Deposits from the non-members	________________
2. Unrefundable Deposit from the Extra income from the Sampat Concessions	________________

3. Expansion/Distillery Deposit (Refundable Deposit) ______

4. Deposit, as per the resolution of Ministerial Committee meeting dated ______ for ______ years with interest refundable deposit (Surplus) ______

______

TOTAL (1 to 4) :

===============

5.5 The factory has to pay 15% rate of interest on the deposits mentioned in 4.

	DEDUCTION		Rs.
1.	Sugarcane Development Fund	Rs.———	per M.T.
2.	Chief Minister's Fund	Rs.———	per M.T.
3.	Small Scale Savings	Rs.———	per M.T.
4.	Earth Quake Fund	Rs.———	per M.T.
5.	Fund for the development of an area	Rs.———	per M.T.
6.	Funds for the Educational institutions/ trusts founded by the factory	Rs.———	per M.T.
7.	Other (Medical Trusts)	Rs.———	per M.T.

______

TOTAL (1 to 7) :

===============

Note : No other deductions be made other than these, no deduction be made in respect of State Agricultural Maha Mandal and Govt. Schools.

5.6 The rate of cash payment is Rs.______ after above cited deductions are made.

5.7 As per the resolution passed in the meeting dated ______ the Ministerial Committee, a sugar factory has to pay cash amount of Rs.____ after making the deductions. The factory is suggested to pay this instalment at its earliest, considering its financial conditions.

6. Factories have to remit the following amounts to the respective Officers immediately — within a month.

6.1 Indira Awas Yojana - Balance
Credit amount Rs. ______

TOTAL : Rs. ______

6.2 Small Savings Balance Rs. ______

TOTAL : Rs. ______

6.3 Chief Minister fund — Balance
Credit amount Rs. ______

6.4 Earth Quake Fund by this order Rs. ______

6.5 Floor Fund — by this order Rs. ______

6.6 Subscription — Deccan Sugar
Institute Balance Rs. ______

TOTAL : Rs. ______

6.7 Education Fund of —
balance Maharashtra
State Coop. Rs.______
By this order Rs.______
TOTAL : Rs.______

6.8 Subscription — Balance State Co-operative Sugar Mills Federation Rs. ________________

By this order Rs. ________________

____

TOTAL : Rs. ________________

6.9 Factories should remit for the loans from the Govt./Financial Institutions upto -/-/199

1. Overdue loans of financial institutions :
2. Govt.'s share of capital :
3. Sugarcane purchase tax loan :
4. Rehabilitation/project expenses/loss :
5. Other Govt. Loans :
6. Sugarcane purchase tax :

7. The factories have to remit this form - refundable / non-refundable deposits and from Rs. ________________ reserved per bag. The bank has to send report by 5th every month.

8. The difference between the rate already paid and final rate is to be paid to the sugarcane producers considering the loans to be paid by each producer as well as deduction, the amount for the completion of the incomplete work of the factory. The amount to be paid to the producers be paid without further delay, considering the arrangements of "Sugarcane Control Order".

9. While making payments to the producer, for the crushing season (year) — loans taken from the co-operative by the producer, be deducted as per the Government circular. If the producer owes any thing else to the factory, it may be deducted.

10. The sugar factories are instructed to complete their accounts and to send their reports to this office upto 19——.

They are further informed to report the undersigned about the implementation of the conditions and suggestions in this order, within 15 days.

Yours faithfully,

Director of Sugar,
Maharashtra State,
Pune - 42.
with permission of

Deputy Director,
(Finance)
Maharashtra State, Pune - 42.

BIBLIOGRAPHY

Attwood, Donald, D. (1993), *Raising Cane : The Political Economy of Sugar in Western India*, Oxford University Press.

Attwood, D.W. & Baviskar, B.S. (1988), *Who Shares? Co-operatives and Development*, Oxford University Press.

Amin, Shahid (1984), *Sugarcane and Sugar in Gorakhpur : An Inquiry into Peasant Production for Capitalist Enterprise in Colonial India*, Oxford University Press..

Baviskar, B.S. (1980), *Politics of Development*, Oxford Press.

Baru, Sanjay (1990), *The Political Economy of Indian Sugar : State Intervention and Structural Change*, Oxford University Press.

Cantanack, I.J. (1970), *Rural Credit in Western India, 1875-1930*, University of California Press, Berkeley.

Dandekar, V.M. (1965), *Minimum Support Prices for Foodgrains : Guidelines for a Policy and Programmes*, Arth-Vijnan Dec. 1965, pp. 273-284.

Gadgil, D.R. (1948), *Economic Impact of Canal Irrigation in Ahmednagar District North of the Nira Canal area.*

Gadgil, D.R. (1955), *Economic Policy & Development*, GIPE Pub. No. 30.

Govt. of India (1996), *Report on Technical Norms for Estimation of Conversion Cost for Sugar Industry - BICP*, Oct.

Govt. of India (1997), *Reports on Price Policy for Sugarcane 1966-67 to 1996-97.*

Govt. of India (1965), *Reports of the Committee on Rehabilitation and Modernisation of Sugar Factories in India.*

Govt. of India (1974), *Report of the Committee constituted to*

Examine the Matters Related to Economic Viability of New Sugar Factories.

Govt. of India (1975), *Report of the Study Team look into the Problems Relating to Inadequate Supply of Sugarcane to Sugar Factories in Maharashtra.*

Govt. of India (1983), *Report of the Committee of Experts for Making Recommendations for Formation of Zones for Drawal of Sugarcane by Sugar Factories in Maharashtra.*

Govt. of India (1998), *Report of the High Power Committee on Sugar Industry.*

Govt. of Maharashtra (1976), *Report of the Study Group for Studying the Yield in Maharashtra,* Ministry of Agriculture and Co-operation.

Govt. of Maharashtra (1999), *Report of the Committee on Co-operative Sugar Factories in Maharashtra (Godbole Committee).*

Inglis, C.C. & Gokhale, V.K. (1928), *Note on the Outturn and Profit from Sugarcane Crops Grown in the Deccan Canal Tracts* : Technical Paper No. 21, P.W.D., GOB.

Jugale, V.B. (1999), *Employment, Wages and Industrial Relations : Farm Sector Workers of Sugar Co-operatives in Maharashtra*, The Classical Publishing Company, New Delhi.

Jugale, V.B. and Jugale, Y.V. (1999), *Delicensing of Sugar Industry in Maharashtra* (Marathi), Samajwadi Prabhodini, Ichalkaranji.

Jugale V.B. and Jugale, Y.V. (1995), *Sugarcane Pricing* (Marathi), Samajwadi Prabodhini, Ichalkaranji.

Kharche, R.M. (1989), *Sugar Co-operatives in Developing Economy*, Parimal Prakashan, Aurangabad.

Kahlon, A.S., Tyagi, D.S. (1983), *Agricultural Price Policy in India*, Allied Publishers Pvt. Ltd.

Laud, G.M. (1986), *Seven Decades of Innovative Banking*, Maharashtra State Co-op. Bank, Mumbai.

Mohite, Y.J. (1974), *Sugarcane Industry in Maharashtra : Blueprint for Progress*, Govt. Central Press, Bombay.

Misra, K.K. (1985), *Sickness of Sugar Industry*, Suneja Publishing Corporation, New Delhi.

Mehta, J.S. (1968), *Indian Sugar Year Book 1967-68*, ISMA.

Narain, L. (1964), *What Price Sugarcane ?* Shri Prakashan, Meerut, 1964.

Patil, P.C. (1927), *Sugarcane Mills and Small Power Crushers in the Bombay Presidency,* Bulletin No. 139, Deptt. of Agricultural, Govt. of Bombay, Poona Yaravada Prison Press.

Patil, P.C. (1928a), *Studies in the Cost of Production of Crops in the Deccan,* Bulletin No. 149, Deptt. of Agricultural, GOB.

Patil, P.C. (1928b), *The Organisation and Cost of Gul (Crude Sugar) Making in the Deccan Sugarcane Tracks,* Bulletin No. 147, Deptt. of Agriculture, GOB.

Rajagopal, S., *Sugar Industry : A Profile*, IBA, Bombay, 1992.

Shrishrimal, W.C. (1967), *The Mechanism of Determining Cane Price in Co-operative Sugar Factories. The Maharashtra Co-operative Quarterly*, Vol. 50, No. 2, April. 1967 (p. 91).

Sahastrabudye, G.N. (1914), *Note on "Indian Sugar Industry and Modern Methods of Sugar Manufacture"* Bulletin No. 60, Deptt. of Agriculture, Govt. Central Press, Bombay.

Visveswaraya, M. (1901), *Memorandum on Irrigation Works in the Bombay Presidency,* Excluding Sing, GOB.

Visveswaraya, M. (1903), *Irrigation on Block System,* P.W.D.

Vasantdada Sugar Institute (1990-91), *Working Results of Sugar Factories in Maharashtra Seasons 1990-91*. Manjari, Pune.

INDEX